VOYEUR NATION

Critical Studies in Communication and in the Cultural Industries
Herbert I. Schiller, Series Editor

VOYEUR NATION

Media, Privacy, and Peering in
Modern Culture

CLAY CALVERT

Westview Press
A Member of the Perseus Books Group

Critical Studies in Communication and in the Cultural Industries

Copyright © 2000 by Westview Press, A Member of the Perseus Books Group

Published in 2000 in the United States of America by Westview Press, 5500 Central Avenue, Boulder, Colorado 80301-2877, and in the United Kingdom by Westview Press, 12 Hid's Copse Road, Cumnor Hill, Oxford OX2 9JJ

Visit us on the World Wide Web at www.westviewpress.com

Library of Congress Cataloging-in-Publication Data
Calvert, Clay.
   Voyeur nation : media, privacy, and peering in modern culture / Clay Calvert.
       p.   cm.—(Critical studies in communication and in the cultural industries series)
   Includes bibliographical references and index.
   ISBN 0-8133-6627-5
   1. Mass media.   2. Voyeurism.   3. Privacy, Right of.   I. Title.   II. Series.

P91 .C28 2000
302.23—dc21   00-43311

The paper used in this publication meets the requirements of the American National Standard for Permanence of Paper for Printed Library Materials Z39.48-1984.

10   9   8   7   6   5   4   3   2   1

Contents

Introduction

A Truman Burbank World

The director Peter Weir's 1998 hit movie *The Truman Show* did more than win three Golden Globe awards and prove that Jim Carrey's acting range stretches far beyond that of a wise-cracking, rubber-faced comedian. The film simultaneously mocked our increasingly voyeuristic society and ridiculed a transparently evident fact—we like to watch other people's private lives and revealing moments, but often care little for actually interacting with them.

In *The Truman Show,* Carrey plays Truman Burbank, a man whose entire life is captured without his knowledge by 5,000 hidden cameras and broadcast live to 1.7 billion voyeuristic viewers as a television show. His every movement, from his birth until he discovers as an adult that his life is played out on gigantic studio soundstage, is caught for the world to watch. His ostensibly private moments are public. Burbank, of course, is the only "true man" in the show; the rest of the people he interacts with, from his best friend to his wife, are merely actors playing roles in his scripted life. Unbelievable? Pure fiction and fantasy?

Not quite. Andrew Niccol, the thirty-four-year–old New Zealander who wrote *The Truman Show* screenplay, remarked that he "used to think this was farfetched and tongue-in-cheek, but I'm not so sure now."[1] Indeed, a host of movie critics lauded the movie's dead-on commentary about today's fascination with peering and gazing into places from which we typically are forbidden and seeing and hearing the innermost details of others' lives. Rita Kempley of the *Washington Post,* calling the film one of the "smartest, most inventive movies in memory," stressed its emphasis on "the rise of voyeurism and the violation of the individual"[2]; Edward Guthmann of the *San Francisco Chronicle* called the movie a "wondrous, thought-stirring parable about privacy and voyeurism."[3]

Voyeurism indeed. The voyeurism depicted in *The Truman Show* and its offspring—Ron Howard and Imagine Entertainment's 1999 film *EDTV* depicted a video store clerk who voluntarily agrees to have his life filmed for a television network—is but a fictitious, over-the-top version of the voyeurism that draws us on a daily basis to watch images of others' lives unfold—frequently, in fact, unravel unceremoniously—on television and the Internet. Summer 2000 brought with it the American network television debut of another voyeuristic spectacle, *Big Brother.* The CBS show features ten strangers residing together in a specially constructed house loaded with hidden cameras. Voyeuristic viewers can watch the housemates around the clock on the Internet. Although voyeuristic content may not be the dominant form of programming today—half-hour situation comedies such as *Friends* and *Everybody Loves Raymond* and hour-long dramas like *The West Wing* and *Judging Amy* still clog prime-time television schedules—it is increasingly popular. Examples of mediated, nonfiction voyeuristic fare are everywhere today on TV and the World Wide Web. They are the focus of this book.

Before we go further, a definition of *mediated voyeurism*—the term given to the phenomenon studied here—is in order. Mediated voyeurism refers to *the consumption of revealing images of and information about others' apparently real and unguarded lives, often yet not always for purposes of entertainment but frequently at the expense of privacy and discourse, through the means of the mass media and Internet.* This definition appears long, yet some may nonetheless find it incomplete or unsatisfactory. Any longer definition, however, certainly would lose its heuristic usefulness and be unwieldy, whereas any shorter version would be nondescriptive and inadequate to capture the nuances of this complex phenomenon.

A few aspects of this definition of mediated voyeurism that will become clearer in later chapters are nonetheless worth briefly unpacking here. The word "revealing" is used strategically to suggest aspects of disclosure and enlightenment that may occur with mediated voyeurism. The phrase "apparently real and unguarded lives" is chosen because the images in question often appear to be or purport to be of the spontaneous, vérité variety. Of course, as Chapter 1 suggests in a discussion of MTV's popular *The Real World* series, it often is hard to distinguish that which is real from that which is contrived. Like the late comedian Andy Kaufman's wrestling forays with women immortalized in the questioning lyrics of R.E.M.'s hit song *Man on the Moon* and the 1999 Milos Forman film by the same title, it may be hard to know what is real and what is fake. As Fox's February 2000 show *Who Wants to Marry a Multi-Millionaire?* proved, a private marriage ceremony can become a public voyeuristic farce.

Likewise, the wording "often yet not always for purposes of entertainment" is carefully chosen. Why is it selected? It is used because, as Chapter 2 reveals, there are a myriad of motivations beyond simple base entertainment and amusement purposes for our inclination to partake in mediated voyeurism. It is not as simple, as Neal Gabler writes in his engrossing 1998 book, *Life the Movie,* as that "life itself is an entertainment medium."[4]

The phrase "frequently at the expense of privacy and discourse" highlights two important interests that often are sacrificed or given short shrift in our desire to be mediated voyeurs. Mediated voyeurism, I argue in this book, thrives when privacy is devalued and privileges spectating over interaction and discussion. The word "frequently" is used in this phrase because later chapters reveal that some of the individuals whose lives we watch willingly allow us to do so. Their privacy thus is *not* sacrificed without their consent and they may be thought of, as the book suggests, as exhibitionists.

Finally, the concluding phrase of the definition, "through the means of the mass media and Internet," taps into the word "mediated" in mediated voyeurism. In particular, this book focuses heavily on content conveyed by and consumed on television and the Internet, as compared to print media such as books or magazines. In some cases, in fact, both television and the Internet provide avenues for watching the same images. New voyeuristic fare such as *Big Brother* and *Survivor* can be both seen on television and tracked on the Internet. Media technologies both capture the images that are the subject of this book and allow us to watch them without ever requiring our interaction with the people we view.

Categories of Mediated Voyeurism

To understand all of the mediated voyeurism described in this book, it may be useful at this early stage to subdivide it into different categories. In particular, nonfiction, reality-based voyeuristic media content can be broken down into at least four categories: (1) *video vérité voyeurism*, (2) *reconstruction voyeurism*, (3) *tell-all/show-all voyeurism*, and (4) *sexual voyeurism*. At times, an individual instance or moment of media content may fit into more than one of these categories. At other times, programs or shows do not fit cleanly into any category. Although this book focuses more heavily on the first and third brands of voyeurism—the video vérité and tell-all/show-all varieties—examples of programs or content that illustrate mediated voyeurism in each of the four categories are set forth below.

Video Vérité Voyeurism

The term "cinema vérité" is sometimes used in film circles to describe a genre or technique of filmmaking that is intended to convey candid, unmanipulated realism, or, as the word vérité suggests, the truth. The camera, sometimes a lightweight, hand-held camera, often tracks or follows the action or individuals in unobtrusive, documentary fashion.[5] The camera is little more than the proverbial fly on the wall.[6] Vérité techniques, such as blurred, grainy visuals, purport to convey an objective window on the world.

The first category of mediated voyeurism—video vérité voyeurism—is derived from cinema vérité. The defining characteristic of this distinctly nonfiction category of voyeurism is un-rehearsed, unscripted moments of real life played out before, and captured by, a video camera. As the title of one Paramount syndicated series suggests, this is *Real TV*. The individuals caught on camera often are unwilling or unsuspecting participants. One need think no further than the videotape of the beating of Rodney King by Los Angeles Police Department officers to get the gist of this category. The beating was unrehearsed and, much to the officers' surprise and chagrin, caught on videotape by George Holliday from his apartment balcony. Holliday's voyeurism purported to capture the truth or reality of the beating, a reality subject to interpretation, of course, by jurors and everyone else who watched the infamous videotape.

Reality crime TV shows like *Cops* also fall into the category of video vérité voyeurism. Unlike the King beating, of course, it is the suspects and not the police who are caught, unsuspectingly and unwillingly, for the camera. Shows such as *Cops, World's Wildest Police Videos,* and *High Speed Chases* take us, via cameras and microphones, on police ride-alongs and high-speed chases, and ultimately they sometimes take us inside people's homes, taping individuals as they are searched, handcuffed, and arrested. We watch all of this, of course, from the safe, comfortable confines of our apartments and homes, without fear of ever having to meet, interact, or talk with the people we are watching. As Mark Fishman, associate professor of sociology at Brooklyn College writes, Cops's "cinema vérité style invites voyeurism. It does not solicit tips, and offers no pretence to catching criminals."[7] As voyeurs, we in the audience simply exercise our right to remain silent while we quench our thirst to see.

Crime shows like Cops and rescue shows like On Scene: Emergency Response are far from the only examples of video vérité voyeurism on television. Real-life courtroom dramas—especially the sexy and sensational ones—are played out daily on Court TV, bringing the legal trials and tribulations of others directly into our living rooms. The format works. As Stephen Easton points out, "The success of the televised trial is based in part upon the audience's voyeuristic thirst for details of others' private lives."[8] Televised trials fit into the video vérité category of voyeurism because nothing in the courtroom is scripted for television; it is captured live by cameras as it happens. The judge, not the cameraperson or television network, directs the action.

Other examples of the video vérité voyeurism category are described in subsequent chapters. This category is of particular importance in this book because efforts to capture the live tape that feeds the video vérité genre often tests, pushes, and strains important social and legal conceptions such as freedom of the press, privacy, newsworthiness, and the public interest. Video vérité voyeurism also is of special significance here because it is a relatively new form of mass-mediated, nonfiction voyeurism, the proliferation of which is made possible largely because of recent advances in technologies such as camcorders and miniature microphones and other improvements in electronic surveillance equipment.

Reconstruction Voyeurism

The defining characteristic of reconstruction voyeurism is the reenactment or dramatization of a real event. Unlike video vérité voyeurism, live videotape is absent or missing and, in its place, are dramatizations and recreations of the sensational or sordid moments that the camera failed to capture. Reconstruction voyeurism thus purports to be nonfiction but remains one degree removed from the voyeurism of the video vérité genre.

Into the reconstruction voyeurism category fall the crime and mystery television programs *America's Most Wanted*, *Unsolved Mysteries*, and *The FBI Files*. As Gray Cavender, professor in the School of Social Justice at Arizona State University writes, this type of show frequently presents "a series of vignettes in which actors reenact actual crimes. Viewers are urged to telephone the police or the program with information about crimes or suspects."[9] The United Kingdom version of this reconstruction voyeurism in the law enforcement realm is *Crimewatch UK*.

These shows are voyeuristic because we are able to watch, albeit by recreation, the sordid and sensational details of others' lives without interacting with them. Reality is recreated and staged for us to watch. If watching *Cops* is like being there on the scene, then reconstructing the scene is the next-best thing. Shows in this category are ostensibly nonfiction television in which we get to take a peek, as if we really were there, at a crime as it occurred or likely occurred.

The ten-part 1993 BBC series *Crime Unlimited*, featuring dramatic and sensationalistic crime reconstructions, faced criticism for its voyeuristic nature. John Getgood, producer of *Crime Unlimited*, admitted the show involved "a sense of voyeurism."[10] A public interest group called Victim Support, in fact, was called in to help with the series. A spokesperson for that group reported that its "interest started after we received a great number of complaints about reconstructions that were voyeuristic and unbalanced."[11]

Tell-All/Show-All Voyeurism

Into a third category of voyeurism fall both the tell-all talk shows and the show-all/investigate-all television newsmagazines such as *Dateline* and *20/20*. Many of the individuals on these shows are *not* unwilling or unsuspecting participants but instead knowingly consent to tell their stories for television. Even when individuals are captured without their consent on camera, the shows package the reality videotape with investigative interviews and commentary from hosts, anchors, or reporters that are counterposed to the video vérité category of voyeurism. Because of both the controversies and criticisms surrounding the tell-all talk show genre and the immense popularity and proliferation today of prime-time television newsmagazines, this category of voyeurism, like that of the video vérité category, is dealt with extensively in this book.

So-called trash-talk television programs like those hosted by Jerry Springer, Ricki Lake, Jenny Jones, and Sally Jessy Raphael bring us a raft of individuals revealing often prurient or titillating facts about their private lives. These exhibitionists provide us yet another opportunity to revel in the joys of others' lives made public. The tabloid talk show genre, writes the Yale sociologist Joshua Gamson in *Freaks Talk Back,* often employs "the low risk strategy of class voyeurism."[12] We get to eavesdrop, in other words, on guests often selected, as Gamson puts it, from the bottom of the social barrel. Hence the derisive name "trash"—as in decidedly classist, elitist, and stereotypic expressions like "trailer park trash" and "white trash"—television.

Television newsmagazines like *Dateline* and *20/20* also fit the mold of tell-all/show-all voyeurism. They pander to our voyeuristic appetite in two ways. First, they specialize in the art of the hidden camera videotape employed by intrepid, undercover reporters and producers to capture alleged wrongdoing on the part of individuals or corporations. We get to see individuals caught in the act as part of this voyeuristic, "gotcha" form of journalism turned infotainment. In addition to playing these voyeuristic-surrogate-for-law-enforcement functions, television newsmagazines often provide viewers with up-close glimpses of others as they experience intensely revealing, private moments. For instance, the proliferating, five-night-a-week NBC newsmagazine *Dateline* broadcast a segment called "Time in a Bottle" in June 1998 that featured three women who allowed cameras and microphones to record their reactions when doctors gave them the news whether their cancer had spread or gone into remission. The law, of course, provides for a doctor-patient privilege to protect against the public dissemination of such disclosures, but the newsmagazines allow us to breach that wall and take a look inside. *60 Minutes* bulldozed that wall when viewers were treated during November 1998—one of the so-called sweeps months in which television stations' advertising rates are determined by the size and demographics (primarily age and income) of the audience watching—to a videotape of the physician Jack Kevorkian assisting in the death of Thomas Youk, a fifty-two-year-old suffering from Lou Gehrig's disease. The segment jacked up *60 Minutes*'s ratings for the week while it simultaneously served up death—some would say murder—voyeuristically. The voyeurism came full circle when Kevorkian's criminal trial stemming from his actions with Youk was played out live for the cameras in the video vérité format on Court TV.

Increasingly, local and national television news programs rely heavily on sensationalistic videotape, packaged with commentary and interviews as news, to capture large audiences. From the smoggy skies above Los Angeles, local news helicopters capture live everything sordid—from the infamous, slow-speed pursuit on Southern California freeways of an allegedly suicidal O. J. Simpson to the actual suicide of Daniel Jones on that same congested freeway system. Jones, a forty-year-old Long Beach maintenance worker, stopped his pickup truck on a freeway in May 1998, unfurled a homemade banner protesting HMOs, and then picked up a shotgun from his truck and blew his brains out. News choppers—voyeuristic eyes in the skies— caught it all live.

Spectatorship of others' lives, in brief, is increasingly paramount in our mediated, must-see TV lives. But television is not the only medium today on which our voyeuristic society preys. Evolutions in technology have introduced new, more intense, and even more intrusive and pervasive forms of voyeurism than at any time in history.

On the Internet, we can watch women such as Jennifer Ringley on so-called girl-cam sites. These popular sites—Ringley's web page at http://www.jennicam.org reportedly receives more than 500,000 hits each day—often feature twenty-four-hour-a-day pictures from the apartments, homes, and even workplaces of women and men who place camera attachments called web cams on their personal computers.

Sexual Voyeurism

The fourth and final category of media voyeurism is distinctly sexual in nature. In contrast to the nonerotic Internet sites operated by budding exhibitionists such as Jennifer Ringley, the World Wide Web is awash in more pornographic and graphic voyeurism pages that feature photographs of unsuspecting individuals in various stages of undress, sexually explicit activity, and bodily function. Try typing in "voyeurism" on a typical search engine such as Lycos and see the hundreds of voyeurism fetish sites, commercial and amateur, that appear. This type of voyeurism is akin to the voyeurism defined as a sexual disorder or form of sexual deviance, as discussed in Chapter 1.

Politics As Voyeurism

In addition to the four types of mediated, nonfiction voyeurism described above, voyeurism today extends to the political arena. We can listen in on tapes of the erstwhile White House intern Monica Lewinsky pouring out her angst and emotions to Linda Tripp. Phrases like presidential semen and oral sex are now part of the political vernacular in the wake of President Bill

Clinton's sexual encounters with Lewinsky. We watched in massive numbers as Monica Lewinsky told all to Barbara Walters in March 1999. And the media perpetuated politics as voyeurism even after President Clinton was acquitted by the U.S. Senate of perjury and obstruction of justice charges. After some initial hesitation, the allegations leveled against Clinton by Jane Doe Number 5—Juanita Broaddrick—received extensive media coverage in late February 1999.[13]

Clinton also was the target of the politics of voyeurism way back in 1992, during his first presidential campaign against George Bush. In this instance, the politics of voyeurism came in the form of an anti-Clinton television advertisement produced by Floyd Brown. Brown was best known at that time for his controversial and allegedly racist 1988 advertisement on behalf of George Bush that featured Willie Horton, a convicted murderer charged with raping a woman while furloughed from prison. That ad, showing a revolving prison gate, was used to attack the prisoner furlough policy of the 1988 Democratic candidate, Michael Dukakis.

Brown's 1992 anti-Clinton ad stunk of voyeurism, not racism. It invited viewers to phone in to a "Bill Clinton Fact Line" to hear actual tape recordings of conversations between Clinton and his onetime alleged paramour, Gennifer Flowers. In the advertisement, Flowers asked viewers to call in and judge for themselves "if this is the way a man talks to a woman who is just a friendly acquaintance." The GOP consultant J. Bryant Smith disowned the ad, calling it "Peeping Tom-style politics" and "voyeurism."[14]

Fast-forward some six years from that advertisement to meet the newest political player in the politics of voyeurism, the infamous *Hustler* magazine publisher Larry Flynt. He takes it on himself to publicly "out" politicians' sexual affairs on a cash-for-trash basis. Flynt purchased a full-page advertisement in the *Washington Post* in October 1998, offering $1 million to anyone who could prove having an affair with a member of Congress or high-ranking government official. Soon his efforts led to information that forced the hand of Bob Livingston, Republican congressman from Louisiana and House Speaker–designate, causing him to admit adultery, relinquish his claim to the speakership, and quit Congress. What is going on here, of course, is more than the so-called politics of personal destruction. More accurately, it is the politics of voyeurism. Although mainstream journalists cried foul, Flynt was merely operating within the politics-of-voyeurism frame those same journalists constructed in covering the Lewinsky affair.

The treatment of politics as voyeurism is an important aspect of this book because it raises questions about what information about the lives of politicians and elected officials is of legitimate concern in a self-governing democracy. It tests notions of personal privacy and ultimately forces consideration of whether there is any information about a political figure that should remain private and out of public consumption.

The Voyeurism Value

What does all of this mediated voyeurism mean? What is happening? More important, *why* is it all happening now?

What is taking place today as we enter the new millennium is the emergence—although not necessarily the creation—of what I call the *voyeurism value* of free expression. The voyeurism value is defined and described in Chapter 7 as a modern-day rationale for protecting expression under the First Amendment. Given the downside of mediated voyeurism in our culture, one may wonder why the word "value" is employed here. Why should voyeurism be *valued?* I use the word value in this book not to suggest that we should or even must prize voyeuristic media content, but to suggest that mediated voyeurism *is* in fact valued by many, from the audiences of television shows that serve up voyeuristic fare to the media corporations that make a healthy profit from producing and distributing that relatively low-cost programming. They value it. To the extent it is valued, perhaps its values should be protected by the First Amendment. Chapter 7 thus contrasts the values of mediated voyeurism with other values—discovery of truth, promoting a better democracy—that often are said to justify protecting expression under the First Amendment.

In this book, I explore mediated voyeurism in its many and varied forms and manifestations today. There is no simple explanation for why mediated voyeurism now takes hold of our society and media fare with such force. As for so many changes in society, there is no one event, incident, or reason that can be identified as *the* critical impetus or cause of the rise of mediated voyeurism or, as Chapter 7 articulates in terms of a theory for protecting expression, a voyeurism value.

Instead, I suggest that the roots of the proliferation of mediated voyeurism today lie at the confluence of a number of developments and changes that have taken place during the past thirty years. The forces pushing the phenomenon of mediated voyeurism to the forefront of society today are multiple—social, political-economic, technological, and legal. These forces, in turn, touch on and sweep up important concepts and values in a self-governing democracy such as privacy, self-realization, discourse, reality, truth, newsworthiness, public interest, and freedom of speech. I argue that all of these concepts either affect or are affected by the voyeurism value.

In the process of describing the forces that give rise to the voyeurism value, I attempt to weigh and expose both the pros and cons of the voyeurism value. Although this book often is critical of both the media content and journalistic practices it describes, it is not an all-out attack on voyeuristic media fare per se. Indeed, we can learn from much of the voyeuristic content we watch, such as shows like *Cops*. As the journalist Douglas Rushkoff wittily writes in *Media Virus,* "How better to see what the heartland of America looks like than barging in unannounced with the camera crew of 'COPS'—and how better to evaluate the role of drugs and alcohol (even TV-network-advertised beer) in contributing to domestic violence, robbery, and homicide?"[15]

On the other hand, much of the voyeuristic fare that we watch reveals a destruction of discourse, privacy, and journalistic standards of news while concomitantly lining the pockets of the megamedia conglomerates that control the cultural industry today. Discussion is replaced by watching. Indeed, the flip side of the so-called death of discourse described by the law professors Ronald Collins and David Skover is, I argue, the birth of voyeurism.[16]

Noble goals of free speech embodied in the First Amendment—discovery of the truth, better government, self-realization—are replaced with a voyeurism value. The First Amendment increasingly safeguards or is called on by media organizations to protect our right to watch—our right to intrude into places from which we once were forbidden and our right to record information with hidden cameras. When ABC employees knowingly lied and used hidden cameras to capture supposedly scandalous footage of food-handling practices at the Food Lion supermarket chain, the media operation invoked the First Amendment to defend its fraudulent conduct. ABC's argument deconstructed? The First Amendment protects fraud in order to protect our right to watch sensationalistic videotape. The First Amendment services voyeurism.

The Organization of the Book

To describe the organization of this book, it is perhaps useful to start off by acknowledging what this book is not. It is not a law book, but it discusses legal issues that affect mediated voyeurism. It is not a journalism book, but it critiques journalism practices that contribute to mediated voyeurism. It is not a sociology or psychology text, but it explores different motivations for our voyeuristic proclivities. It is not a technology tome, but it describes technological forces propelling the capture of voyeuristic images. To the extent that readers approach this book looking for an in-depth, single-minded explication of one of those areas—law, journalism, sociology, technology—they will no doubt be sorely disappointed.

This book also is not intended as a neutral textbook review of a media and cultural phenomenon. The book does take a stand at various points and it can at times be quite sarcastic, if not flippant, in tone. Those seeking complete objectivity and fairness are strongly encouraged to search for other books to balance out the perspective set forth here.

What is this book then? It strives to be scholarly and interdisciplinary yet at the same time accessible to a general lay audience. It touches on and attempts to connect many different approaches to the study of mediated voyeurism. Multiple perspectives thus are taken on one subject in an effort to provide a well-rounded look at this complex phenomenon. Of course, as Duke University's Stanley Fish once put it so well, "being interdisciplinary is so very hard to do,"[17] and I am sure that experts in one field or another—law, journalism, sociology, technology—will find shortcomings in this endeavor. With those caveats in mind, however, the book approaches the subject of mediated voyeurism as follows.

Chapter 1 initially describes, defines, and provides examples of our voyeuristic culture. It contrasts the concept of mediated voyeurism used in this book with both the psychological definition of voyeurism as a form of sexual deviance and the related concept of exhibitionism. As the chapter suggests, much of our voyeuristic pleasure occurs either at the expense of individuals whose images and words are captured by surprise and without their knowledge or at the expense—in some cases perhaps for the benefit—of the exhibitionists who freely consent to have the intimate moments of their lives put on public display. Other important communication concepts—spectatorship and gaze—are introduced in relation to mediated voyeurism. The opening chapter also provides a brief history, including examples, of voyeurism in the mass media, from the voyeurism in medieval literature to that on the old television show hosted by the late Allen Funt, *Candid Camera*. Perhaps the original form of mediated voyeurism on television, *Candid Camera* was—not surprisingly—reborn in the 1990s on CBS and was still going in 2000 with Peter Funt, its creator's son, as the host.

Chapter 2 describes social forces behind the emergence of the voyeurism value. These include the rise of an image-based, video-literate society and a sound bite culture in which the value of speech is secondary to the value of the image. The chapter also explores the uses and gratifications of mediated voyeurism that sustain its audience, from a search for truth and reality in a mediated world to a need to feel superior to or more fortunate than others to the more hedonistic aims of diversion, entertainment, and other visual pleasures. In addition, the chapter describes the social and psychological interests of the exhibitionists who sometimes provide the subject matter of the mediated voyeur's delight. Finally, this chapter offers up a conservative perspective, one framed in part by the work of the erstwhile United States Supreme Court nominee Robert Bork, on the forces that drive mediated voyeurism.

Chapter 3 analyzes the political-economic forces behind the rise of mediated voyeurism. From the bottom-line needs of media corporations who feed our desire to watch to economic deregulation in the marketplace of ideas—today, really, the marketplace of *images*—a number of economic and political forces fuel voyeurism in the media. Politics itself today is voyeuristic, growing from the combination of political apathy, spectatorship, and the collapse of discourse into political sound bites and photo opportunities. The Lewinsky affair and so-called Flynting of politicians embody politics as voyeurism. In addition, a more subtle political influence pushes the voyeurism value—the growing acceptance of surveillance cameras in cities and towns, in parks and stores, as a means of law enforcement.

Chapter 4 is the briefest chapter in the book. It provides an overview of the technological forces driving mediated voyeurism today. It explores both prying technologies—hidden cameras and tiny recording devices—and viewing technologies such as the Internet and television. In the process, this chapter gives examples of some of the voyeuristic content that we see today in the media.

Chapter 5 explains the legal forces that help to propel (and hinder) mediated voyeurism. This chapter examines two critical concepts in the law—public interest and newsworthiness—that have been reduced, collectively, to mean little more than whatever the public wants to watch or see. Thus a federal judge in California can conclude—keeping a straight face all the while—that nude photographs of former *Baywatch* turned *VIP* star Pamela Lee and Motley Crüe drummer Tommy Lee and an accompanying article about their sex life in an adult magazine, *Penthouse,* are newsworthy as a matter of law.[18]

In addition, Chapter 5 addresses a critical issue: Should the megamedia corporations that fuel mediated voyeurism receive First Amendment protection coextensive or equal to that given to individuals? Parsed differently and surely more explosively, why should these wealthy corporate entities be able to hide behind the freedoms of speech and press to protect their ability to make a profit by purveying voyeuristic content that often has very little to do with lofty First Amendment goals of serving democracy or discovering the truth?

Chapter 6 then explores the legal issues behind the so-called media ride-alongs—situations in which news or entertainment media personnel ride along with law enforcement officials and capture videotape and sound recordings that are used voyeuristically on shows such as *Cops.* In particular, the chapter analyzes a 1999 United States Supreme Court decision—*Wilson v. Layne*[19]—that dealt a severe but nonfatal blow to mediated voyeurism of the ride-along variety. This chapter concludes by describing what may be a growing legal backlash cropping up against some forms of mediated voyeurism. It addresses the new wave of anti-paparazzi legislation that arose in the wake of Princess Diana's death as well as new laws designed to tackle video voyeurism.

Finally, Chapter 7 compares the voyeurism value as a rationale for protecting freedoms of speech and press with more traditional, established theories in First Amendment jurisprudence for safeguarding expression. In particular, the chapter contrasts the voyeurism value with the marketplace of ideas metaphor, theories of speech and press in service of democratic self-governance, and the self-realization and human dignity rationales for protecting speech.

Taken as a whole, the chapters suggest what might be thought of as a voyeurism vortex—a maelstrom of forces that drive the voyeurism value to the forefront of our mediated culture and First Amendment jurisprudence in the new millennium. Let us now consider mediated voyeurism and those forces, trying to keep in mind the increasingly fine line between the world inhabited by Truman Burbank and the world in which we live and are watched.

Peeping Tom Meets Jennifer Ringley

The Emerging Culture of
Mediated Voyeurism

When President Bill Clinton was acquitted by the U.S. Senate in his impeachment trial in February 1999, the noted right-wing strategist and conservative leader Paul Weyrich lamented the outcome. For Weyrich, the Senate's decision not to convict on counts of perjury and obstruction of justice stemming from Clinton's admittedly "not appropriate" relationship with "that woman"—Monica Samille Lewinsky—was symptomatic of what he called "the collapse of the culture."[1] Weyrich explained that culture in the United States was becoming, at least metaphorically, an ever-wider sewer.

Weyrich's statements, besides revealing an elitist, value-laden perspective of the concept of culture in which the term is used narrowly to refer to a set of practices and mores that comport with a fixed belief system, miss the mark. Culture has not collapsed or disappeared. It has not gone away. Culture, instead, simply has changed and shifted, as it often does, with the ample assistance of the mass media, over time. It has, depending on one's point of view, evolved or devolved into a culture of mediated voyeurism—a culture that values watching electronic images of other people's private and revealing moments, especially those that are sordid and sensational or simply strange and unusual.

As the Introduction to this book suggests, the images of arrests, busts, and car chases on reality television shows like *Cops* and the tales of prurient sexual activities, practices, and relationships on tabloid talk programs such as *The Jerry Springer Show* are voyeuristic. They are both revealing and personal, and they lean heavily toward the sensational in terms of the actual lives of most of the audience, assuming, of course, that most people watching never have been arrested in a raid on a crack house or publicly exposed for sexual practices society deems deviant. As the attorney and Pennsylvania State University journalism and law professor Robert D. Richards writes about tell-all shows like Jerry Springer's, "guests' willingness to air their 'dirty laundry' on these programs feeds the tastes of *electronic voyeurism* that seems to be prevalent in daytime television markets throughout the United States."[2]

Perhaps most important, the video vérité shows like *Cops* and the tell-all/show-all programs like *Springer* are voyeuristic because those of us in the television audience never need to interact with the people we observe handcuffed, ambushed, surprised, and exposed on the television screen. The people are simply "others" out there. We are safely separated and distanced from them. They will not show up, at least not in person, in our living rooms or dens and force us to have a discussion with them or to share a beer. They will not walk off the screen and into the audience like the characters in Woody Allen's *Purple Rose of Cairo*. Their problems disappear from our voyeuristic vantage point when the set is clicked off with a wave of the remote control wand. Electronic voyeurism is just that easy today. Thus, as the definition of mediated voyeurism offered in the Introduction and reiterated here suggests, mediated voyeurism frequently thrives on the denigration of discourse and interaction with others.

It may be useful before going further to unpack the phrase "culture of mediated voyeurism," much as the Introduction both defined mediated voyeurism and unraveled and identified four distinct categories of voyeuristic media content. When explicating a concept that links two complex words or phrases, it is useful to consider the two components—in this case "culture" and "mediated voyeurism"—both separately and in conjunction.

Trash Talking: Contesting Culture

The word "culture" is used here not to make value judgments, such as whether mediated, reality-based voyeurism constitutes either "high-brow" or "low-brow" culture. Culture, for instance, is sometimes used to classify one form of music, such as opera, as "high" culture, whereas another form, such as Top 40 FM radio, is derisively labeled as "low" culture. That judgmental approach to the concept of a voyeuristic culture is not the one I employ in this book. Resolving whether mediated, reality-based voyeurism, in other words, is symptomatic of a culture that is an ever-wider sewer, as Paul Weyrich might have it, is not the point of this book or the way in which I evoke the term culture. I strive, instead, to show the causal forces behind this culture, as well as to uncover the implications and ramifications—both pro and con—of the voyeuristic culture in which we live on important social and legal conceptions such as freedom of the press, privacy, newsworthiness, and the public interest.

The negative critique of our voyeuristic culture until this time has been left largely—and perhaps unfortunately—in the hands of politicians ready to blame the media as an ever-easy target for society's problems. A case in point is the view taken by Joseph Lieberman, the Democratic senator from Connecticut. A frequent critic of voyeuristic or exhibitionist tell-all talk shows, Lieberman lamented in a recent speech, "We've watched day-time trash TV talk shows sink ever lower in a competition to see who can become more outrageous, salacious and offensive, thrusting the worst of the bedroom into our living room, as nine million children watch on a daily basis."[3] Jerry Springer, Lieberman argues, brings "daily new lows in tastelessness."[4] Critics of daytime talk shows, the Yale sociology professor Joshua Gamson observes in *Freaks Talk Back,* "point adamantly to the dangers of exploitation, voyeurism, pseudotherapy, and the 'defining down' of deviance, in which the strange and unacceptable are made to seem ordinary."[5]

Many of those fears, it is worth noting, may be exaggerated. Recent social science research preliminarily suggests that fears about the negative impact on teens of viewing the tell-all talk shows are overly pessimistic. One study of 292 high school students published in a peer-reviewed communications journal concludes, "The sweeping condemnation of talk show viewing is rather extreme. Although talk shows may offend some people, these data do not suggest that the youth of the U.S. is corrupted by watching them."[6] The researchers found "no support for the desensitization hypothesis. Heavy talk-show viewers were no less likely than light viewers to believe that the victim of antisocial behavior had been wronged, to perceive that the victim had suffered, or to rate the antisocial action as immoral."[7]

If the concept of culture is not used in this book in a pejorative sense, then how is it used? Culture is used here more broadly—and less judgmentally—in the manner defined by the scholar Graeme Turner. Turner defines culture as the place "where meaning is generated and experienced" and the location where "social realities are constructed, experienced, and interpreted."[8]

Much of our social reality today—much of the meaning in our lives that we experience—is generated through mass-mediated content, such as television shows and motion pictures, rather than by direct, firsthand experience with people, places, and practices. Much of that mediated content, in turn, increasingly is voyeuristic in nature. The voyeuristic media messages and images that we view and absorb tend to create, maintain, and transform our social reality—our culture. The media construct a social reality for us, cultivating our images of and beliefs about the real world and reality.

The media environment—our pseudo-environment as Walter Lippmann put it in 1922 in his book *Public Opinion* in an effort to distinguish it from our world of direct experiences[9]—is filled with images that allow us to take part in voyeurism. The "pictures in our head," to use Lippmann's famous phrase, are those that allow us to play the role of voyeur on others' lives.

I'll Be Watching You: Mediated Voyeurism

I use the term "mediated voyeurism" here in a rather generic sense, one to be distinguished from the psychological definition of voyeurism described later in this chapter as a sexual disorder or form of sexual deviance. I borrow here from the definition used by Peter Keough in relationship to the viewing of violent and sexually explicit movies—as an "urge to gaze at the alien and the intimate."[10] The alien and the intimate tend to be sordid or sensational, but they need not be. Our voyeurism may be as simple as watching the home movies of others' lives and knowing that we could be "the star of the next show."[11]

Building on Keough's definition of voyeurism, I defined mediated voyeurism in the Introduction as *the consumption of revealing images of and information about others' apparently real and unguarded lives, often yet not always for purposes of entertainment but frequently at the expense of privacy and discourse, through the means of the mass media and Internet.*

America's Funniest Home Videos fits this definition of mediated voyeurism. It is a voyeuristic and exhibitionist television show that features a collection of amateur videotapes of people revealing often embarrassing or funny moments to the world. Someone is surprised, captured off guard, embarrassed. The audience's laugh is at the expense of the person caught on videotape. We never need to interact with these individuals—that is part of the thrill of the "mediated" aspect of mediated voyeurism. We do not need to be physically present to see the revealing moments. The media convey the information to us.

The formula works—the show hit number one in the national ratings in February 1990, less than four months after it debuted, and it lasted for nearly a full decade in first-run production until it was axed by ABC in 1999. *America's Funniest Home Videos* featured a great formula for corporate profit, given that the amateur videotape was generated at someone else's time and expense and then cannibalized by the producers of the television show. That was far cheaper, of course, than paying high-priced Hollywood actors like those in the cast of *Friends* to play the roles. The economic incentives and forces driving electronic voyeurism are discussed in greater detail in Chapter 3.

Uniting the concepts of culture and mediated voyeurism, the culture of mediated voyeurism is one in which our proclivity and affinity for mediated voyeurism rises to the forefront of our media consumption. The culture of mediated voyeurism is characterized by a number of attributes. It values watching over discourse, sacrifices privacy for others' enjoyment and enlightenment, and demands protection for often aggressive and intrusive gathering of visual images and information. Chapter 7 contrasts these values associated with voyeuristic expression with other, more traditional values asserted for protection of speech, such as discovery of truth and promoting democracy.

Upping the Voyeuristic Ante?

The often shaky, handheld camcorder footage of family mishaps featured on *America's Funniest Home Videos* looks almost quaint today as the degree and severity of our mediated voyeurism is steadily ratcheted up. In March 1999, NBC premiered a more intense, weekly form of the video vérité voyeurism genre described in the Introduction with the show *World's Most Amazing Videos*. A single episode of this video clip–stapled show is all one needs to watch to understand its voyeuristic nature. The March 10, 1999, episode, for instance, allowed a national television audience to watch a pregnant woman leaping from a burning building, a bungee jumper falling to the ground when his cord snaps in midleap, and a race car skidding directly into a trackside TV cameraman—all moments captured live, all exposing someone else's tragedy or, as Chapter 2 suggests, someone's moment of truth or reckoning, in a sensationalistic and sordid manner. The show features prime examples of the content symptomatic of the culture of mediated voyeurism in which we live.

Of course, the list of video vérité voyeurism television programs goes far beyond *America's Funniest Home Videos* and clip shows like *World's Most Amazing Videos*. It includes the reality-based shockumentary—some would derisively say "schlock reality"[12]—shows titled *World's Scariest Police Chases, World's Wildest Police Videos, When Good Pets Go Bad, When Animals Attack, When Stunts Go Bad, World's Worst Drivers Caught on Tape,* and *Cheating Spouses Caught on Tape.* It is, as the titles of the last two shows in this list suggest, the "caught on tape" aspect of all of these programs—the video vérité format described in the Introduction, packed with short bursts of reality strung together over the course of thirty minutes to an hour—that fuels the voyeurism we value and satiates our visual appetite. Nothing is staged, all is real, and the moments captured are sensational and alien to most of the audience. As the on-line Internet promotional literature for *World's Wildest Police Videos,* a Fox television program produced by Paul Stojanovich Productions, promises, "a combination of real and never-before-seen videos acquired from law enforcement agencies, news bureaus and other sources from around the world. Riveting dramas unfold as video cameras catch full-throttle action of an array of police activity, including high-speed chases, robberies in progress, SWAT team raids and deadly shoot-outs."[13]

John Langley, executive producer and creator of *Cops*, recognizes the appeal of voyeuristic video vérité: "I've always believed that there's nothing more exciting than reality if you can somehow manage to capture the moment, or be in the moment."[14] On *Cops*, the goal is simple—"We wanted to put the viewer in the passenger seat." Langley claims the "best episode is the one that has no cuts, no editorials, no interference—when the camera simply rolls and captures what happens as it happens."

We revel rather perversely in others' embarrassment and pain in voyeuristic fashion. When those good pets do go bad, we are fortunate that someone had the good sense to have a video camera handy so that we can watch as pit bulls tear into children and old women. When those unfaithful spouses do cheat, we are grateful some intrepid private detectives had their camcorders at the ready.

The Voyeur's 20/20 Vision

Mediated voyeurism, as noted in the Introduction, also sweeps up much of the content on television newsmagazines. It may be useful at this stage, then, to explore some specific examples that illustrate this point. Two consecutive months—February and March 1999—alone provide plenty of evidence of voyeuristic fare on the newsmagazines.

Individuals who tuned in to Barbara Walters's *20/20* interview of Monica Lewinsky in March 1999 were participating in media voyeurism. And the number of individuals tuning in was enormous—the interview drew an audience second only to the Super Bowl.[15] We basked for two hours in a voyeur-fest as the sordid details, such as Lewinsky showing her thong underwear to President Clinton to suggest, as she put it so aptly, "I'll play," were broadcast.

The voyeurism in the Walters-Lewinsky *20/20* interview was transparent, if not over the top. Heather Svokos, the pop culture writer for the *Lexington Herald-Leader,* wrote that the interview "went beyond casual voyeurism. It made me feel like diving into a reservoir of lemon-fresh Clorox."[16] Kathy Kiely of *USA Today* called the Monica mania surrounding the interview a symptom of a national tendency to practice voyeurism.[17]

Less than two weeks after the Lewinsky chat session, *20/20* was at it again with more voyeurism—Diane Sawyer behind bars in a women's prison for forty-eight hours, video camera in hand, for what she called "a rare and compelling glimpse into an extraordinary world hidden behind bars."[18] That description itself, from the standpoint of mediated voyeurism, is worthy of further consideration. The word "extraordinary" is important in Sawyer's statement. It suggests, in line with the concept of voyeurism described earlier in this chapter, that we are witnessing something that is *not* ordinary. It is, instead, something unusual, something alien, something we do not usually see; it is something *extra*ordinary. The other key word in Sawyer's description of the episode is "hidden." Sawyer's exposé transports us voyeuristically into a world we do not ordinarily see, that typically is out of our view. What is more, she also played up the prurient or sexual voyeurism angle mentioned in the Introduction with her discussions of allegedly rampant lesbianism and the coupling up of women behind bars, as if this were some low-budget pornographic women's prison movie rather than a newsmagazine.

The *20/20* prison segment put to shame the voyeurism inherent in the rival newsmagazine *Dateline*'s feature from just a month before on the then–two-year-old mystery behind the murder of JonBenet Ramsey. The Ramsey murder is, was, and always will be a perfect story with all of the features of voyeurism. We are taken into the home (at least via blueprints on the *Dateline* segment) and sordid lives of the rich and elite and allowed to gaze at amateur videos of a very young girl dressed up like a Las Vegas showgirl, and, best of all, we never need to deal with these freakish people in our lives. That the Ramsey story is the stuff of which voyeurism is made was confirmed when *Dateline*'s February 1999 report was followed up in April 1999 by *48 Hours*'s own, Dan Rather–hosted feature on the murder mystery. When in October 1999 the grand jury in Boulder failed to indict anyone, *Dateline* predictably returned to the story with yet another Ramsey voyeur-fest broadcast shortly thereafter. In 1999—more than two full years after it occurred in December 1996—the JonBenet Ramsey murder was the third most covered newsmagazine story.[19]

20/20 rebroadcast a story in March 1999 that featured multiple layers of voyeurism. The segment, called "Sex, Lies and Videotape," involved a man who installed a tiny hidden camera device in a television set to catch his wife sleeping with his next-door neighbor. That is the first layer of voyeurism. The segment then allowed us in the television audience to watch snippets taken from the videotape that indeed caught the two in the act. That is the second layer of voyeurism. As subsequent chapters of this book suggest, this and similar forms of video surveillance used in the name of protection, revenge, or justice are becoming more prevalent. We increasingly use surveillance equipment to eavesdrop or spy on others—the baby-sitter taking care of the children, for instance—to the point that it tends to make voyeurism more and more an accepted and less and less a controversial practice.

Not even staid *60 Minutes*—at least not its Wednesday night offspring, *60 Minutes II*—was above joining the voyeuristic fray. For instance, the March 24, 1999, episode featured a Bob Simon segment, "The Lost Children," that dealt with the approximately 10,000 children from England who were deported to Australia in the two decades after World War II. The youths, many allegedly orphans or otherwise abandoned by their parents, were shipped off in an effort to help populate Australia with Anglo-Saxons while simultaneously clearing out Britain's overcrowded children's homes.

One of those children interviewed by Simon was an adult woman now in her fifties. She had not seen her mother since she was, literally, shipped off to Australia decades before. Thanks to *60 Minutes II*, however, the woman was able to fly home to meet her now frail, eighty-year-old mother in person for the first time in many, many years. All of this reuniting is fine and good, of course. But the segment ended up reeking of voyeurism when both camera and microphone captured the initial, tearful meeting between mother and daughter. Perhaps the voyeuristic intrusion was the quid pro quo the woman paid for *60 Minutes II* purchasing her airplane ticket home.

As this book suggests in later chapters, the idea that watching others' lives voyeuristically constitutes news—the episodes described above appeared on shows called *news*magazines—is an important force behind the rise of voyeurism. Our notions of news and human interest stories have shifted over time. Today, voyeurism passes as news.

I Want My Voyeur TV

Starting in the early 1990s, a young generation of television viewers was weaned on the ways of video voyeurism, thanks in large part to the cable station that gave us the music video, MTV. In 1992, MTV premiered the still-running hit series *The Real World*. It featured seven young men and women, five white and two black, ranging in ages from nineteen to twenty-five, and in occupations from poet to model.[20] These individuals were selected from the more than 500 people who auditioned to share a four-bedroom loft in the trendy SoHo area of Manhattan for thirteen weeks.

The price they paid in exchange for free room and board, as well as weekly walking-around money and a check for $1,300 at the conclusion of the thirteen weeks, was their privacy. Their interactions were caught on camera and microphone. Fourteen microphones were set into ceilings and night tables. The show's "cast members" each wore wireless microphones. The telephones were tapped to allow viewers to hear both sides of their conversations. All of this was edited and packaged up by the co-executive producers Jon Murray and Mary-Ellis Bunim into half-hour segments of a postmodern combination of reality-based documentary and soap opera.

Murray and Bunim described their goal for that first season this way: "Find seven young adults from diverse backgrounds, move them into a fantasy loft, film their every waking moment, and cut the results into thirteen weekly episodes of a 'reality soap opera' for MTV."[21] As for casting, their criteria were "diversity, intelligence, humor, verbal ability, willingness to share themselves, charisma, and a desire to grow through experience."[22]

The formula worked. Each year since the original season, the show has assembled a new cast—a cast seemingly selected to generate the conflict and controversy that plays so well to an audience of voyeurs—in a new city. After starting in New York, the show next moved to Los Angeles, and then on to San Francisco, London, Miami, Boston, Seattle, Hawaii, and New Orleans. The Los Angeles version featured a cast that included an AIDS care specialist and a stand-up comic, all living in a posh, 6,000-square-foot house in Venice Beach.[23] The 1998–1999 season, shot in a Seattle, featured a younger cast of seven college undergraduates—no one was older than twenty-two—and consistently ranked in the top fifteen cable programs among viewers in the twelve- to thirty-four-year-old demographic group.[24] It featured eighteen half-hour episodes culled from 1,894 hours of videotape.

The name *The Real World* is highly ironic, of course. Even though the camera captures action as it occurs and no scripts are used, the individuals know they are being filmed. Sometimes they even talk directly to the cameras. The show features weekly confessionals in which the individuals go into a room alone and talk directly to the camera, often about the other people in the show that they despise. There are many willing exhibitionists each season to fill the roles—Murray and Bunim now receive 14,000 to 15,000 videotapes each year from people auditioning. So much is edited out that what is left is only the most interesting and sensational material. The settings are also highly unrealistic. The Seattle season, for instance, took place in posh digs on Pier 70 that featured sixty-seven donated artworks, a rock-climbing wall, exercise machines, a pool table, a hot tub, an aquarium, and a library filled with books—not too bad digs for a group of college kids. As one of my undergraduate students at Penn State told me, "It's like a fantasyland, not reality."

Despite the contrived, formulaic nature of the voyeurism and the criticisms that the individuals play to the cameras, the show thrives on the kind of tension—sexual and relationship-based tension, in particular—and conflict (during the Seattle season one cast member actually struck another cast member) that allows us to gaze at others' lives. As Caryn James of the *New York Times* wrote, "the revolving door of characters works because the series' appeal is the irresistible pull of watching lives, any lives, unfold without a script."[25] She adds astutely, "Dipping in and out of other people's lives is precisely what the current television culture is all about." Indeed, the individual who struck the other person was forced to go to counseling sessions—counseling sessions that were taped for our voyeuristic enjoyment.

The Real World is still going strong today. The season beginning in June 1999 saw the show hit record ratings. The percentage of households watching during the 1999–2000 season rose an astounding 41 percent from the previous season and more than doubled the program's ratings from its inaugural season back in 1992.[26] That a show's ratings are still growing after it has been on for seven years is extremely rare. By that stage, most long-running series are beginning to experience a gradual ratings decline.

Building on the success of the formula of *The Real World* and the television formula of copycat television programming, MTV launched a cloned, mobile version of the show in 1995 called *Road Rules*.[27] Also produced by Jon Murray and Mary-Ellis Bunim of *The Real World* fame, this still-successful show packs young people in a recreational vehicle for a series of adventures, called "missions," across the United States and, in 1999, Latin America.

It is easy to see that the influence of MTV stretches far beyond the rise of the musical video and Madonna. The network propagates and disseminates video voyeurism, nurturing a new generation on the ways of watching others' lives unfold. Ultimately, this generation comes to accept as normal and takes for granted the presence of cameras. Far from fearing the prying presence of the lens, a new generation longs to live its life out in full view for all to see.

As Chapter 2 discusses, one of the social forces that makes shows like *The Real World* possible is a changing conception of what is private and what is public. The voluntary surrender of privacy to appear on *The Real World* apparently is well worth the spoils of living rent free and attaining a moment of television fame. Although the generations that came of age in the 1970s and 1980s grew up *on* watching television, the youth of today now crave growing up *in* television.

The Real World's blurring of the lines between reality and acting—the individuals who appear are carefully chosen to play parts in front of cameras that they know are omnipresent—also suggests another social force behind mediated voyeurism that is explored in Chapter 2. It indicates a quest on the part of audience members for reality in an increasingly mediated world in which fact and fiction—acting and being—are hard to distinguish.

The 1999 season of *The Real World* featured a disturbing incident that revealed how mediated voyeurism sometimes may go too far in the name of high ratings: One of the individuals featured on the show got behind the wheel of a van after drinking heavily. Although officials from MTV maintain that a director warned the young woman not to drive in her apparently intoxicated condition, she drove off anyway, cameras rolling.[28] The MTV film crew followed her and when they eventually caught up with the woman, found the good sense and decency to order her out the van.[29]

The trials and tribulations of this twenty-one-year-old woman with an alcohol problem—she is seen in one episode falling down drunk in a disco and throwing up half-naked in a shower—may be partly responsible for *The Real World*'s hefty ratings in 1999. All of this raises important ethical questions about whether the producers of mediated voyeurism should exploit and profit from others' troubles, whether they have a duty and responsibility to step out of the role of voyeur and actually intervene when things go too far, and whether there is a privacy line that is crossed when an individual's serious problems are given widespread publicity to a nation of mediated voyeurs.

The coproducer Jon Murray apparently felt few qualms in bringing the MTV audience the young woman's problems. He told a reporter from the *Wall Street Journal*, "We're documentarians who want to document young people's lives. If we, as older, perhaps wiser adults, step in to every situation and try to solve it for them, we're not going to wind up with a program that deals with these problems."[30] Murray added that the cast members "know very much what they are getting into."[31]

Although this book focuses heavily on legal issues surrounding mediated voyeurism, *The Real World* reveals that ethical issues also abound with this form of programming. Even if the law may not prohibit mediated voyeurism, this does not make it ethical. In journalism, there sometimes is a tension between exposing the truth and the harm that the truth may cause.[32] This tension certainly exists in the mediated voyeurism involving the MTV hit series. In bringing the viewers of *The Real World* the truth about a young woman's alcohol problems, the show's producers may have exacerbated the woman's troubles by exposing them to the world at large.

From *The Real World* to *Big Brother*

In television, genres, or formats, of programs typically move through three stages, or steps. First, there is the *invention* stage, in which a new type of program emerges. If the "invented" genre or format is a success—meaning that it attracts a large audience composed of people whom advertisers want to reach with their commercials—it is followed by the second step, *imitation*. In the imitation stage, programs that fit in the successful genre proliferate. Once the market is saturated with imitations of a successful format, there comes the final stage, *decline*.

The first two stages were clearly evident in January 1999, when the Lifetime Television cable network turned to Jon Murray and Mary-Ellis Bunim, the producers of MTV's *The Real World* and *Road Rules,* for a new television series. They ordered a pilot of a new show called *Real Families.* Dawn Tarnofsky-Ostroff, senior vice president of programming and production at Lifetime Television, described the format of *Real Families* this way to *The Hollywood Reporter:* "Cameras will go in and live with a family through some period of their lives that revolves around some issue or crisis or something that's about to change."[33]

Sound familiar? It smacks of the contrived voyeurism in *The Real World* and *Road Rules,* but this time it targets a different, older audience with a different cast of characters. Said Tarnofsky-Ostroff, "We have a goal of trying to find a reality show that our viewers will find irresistible. There's something about seeing real people overcoming situations that makes it hard not to root for them." Ah, yes, formulaic voyeurism at its finest.

In summer 2000, the imitation stage continued when CBS debuted the U.S. version of *Big Brother*, a show featuring ten people living together in a house loaded with cameras and microphones and constructed on a television studio lot in California. Also in summer 2000, CBS launched another voyeuristic program called *Survivor*. *Survivor* follows the happenings of real people put together on a tropical island off the coast of Borneo.

Mediated Voyeurism Everywhere

It is important to understand that ours in the United States is not the only mediated culture that apparently revels in and values reality-based voyeurism. Reality television programming, for instance, has become an accepted, if controversial, feature of television programming in France and elsewhere in Europe.[34] In Australia, a top-rated program that also airs in the United States is *Real TV*. It brings viewers footage of, for example, the late Margaux Hemingway undergoing bulimia therapy and of a man attempting to escape from his burning vehicle.[35] In Russia, a highly rated show called *Perehvat* ("to nab") takes the premise of Fox's *Cops* for a spin, literally, in a different direction—it involves actual traffic police chasing cars driven by contestants, not suspects, across the frozen streets of Moscow.[36] When contestants elude the police for the duration of the show, they win a new car. All of this suggests, as Chapter 2 later explores, that certain social forces that transcend geographic boundaries are driving, in part, the ascendancy of a mediated voyeuristic culture.

Throughout this book, other examples of voyeurism will be discussed to further illustrate the voyeurism value and our voyeuristic culture. Before going further, it may be useful to provide a brief historical perspective of mediated voyeurism. As will become clear, some of the voyeurism described in the following sections is readily distinguished from the voyeurism that is the focus of this book. In particular, this book focuses both on the reality-based, video vérité voyeurism defined in the Introduction in which real people—not paid actors playing roles—are caught on camera, tape, or film engaging in real, unstaged activities, and on the tell-all/show-all variety of voyeurism in which real people knowingly and willingly reveal all about their private lives to an eager audience. In contrast, much of the voyeurism discussed below, in films such as Alfred Hitchcock's *Rear Window* and *The Truman Show* and literature such as the *Canterbury Tales,* is fiction. It is scripted or staged. With this difference in mind, in the next section I look at the historical evolution of mediated voyeurism, beginning with its roots in legend and literature, continuing in print journalism, and then going into the electronic eras of television and film.

History of Media Voyeurism

The Ride of Lady Godiva

Mediated voyeurism historically transcends both the broadcast medium and reality-based content to sweep up fiction and legend in both literature and films. The legend of Lady Godiva, for instance, dating back nearly 1,000 years to around 1050 and since recaptured and retold in print and on canvas and carved in stone, features perhaps the best-known example of voyeurism in legend and folklore.[37] According to some versions of the tale, when Lady Godiva rode naked on a horse through the city of Coventry to protest taxes, a young man named Tom—known today as the Tom behind the moniker Peeping Tom—dared to gaze at Godiva. For this, he was, depending on the particular account or version of the retelling, killed or blinded. The Peeping Tom character became an essential part of the Godiva story after 1700 and today the name is synonymous with a voyeur.

Today, of course, Peeping Tom of Coventry would not need to steal a peak at Lady Godiva on the streets of Coventry and risk blindness for his action. Instead, he could flip on his computer, type in the address http://www.jennicam.org and catch photographs twenty-four hours a day of the apartment of Jennifer Ringley. He might even catch her, as he did Lady Godiva, naked.

Voyeurism, of course, can be found in other forms of literature and legend besides the story of Lady Godiva. A. C. Spearing, the William R. Kenan Professor of English at the University of Virginia, writes in *The Medieval Poet As Voyeur*, "Within medieval love narratives, secret observers, concealed from the lovers as the lovers are from society at large, are frequently represented as responsible for exposing private experience to the public gaze; as readers or listeners to such narratives, we too can be made to feel that we are secret observers."[38] Spearing calls Geoffrey Chaucer a poetic voyeur who spectates on lovers, private life, and its violation in works such as the *Canterbury Tales* and *Troilus and Criseyde*.

Boston University's Dorothy Kelly explores voyeurism in the French novels of the seventeenth, eighteenth, and nineteenth centuries in her book *Telling Glances*.[39] She examines voyeurism in, for example, the works of Honoré de Balzac (1799–1850) and Denis Diderot (1713–1784). Kelly summarizes the basic plots of many French novels of the period:

> A man desires a woman who is enigmatic and unobtainable. He not only desires to possess her; he also experiences an irresistible need to see her and to understand her, to know exactly what she is, or what she desires. But since this information remains hidden, the man resorts to spying on her in order to obtain the information; he resorts to an act of voyeurism.[40]

How is this sexual voyeurism drawn from romantic fiction of another time period and country useful for exploring and analyzing the video vérité voyeurism or the tabloid talk show voyeurism of the electronic era of the twenty-first century? Kelly suggests that much of the voyeurism in the French novel, as well as much of psychoanalysis, focuses on quests for truth and knowledge, as well as searches for identity and desire.[41] These same social forces, as Chapter 2 suggests, may be in part responsible for our insatiable appetite today for electronic voyeurism. Thus, although the aim of the voyeur in the French novel may have been to gain sexual knowledge from his gaze, as Kelly suggests, today we are voyeurs perhaps because we hope to learn something about ourselves, our society, and our own place or places in that society. We strive to learn what truth and reality are in our mediated, jump-cut world by watching others, the next chapter suggests.

The Print Media Roots of Electronic Mediated Voyeurism

The electronic voyeurism present today in reality-based television shows, shockumentaries, newsmagazines, and tell-all talk shows can be traced back at least to the ages of yellow and jazz journalism. These periods, known for sensationalism in an effort both to attract readers and, in some cases, to bring reform to real-world problems, stretch from the 1880s through the 1920s. Two famous examples from this era illustrate the roots of today's voyeurism.

Elizabeth Cochrane, better known under her pseudonym Nellie Bly, worked for Joseph Pulitzer's *New York World* and in the 1880s feigned mental illness to enter an insane asylum. She came out with horrific tales of abuse and atrocious conditions. Unlike Diane Sawyer and her trek behind bars in a women's prison for *20/20,* however, Bly did not have a video camera to capture these moments.

Tom Howard did have a camera in 1928, about thirty years after halftone technology first brought to a mass audience the realism of photography. Howard brought a miniature camera, taped to his left ankle and hidden from general view, into an electrocution room in New York to capture the moment as a

2,200-volt current shot through the body of the condemned murderer Ruth Snyder. The famous photograph was splashed across the front page of the New York *Daily News* on January 13, 1928, under the headline "DEAD!" The paper sold one million extra copies that day.[42] The very next day, the *Daily News* again printed on its cover a full-page picture of Snyder in the Sing Sing electric chair, this time under the heading "FUNER-ALS HELD."[43] Sixty years later, as described in the Introduction, we would be treated to pictures of another death—a videotape on *60 Minutes* of Jack Kevorkian assisting in the suicide of Thomas Youk, a man suffering from Lou Gehrig's disease.

Notably, the tabloids of the jazz journalism era of the 1920s and 1930s were heavily image based in the voyeuristic tradition. Writing in 1938, Simon Michael Bessie observed that tabloids of the era often devoted the entire front page to a giant "arresting picture" and a single huge, boldface headline.[44] The photograph of Ruth Snyder, dead in the electric chair, under the single word "DEAD!" illustrates this point. The extensive use of photography in the tabloids of the jazz journalism period was a precursor to the more intense photographic voyeurism of tabloids today that make use of high-powered camera equipment to capture voyeuristic pictures of celebrities on beaches and in their yards.

Even before the advent of the halftone screen technology that made such photographs possible, Joseph Pulitzer played up the use of sensational illustrations during the 1880s and 1890s in the era of yellow journalism. As Bessie writes, "Acting upon the truism that 'pictures speak a universal language which requires no teaching to comprehend,' Pulitzer ordered a great increase in the use of illustrations to brighten his pages."[45] Pulitzer used technology to extend a tradition of voyeuristic illustrations that dates back at least to 1823, when the *Illustrated London News* used five illustrations of a murder, including ones of "the scene of the murder" and the "pond in which the body was found."

This was not a far cry from the death-on-camera of Ruth Snyder 100 years later in 1928 or the death on videotape of Thomas Youk in 1998.

The *New York Evening Graphic* used a technology and technique called the composograph in the 1920s that appealed to voyeurism.[46] This method featured staged scenes—some involving staff members of the tabloid—reenacting events such as hangings or medical operations. This approach to voyeurism fits in the category of reconstruction voyeurism described in the Introduction and present today on television on shows such as *America's Most Wanted*.

Some contend that the mediated voyeurism of today can be traced back even before the eras of yellow and jazz journalism described above to the early days of the penny press in the 1830s—long before the advent of halftone technology—when newspapers began to sell for a penny and often relied on entertaining, human interest stories to attract mass readership. Andie Tucher, currently an associate editor of the *Columbia Journalism Review* and the author of *Froth and Scum: Truth, Beauty, Goodness, and the Ax Murder in America's First Mass Medium,* makes this argument. She asserted in the *New York Times* in 1985, "The modern electronic media did not invent mass voyeurism; that's been around since at least 1836, when James Gordon Bennett, determined to make his *New York Herald* the best-selling penny newspaper in the city, achieved this goal with help of lurid and exhaustive coverage of the ax-murder of a prostitute."[47] As Simon Michael Bessie writes about the sensationalistic coverage of the murder of this prostitute, Helen Jewett, "Whores and murders were just as fascinating then as they always have been and no tabloid could abandon itself more gleefully to sordid details than did the 'quaint' penny press in exploiting this now forgotten tragedy."[48]

Regardless of precisely which era—penny press, yellow journalism, or jazz journalism—one pinpoints for the origin of modern-day, reality-based electronic voyeurism in the United

States, it should be clear from this brief history that sensational, mediated voyeurism, including the reality-based and tell-all variety that is the focus of this book, is not new. What is new, however, is the medium, quantity, and intensity of vérité voyeurism. It is a pervasive presence today in the media, due to the confluence of social, political-economic, technological, and legal forces described in Chapters 2 through 6. Before turning to those forces, it may be useful to trace the evolution of mediated voyeurism from the print medium described above to the electronic realm described below.

Smile, You're on Candid Camera

"One of the luckiest discoveries I ever made, as far as camera concealment is concerned" wrote Allen Funt nearly a half century ago in 1952, "was a small wonder known as a two-way mirror."[49] Funt, who passed away in 1999, was a progenitor of the television voyeurism genre. Called everything from a dirty snoop to an ingenious sociologist, Funt was the force behind the television show *Candid Camera* and, before that, a radio program called *Candid Microphone*. It was the "candid" part— the surprise of the unwitting individual caught on camera—that played so well in the late 1940s and the 1950s on a new medium to an audience that fifty years later would become fully trained electronic voyeurs. Indeed, in 1997 CBS brought back the show with its tried-and-true formula of ambushing ordinary citizens with odd situations. The new version, firmly entrenched in CBS's 1999 lineup in a Friday evening time slot, is cohosted by Peter Funt, Allen Funt's son, and the former *Three's Company* star turned infomercial exercise equipment queen, Suzanne Somers.

One important difference between *Candid Camera* and the video vérité voyeurism of *Cops,* of course, is that the producers on the former show set up scenes in which to ensnare unsuspecting individuals for the viewer's pleasure. A March 1999 episode of the new version of *Candid Camera,* for instance, created "its own version of Andy Warhol's '15 minutes of fame' as unsuspecting travelers outside an airport are swarmed by television news crews and autograph-seekers who believe they are famous television stars."[50] On *Cops,* in contrast, the events unfold spontaneously; one never knows what the next call over the police radio will bring. Despite this difference, one can see—literally—the beginnings of television voyeurism in *Candid Camera.*

Another early and extremely more controversial and serious form of reality-based television voyeurism involved a twelve-hour documentary series broadcast on public television in the early 1970s called *An American Family.* It was, as the Brown University professor Philip Rosen observes, "planned as an unprecedented documentary observation of everyday family life over an extended period of time."[51] The show chronicled, on film, the real-life problems of the Louds, a family from Santa Barbara, California. "Starring" William and Pat Loud, along with their five children, the show featured son Lance coming out of the closet and his parents' apparent refusal to acknowledge that their son was homosexual. The cameras also captured the sad breakup of the Loud family, including one infamous scene in which Pat told her husband, William, that she wanted a divorce. It took a camera crew that lived with the Louds seven months to film enough of this material to fill the twelve-hour series.

William Loud felt his family was misled in the end result, alleging that the editors focused on the negative aspects of his family's life and that they had a preconceived liberal, leftist view. Twenty-five years after *An American Family* was first broadcast, PBS aired a powerful *Frontline* documentary, *The Farmer's Wife,* that focused on a Nebraska family's fight to save its farm. As *Candid Camera* and *An American Family* make clear, voyeurism on television—be it the contrived voyeurism in which humorous gags are created or the vérité voyeurism in which reality unfolds unscripted and unceremoniously—is not necessarily a new phenomenon but one that is today more prevalent, more ambitious, and more sensational.

Cinema Voyeur:
Visual Pleasures in the Dark

Not only is there a long tradition of voyeurism on television, but there is a history of voyeurism in film. That cinematic voyeurism is at least twofold. First, there may be voyeurism in the content of films, as when one character watches another character or a camera watches a character. Second, there is voyeurism in the relationship between the audience and the film—the audience watches the characters on the screen, gazing at them without interacting with them or interfering with the action as it unfolds. As the Chicago-based movie critic Roger Ebert writes, "The movies make us into voyeurs. We sit in the dark, watching other people's lives. It is the bargain the cinema strikes with us, although most films are too well-behaved to mention it."[52]

Norman K. Denzin, a professor of sociology at the University of Illinois, succinctly observes in *The Cinematic Society,* "The postmodern is a visual, cinematic age; it knows itself in part through the reflections that flow from the camera's eye. The voyeur is the iconic, postmodern self. Adrift in a sea of symbols, we find ourselves, voyeurs all, products of the cinematic gaze."[53] Watching films is a voyeuristic activity. Laura Mulvey writes in one of the most influential feminist essays in film criticism, "Visual Pleasure and Narrative Cinema,"

> The mass of mainstream film, and the conventions within which it has consciously evolved, portray a hermetically sealed world which unwinds magically, indifferent to the perspective of the audience, producing for them a sense of separation and playing on their voyeuristic fantasy. Moreover, the extreme contrast between the darkness in the auditorium (which also isolates the spectators from

one another) and the brilliance of the shifting patterns of light and shade on the screen helps to promote the illusion of voyeuristic separation.[54]

By Denzin's count, Hollywood produced over 1,200 films between 1900 and 1995 involving voyeuristic activities by one or more of the main characters. Voyeurs in film often take the role, Denzin suggests, of journalists, spies, sexual perverts, and psychoanalysts, among others. Alfred Hitchcock, Denzin observes, is the "voyeur's director," and he cites a bevy of voyeuristic Hitchcock films, from *The Man Who Knew Too Much* to *Rear Window,* which Denzin calls an ode to voyeurism.[55]

In *Rear Window,* Jimmy Stewart plays a photographer, Jeff, who observes from the vantage point of his apartment window the goings on across a courtyard in another apartment building. In doing so, Jeff ultimately solves a murder. Along the way, Jeff is specifically called a Peeping Tom, a reference to the Lady Godiva story referred to earlier. The very title of the movie, Denzin suggests, "asks the viewer to appropriate the identity of the voyeur."[56]

Perhaps in a tribute to our love of this voyeuristic film or possibly because of our voyeuristic curiosity to watch a famous leading man now confined to a wheelchair and life-sustaining breathing apparatus, the Hitchcock classic was remade in 1998 into a television movie starring Christopher Reeve. Our former *Superman* Reeve is turned into a supervoyeur. As discussed in the Introduction to this book, voyeurism in film was taken to new levels in 1998 with *The Truman Show* and then again in 1999 with *EDtv,* in which individuals' entire lives are lived on camera for the world to watch. It is worth noting here that this scenario is not too far from a dream of Allen Funt, founder of the *Candid Camera* show described above. Funt wrote in 1952, "Someday we want to make a photograph of the way a man spends his entire working day—every public minute of it. This may not be great entertainment, but it certainly should have a place in the time capsule of this civilization."[57]

Voyeurism in the modern horror film genre is common. As Isabel Cristina Pinedo writes in *Recreational Terror,* horror movies often employ "a series of voyeuristic shots, either tracking or stationary, taken from assorted angles and points in narrative space, and placed behind a window, doorway, or other framing device to create the keyhole effect of surveillance by an unseen or partially seen other."[58] The monster or murderer is off-screen, watching from a distance. It is the "inability to see what is not shown [that] heightens the power of the image to horrify," writes Pinedo.[59]

Peeping Tom, in fact, would turn out to be the name of the one of the most controversial horror films ever made.[60] Not surprising, the protagonist of this 1960 release by Michael Powell uses a camera equipped with a hidden knife to capture the moment of death of his victims. The gazing at the morbid—the voyeurism that occurs in watching death and capturing it on camera—suggests quite literally that looks can kill. The voyeurism portrayed in this film is of the sexual perversion variety that ultimately results in crime, in contrast to Jimmy Stewart's use of voyeurism as a crime-solving tool in *Rear Window*.

As this brief history illustrates, mediated voyeurism exists in many varieties and media. This book focuses on the reality-based, electronic voyeurism of today and, in particular, on the video vérité and show-all/tell-all varieties defined in the Introduction. A concept closely related to and often prevalent in some of this reality-based voyeurism today is exhibitionism. It is discussed in the next section.

Letting It All Hang Out:
Exhibitionism and Mediated Voyeurism

Exhibitionism, as defined in *Webster's Ninth New Collegiate Dictionary,* is in part "the act or practice of behaving so as to attract attention to oneself."[61] It is also "a perversion marked by a tendency to indecent exposure."

Exhibitionism, under these definitions, clearly is present in some of the voyeuristic content that we watch today. Tell-all television talk shows like *The Jerry Springer Show* and *Ricki* feature guests who routinely make revelations about their private lives that titillate or infuriate both the studio audience and the audience of voyeurs watching at home. The guests behave so as to attract attention to themselves, and, in particular, in a manner that many would find to be indecent exposure in a mediated public venue. The social forces that drive this exhibitionism-in-service-of-voyeurism are described in more detail in Chapter 2.

Shows like *Cops* at first appear to lack exhibitionism. The suspects busted on camera did not volunteer to be arrested or searched. They did not know before the moment of arrest or interrogation that they would be taped during those moments. Exhibitionism thus appears absent from *Cops* and its kin such as the now-defunct *Real Stories of the Highway Patrol*. On closer inspection, however, *Cops* is a model of exhibitionism-in-service-of-voyeurism. The exhibitionists are the law enforcement officials who agree in the first place to allow the media to ride along with them while on duty. The hope is clear—to call public attention to the exploits of law enforcement personnel and agencies. Viewers of *Cops* come to expect to see the bad guy nabbed. The foibles of law enforcement are not the focus of this show.

Not all vérité videotape voyeurism involves exhibitionism. Shows such as *World's Most Amazing Videos* catch on tape shocking moments that no one who actually appears on tape could have expected. The pregnant woman who leaps from the burning building is not an exhibitionist. The cheating spouses are certainly not exhibitionists. These individuals are the unwitting subjects of our voyeurism.

On the World Wide Web, some of the voyeurism involves blatant exhibitionism, and some focuses on subjects photographed without their knowledge. Into the exhibitionism category falls

Jennifer Ringley, a twenty-something graduate of Dickinson College in sleepy Carlisle, Pennsylvania. Ringley currently has cameras attached to computers in both the bedroom and the office of her Washington, D.C., apartment, from where she does freelance web design projects. The cameras take pictures around the clock—a MacWebCam takes one new picture every minute—except when Ringley has camera-shy friends over to her place. Even when she is not home, the camera takes pictures that appear on her web page.

Ringley has no fear that any of this invades her privacy. As she writes in the Frequently Asked Questions (FAQ) section of her web page, "I don't feel I'm giving up my privacy. Just because people can see me doesn't mean it affects me—I'm still alone in my room, no matter what. And as long as what goes on in my head is still private, I have all the space I need."[62] In a demonstration of exhibitionism, she writes, "I never feel a need to hide anything going on anyway."

Ringley's statements raise important questions about the social forces that drive the voyeurism value, including issues about the concepts of privacy and individualism that are central to American culture. Our desire to watch and the willingness of others to be watched suggests that notions of privacy are shifting and that our sense of individualism is in a state of decline as we desire to live our lives "watched" by others. Our sense of self is fulfilled by others watching our actions. The social forces that drive the voyeurism value are explored in Chapter 2.

Consider another example of web-based exhibitionism that allows the audience to play the role of mediated voyeur. It is a site appropriately called Voyeur Dorm.[63] In this corner of cyberspace, a collection of young women live together in a house loaded with cameras. As the site's own home page describes it, Voyeur Dorm provides a chance to "peer into the lives of seven real college coeds" and there "are no taboos. The girls of Voyeur Dorm are fresh, naturally erotic, and as young as 18."[64] All of their actions, including intimate ones, are captured by the cameras. The women know they are being watched—they are exhibitionists.

Voyeur Dorm proved popular and profitable in 1999. It reportedly had about 5,000 subscribers, each paying thirty-four dollars each month.[65] Apparently the subscribers did not mind, according to one report, that only three of the seven women who lived in the house/dorm were really college coeds.[66] Unfortunately for its fans, however, Voyeur Dorm was declared a sexually oriented business by the Tampa City Council.[67] The problem? The house was located in an area zoned exclusively for residential property, and the council's decision jeopardized its future as a business.[68]

In contrast to Ringley's site and that of Voyeur Dorm, much of the voyeurism on the web involves sites that feature pornographic hidden camera photographs of women and men in various stages of undress or sexual activity. These unsuspecting individuals, some caught by a hidden camera in the shower or changing room and others in the bedroom or tanning booth, are certainly not exhibitionists. Voyeuristic "upskirt" pages likewise feature photographs taken by tiny cameras placed in shopping bags at mall stores. As the term upskirt suggests, photographers strategically drop camera-carrying shopping bags immediately next to women wearing short skirts, hoping to capture images of their underwear. The women whose undergarments are exposed are decidedly *non*exhibitionist. They do not know they are being watched. As Chapter 6 suggests, laws are springing up across the country that criminalize such video voyeurism. In the meantime, pornographic voyeurism sites that capture decidedly nonexhibitionist individuals are plentiful on the web.

In summary, exhibitionism is present in much, but certainly not all, of the voyeuristic media content that we devour today. In the next section, the terms voyeurism and exhibitionism are examined from the psychological perspective of sexual deviance. Although the generic definition of voyeurism used in this book is different from the definition set forth below, the fact that voyeurism is considered a deviant behavior perhaps in some way explains our current fascination with seeing others' lives unravel on tape.

The Dark Side of Looking: Voyeurism As Sexual Deviance

Voyeurism may be thought of as a sexual disorder or form of sexual deviance. Sigmund Freud, in an essay on sexual aberrations, wrote that the

> pleasure in looking [scopophilia] becomes a perversion (a) if it is restricted exclusively to the genitals, or (b) if it is connected with the overriding of disgust (as in the case of *voyeurs* or people who look at excretory functions), or (c) if, instead of being preparatory to the normal sexual aim, it supplants it.[69]

The fourth edition of the *Diagnostic and Statistical Manual of Mental Disorders* (DSM-IV) defines voyeurism as a sexual disorder, or paraphilia, that "involves the act of observing unsuspecting individuals, usually strangers, who are naked, in the process of disrobing, or engaging in sexual activity. The act of looking ("peeping") is for the purpose of achieving sexual excitement, and generally no sexual activity with the observed person is sought."[70] Diagnostic criteria include both recurrent behavior of the kind described above over a six-month period coupled with intense sexually arousing fantasies or sexual urges, as well as significant distress or impairment in one's social, occupational, or other important areas of functioning caused by the fantasies, urges, or behavior.

This definition of voyeurism is inapplicable for much of the mediated voyeurism on television newsmagazines and reality-based shows. The bulk of our broadcast voyeurism is nonsexual and has nothing to do with observing unsuspecting people in a state of nakedness. On reality television shows like *Cops,* we observe unsuspecting people in a state of *distress* rather than a state of *undress.* They are in a state of distress as they are chased, arrested, or interrogated by law enforcement officials. Likewise, on shows such as *World's Most Amazing Videos,* we observe individuals in a state of distress. The March 17, 1999, episode of this NBC program featured a airplane wing walker in a state of distress when he slips during a stunt exhibition and is dragged by his safety cable with, as the NBC web page description of the show put it, "only one chance to survive." The same episode also featured a woman visiting an Alaskan zoo in a state of visible distress as she is grabbed through the bars of a pen by a polar bear.

On the other hand, some of our mediated voyeurism carries distinctly sexual overtones. As described above, we can hear Monica Lewinsky on *20/20* describing sexual acts with the President of the United States. Newsmagazines have focused on the effects of Viagra, the erectile dysfunction wonder drug, not only on men but on women. On tell-all talk shows, guests frequently describe their sexual proclivities, exploits, and conquests. One recent study of eleven different talk programs, including those hosted by Jerry Springer, Jenny Jones, and Ricki Lake, found that sexual activity was a major issue on 36 percent of the episodes studied, sexual infidelity on 21 percent, and sexual orientation on 12 percent.[71]

On the World Wide Web, of course, much of the mediated voyeurism that can be found simply by going to a search engine such as Excite or Lycos and typing in the word "voyeurism" appears to be fodder for individuals who may be subject to the sexual disorder of voyeurism. Multiple sites are stocked with pictures of unsuspecting women undressing or showering or even engaged in sexual activities with their partners. One such site, available in May 2000, from which such voyeuristic images could be downloaded at no cost was The VoyeurWeb at http://www.voyeurweb.com. The pictures are sometimes taken through windows or through hidden cameras placed inside gym bags in women's locker rooms. In these voyeurism sites are further levels of sexual, voyeuristic fetishes—pictures of unsuspecting women taken while they sit on a toilet, pictures of women's underwear shot from underneath their skirts (so-called upskirt voyeurism), and pictures taken from above women looking down their blouses ("downblouse" voyeurism). Women, however, are not the only targets of this sexual voyeurism on the Internet.

In April 1999, the *Philadelphia Inquirer* published a story that hidden camera videotapes showing members of the University of Pennsylvania men's wrestling team changing and showering in locker rooms at Northwestern University and Penn were displayed as pornography on the Internet.[72] One tape probably was made with a hidden camera placed in a gym bag that featured a mesh opening. The videotapes were sold on a web site called "Young Studs Online" that boasts "the Internet's largest collection on the web of hidden camera locker room photos!"

Unlike the wrestling videos, some of the sexual voyeurism on the web happens by accident. In March 1999, the sexual and medical histories of a psychiatrist's patients were posted on a public Internet site due to a computer glitch.[73] The psychiatrist, a certified sex therapist from Indianapolis, Indiana, engaged in the on-line treatment of sexual dysfunction, suspects a computer hacker gained access to the server he was using to gain access to the files. All in all and whatever the cause may have been, the intimate details of the sex lives of some ninety patients were exposed on the Internet in this one incident. The doctor's web page administrator said the information could have been posted for months before it was discovered by newspaper reporters who were researching an article about computer security.

Although much of our mediated voyeurism today on television does not fit the definition of voyeurism as a sexual disorder, it is important to keep this "deviant" definition in mind. Why? It suggests that there are some forms of "looking" or "watching" that are not appropriate and that fall outside the boundary of acceptable conduct. It implies that there may be some socially or perhaps legally imposed limitations on the images of others that we should watch, be they on television or the World Wide Web. This, in turn, forces us to confront the issue of whether our own societal definitions of what mediated content is or is not permissible to view have changed over time.

Subsequent chapters in this book consider the social and legal forces that suggest that limitations on "inappropriate" lookings have indeed changed and loosened or relaxed today. Although these forces have made looking and watching others' lives easier, there still exist limitations on how far the law is willing to protect our right to look. By placing legal limits on our right to look at and to gather images of others, society implicitly deems some forms of looking deviant or not appropriate. That is why it is important throughout this book to keep in mind that voyeurism can indeed be classified as a type of disorder or deviant watching of others.

As noted earlier in the chapter, the concept of exhibitionism often is linked with mediated voyeurism today. The tell-all talk show guests who willingly expose their sexual predilections are exhibitionists, as are the law enforcement officials on *Cops* who agree to have their exploits captured on tape for the rest of the world to see. These exhibitionists must be distinguished from those who suffer from exhibitionism as a type of sexual disorder. The fourth edition of the *Diagnostic and Statistical Manual of Mental Disorders* makes it clear that the paraphiliac focus of exhibitionism "involves the exposure of one's genitals to a stranger." Such behavior easily can be located on the World Wide Web by typing the word "exhibitionist" into a search engine. Many voyeurism sites feature separate sections devoted to exhibitionists, such as women pulling up their dresses or taking down their tops for the camera.

Before moving on to explore the social forces that drive the voyeurism in the new millennium, it may be helpful to consider two related concepts from film and cultural studies—gaze and spectatorship—that relate to the topic of media voyeurism. Those concepts are described in the next section.

In Your Eyes: Gaze and Spectatorship

The concept of gaze is a major area of study in film criticism. It often focuses on examining which characters on screen have the privilege and the power of doing the gazing—the looking—and which characters are the object or spectacle of that gaze. A feminist, critical critique argues that more often than not the male gaze—the male holding the power of looking at and defining women as spectacles or objects to be stared at—dominates movies. It is the male who enjoys the pleasure of spectating and the woman who is looked at, as Laura Mulvey considers it in her essay "Visual Pleasure and Narrative Cinema." This perspective allows the male to construct female identity and sexuality. In the audience, we are spectators who also look or gaze, and our gaze is from the perspective of the individual on screen who does the looking.

The notion that there is or may be power and privilege in looking and spectating is important. It suggests, as is explored in more detail in Chapter 2, that part of our voyeuristic fascination with watching others relates to a sensation of power that we possess by watching them. This may be one of the social forces driving mediated voyeurism today. With that in mind, let us turn to Chapter 2 to unpack the multiple social and psychological motivations that, in part, give rise to the emergence of a culture of mediated voyeurism.

The Social Forces Driving Mediated Voyeurism

In the world of television everything is everyone's business and the viewers are curious, invisible, silent third-party voyeurs peeking into other peoples' lives.
—Robert Abelman, *Reaching A Critical Mass,* 1998

The communications scholar and popular culture pundit Robert Abelman's cogent comment reflects well the relationship today between voyeurism and television viewing. Another observation by Abelman on the voyeuristic nature of television viewing also is on point—"On television, the private sphere of intimate relations, personal problems, illicit and illegal acts, embarrassing behavior, and confidential activities remain magically open to the viewer."[1]

Abelman's remarks raise numerous and important questions about our desire to play the role of mediated voyeur at a time when shows such as *The Real World, Survivor,* and *Big Brother* proliferate. Why are we fascinated today with reality-based, mediated voyeurism? What is its appeal? What are the forces that drive it to the forefront of our mediated culture?

There are, of course, no simple answers to these questions. The forces that propel mediated voyeurism are multiple and complex. They include social, economic, political, technological, and legal factors. This chapter explores the social forces that suggest reasons why we are so attracted to mediated voyeurism. As will become clear, there also is not a single social force at the heart of our urge to watch others' lives on television or the World Wide Web. Instead, there is a multitude of social forces—some overlapping, others distinct—that explain why we watch the different forms of mediated voyeurism described in the Introduction and in Chapter 1.

Why We Watch:
Media Uses and Gratifications

In the academic discipline of media studies, one area or focus of study is known as *uses and gratifications* research. This approach differs from the traditional study of media messages in an important way. Typically, communications researchers study the impact or effect of media messages on members of an audience. For instance, one might study whether viewing a violent television program such as Chuck Norris's *Walker Texas Ranger* increases one's propensity to commit acts of violence or whether watching a pornographic video or reading a magazine like Larry Flynt's *Hustler* causes men to treat women as sex objects or to aggress against them.

Uses and gratifications research, however, takes the opposite approach. It focuses not on what messages do to people, but instead on how people use and select messages. This approach, as the San Jose State University communications professor Stanley Baran points out, emphasizes audience members' motives for making specific media consumption choices and the consequences of those intentional, deliberate choices.[2] Communications researchers have suggested that people choose to attend to media messages for a number of reasons.

For instance, people may watch television situation comedies such as *Friends* or *Frasier* as a form of entertainment to escape, even if just temporarily, from their problems in the real world or to put them in a good mood. This function of a television program sometimes is referred to as a *diversion* use of the media. It may be that we watch the sensationalistic video vérité voyeurism of *World's Most Amazing Videos* for precisely this reason—to be entertained by others' misfortunes and to laugh at their expense. It also may be the reason we watch the tell-all voyeurism of *The Jerry Springer Show*—to escape from our own problems and to revel in others' predicaments.

Alternatively, people may attend to media messages for more cerebral or cognitive reasons. They may want to acquire information about the stock market from a newspaper to make sound investment decisions. They may want to learn what the weather will be like tomorrow so they can dress appropriately. These instrumental uses sometimes are referred to as *surveillance* functions of the media because we use the media as a type of surveillance tool to gain information about the world. We may engage in the voyeurism of Court TV, for instance, to learn about how the legal system works, just in case we are ever caught in its trap. We may partake in the video voyeurism of watching *Cops* to learn about both the world and the work of law enforcement personnel.

In addition, people may watch media messages for the social utility those messages carry. Individuals who watch the same television show on Monday night find they have something in common to talk about on Tuesday morning at work. The television show helps to sustain a sense of community, create a topic for shared conversation, and provide a mechanism for bonding and friendship. Thus people who separately watch the same hidden camera report on an episode of *Dateline* can talk about that together and share their feelings on the subject. Viewing television may also play a social function as a companion to occupy time and to fill the silence in one's life when no one else is around. The characters on the screen simultaneously disrupt the quiet and provide companionship and parasocial interaction to dissipate the loneliness. With programs such as *The Real World* and *Survivor,* we may find ourselves relating to particular individuals.

Finally, watching television or reading a newspaper may help to shape a person's sense of self, or individual identity. We may watch television to learn values and self-understanding or, alternatively, to reinforce or solidify our preexisting values.[3]

In summary, people may have very different motives for attending to or watching different media messages. The motives may even overlap when we watch a given television program. For instance, one may watch an episode of *Dateline* not only to learn about a new medical procedure described by the physician Bob Arnott, the newsmagazine's medical correspondent, but also to relax from the stresses of the workday by engaging in the essentially passive activity of television viewing. Likewise, one may watch *World's Most Amazing Videos* not only to be entertained or to laugh but also to gain a point of common reference or conversation with others who watch the show. Given these various functions of media use, the remainder of Chapter 2 suggests a number of different motives people may have for engaging in a specific activity—voyeuristic media consumption.

Searching for Truth and Reality

The popular Fox television series *The X Files* admonishes viewers that "the truth is out there." Although viewers of science fiction shows that target the reality challenged may believe that the truth lies in outer space or in a top secret, sealed government file on UFOs, viewers of reality-based voyeurism instead may believe that the truth is out there—on television and the Internet—on videotape.

The wave of mass-produced, technologized images that flood the modern mind in our image-immersed culture often cause people to "feel themselves teetering between a world of reality and a world of imitation and illusion."[4] So much, after all, is staged for the camera today. From the photo opportunities carefully crafted on behalf of politicians to the bulk of television entertainment fare that is created on soundstages and back lots in Southern California, there appears to be much in the media that is fiction and little that represents reality or the truth.

Truth, of course, is an extremely elusive concept. To understand the slippery and subjective nature of truth one need look no further than to President Clinton's claims to be telling the truth during his deposition in the Paula Jones sexual harassment case and again during his finger-pointing press conference performance in which he denied having sex with "that woman . . . Miss Lewinsky." Was President Clinton telling the truth? Or to paraphrase Clinton's statement during his taped grand jury testimony that the veracity of his responses depended on the meaning of the word "is," does it depend on what the meaning of truth is?

The quest for the meaning of truth or what the truth is is far from a new phenomenon. The philosopher Sissela Bok writes in her book *Lying,* "From the beginnings of human speculation about the world, the questions of what truth is and whether we can attain it have loomed large. Every philosopher has had to grapple with them. Every religion seeks to answer them."[5] Maybe it is even correct, as Bok suggests, that "the whole truth *is* out of reach."[6]

Despite the illusive nature of truth, the media often do purport to convey it to the public. Telling the truth, after all, is one of the bedrock principles of journalism as it is preached and practiced in the United States. For instance, the most recent revision of the ethics code adopted by one of the country's most important and influential journalism organizations, the Society of Professional Journalists, admonishes journalists to seek the truth and to report it.[7] Indeed, the University of Illinois professor Clifford Christians and his colleagues write, "The press's obligation to print the truth is a standard part of its rhetoric."[8] Journalists thus claim to convey only the facts and to do so in an objective, detached, and impartial manner.

But as the communications professors James Ettema and Theodore Glasser write in their recent critique of investigative journalism, "The separation of fact and value is inevitably breached by all but the most elementary and isolated bits of information about the social world."[9] Despite this, they contend that journalists often speak of truth "in the form of the one and only account that corresponds to the things and events of a determinate world, an account free of individual interest, social value, and even language itself."[10]

The standard definition of truth in journalism tends to take a naïve form of realism, in which truth is viewed as a one-to-one correspondence between what a reporter writes and what really happened. Truth, at least in this light, is akin to accuracy—a story is "true" if the journalist accurately reported what the source said. As Jeremy Iggers of the *Minneapolis–St. Paul Star Tribune* writes in *Good News, Bad News,* the commitment to a correspondence theory of the truth suggests that journalists must paint a picture of the world that corresponds to a set of facts that exist independently of the journalist.[11]

Perhaps because we recognize that journalists in fact construct or create a particular version of the truth with the words they choose to use and the sources they choose to quote, we are not always satisfied today that the news, as it is reported, is in fact a representation of the truth. Or perhaps our dissatisfaction arises from our recognition that journalistic facts are, as Carlin Romano of the *Philadelphia Inquirer* once put it, little more than assertions with visiting rights.[12] Alternatively, it may be that we recognize that what passes for news today often is little more than infotainment, slickly packaged to reach a large audience, not to inform the public or give us the truth, as Chapter 3 suggests. In brief, even if the truth is out there, as *X-Files* fanatics would have it, there is little reason to believe that journalists today give it to us.

Perhaps this is why we turn away from journalism and toward reality-based, mediated voyeurism—to give us the truth about what takes place in a mediated world. Shows that feature unscripted, unstaged videotape—be it the hidden camera work of investigative reporting on television newsmagazines like *60 Minutes II* or the ride-along camera work of crime shows like *Cops*—offer viewers a glimpse at what *appears* to be the truth. The shows make it appear as if a camera or video recorder is an objective observer, free from the interference of a human hand, in the tradition of cinema vérité documentaries. The pictures tell the story, not the journalist. The shows, after all, are frequently referred to as reality television—they claim to represent reality. The title of one program is even *Real TV*. If the cliché that a picture is worth a thousand words is at all accurate, then it must be exponentially valid for the multiple frames of videotape featured on these shows. The proof and verification of what life is like—what takes place in lives and locations other than our own—is captured by the camera for us to watch.

That, at least, is the theory. Much of the mediated voyeurism—even that in the vérité video genre described in the Introduction—does *not* reflect or correspond with reality, even if one adopts that as a definition of the truth. Mary Beth Oliver, a professor of communications at Pennsylvania State University, for instance, reports that reality-based crime programs overrepresent the occurrence of violent crime.[13] They also overrepresent the extent to which police officers succeed in capturing criminals. She further contends that reality-based shows tend to cast the majority of African Americans and Hispanics as criminal suspects rather than police officers, but cast the majority of Caucasians as police officers rather than criminal suspects.

Cops may also present a skewed picture of the truth about crime because the locations that tend to be showcased are predominantly lower class. "Wealthy areas, while often host to the same domestic abuse and robbery problems that make up the program's stable of policing situations, are disdained as not crime-ridden enough," writes the sociologist Aaron Doyle in a study of *Cops*.[14]

In addition to doubts that shows like *Cops* tell the truth, the hidden camera investigations of newsmagazines that purport to show the truth about conditions in everything from grocery stores to nursing homes cannot be trusted to convey the truth. For instance, when ABC's *PrimeTime Live* broadcast an exposé with hidden camera footage depicting allegedly unsanitary food-handling practices at the Food Lion grocery chain in November 1992, the show's producers subjectively and selectively chose a total of about ten minutes of videotape to illustrate its story. In fact, ABC employees had about forty-five hours of hidden camera videotape from which to choose those ten minutes. In other words, 10 minutes of 2,700 minutes—less than one half of one percent—was used. What is left on the cutting room floor may also be the truth, but it does not make it onto television to tell a more complete version of the truth. This is not surprising for videotape voyeurism. It will be recalled from Chapter 1 that the 1998–1999 season of *The Real World* in Seattle, Washington, on MTV featured eighteen half-hour episodes culled from a reported 1,894 hours of videotape.

Tell-all talk shows such as those hosted by Jerry Springer and Ricki Lake allow us to dip voyeuristically into the sordid, private details of others' lives. Yet whether these shows in fact convey the "truth" about real people is sometimes suspect. Allegations that the fights and arguments between guests—more accurately, perhaps, combatants—on *The Jerry Springer Show* are staged have floated for a long time.[15] The shows are also criticized for sometimes letting individuals get on television who fake or make up their stories. For instance, on the *Ricki* show in 1993 one guest claimed to have AIDS and told Ricki Lake and an audience of voyeurs that she tried to have unprotected sex with as many people as possible before she died so that they too could die. A few days later, it turned out she made up her story just to get on television.[16]

As with *Cops,* the topics and people chosen for discussion on the tell-all talk shows also may not represent reality, because some subjects or individuals are overrepresented and others are ignored. As Vicki Abt and Leonard Mustazza, American Studies scholars at Pennsylvania State University, write in their recent book *Coming After Oprah: Cultural Fallout in the Age of the TV Talk Show,*

> Talk shows give us glimpses of what are purported to be real people with representative problems from which we can learn to live our own lives. But if an episode of Ricki Lake's show, say, were to be placed into a time capsule and discovered in a millennium, would it be anything but a grossly distorted reflection of American social reality in the 1990s?[17]

Despite this criticism, it appears that one social force driving the voyeurism of tell-all talk shows *is* the fact that the guests are real people with what appear to be real problems—they are not movie stars. Some members of the audience may be able to relate to the people they watch on talk shows and to the stories those people tell. The real experiences faced by others may help those in the audience to better understand their own life situations. There is a certain authenticity and reality, then, that may attract some in the audience to watch these shows.

In summary, we may turn to mediated voyeurism for truth and reality. It should be clear, however, that this is not necessarily the end result of watching so-called reality television and voyeuristic tell-all talk shows. Despite this fact, our age-old fascination with and quest for the truth described earlier by Sissela Bok, when coupled with the *perception* that shows such as *Cops* and *Dateline* bring us the unadulterated truth, may be one of the driving forces that attracts us today to the plethora of voyeuristic media content.

Fighting Bulls:
The Moment of Truth and Reckoning

Much of the writing of Ernest Hemingway—*Death in the Afternoon, The Short Happy Life of Francis Macomber,* for example—involves individuals who face a test of their mettle, a moment of truth or reckoning. They may founder and so reveal their cowardice or they may flourish and so reveal their courage and grace under pressure.

The chance to observe real people as they face their moments of reckoning may be one point of appeal of some varieties of video voyeurism on television. The on-line promotional literature for NBC's *World's Most Amazing Videos* suggests this opportunity is, at the very least, a selling point for that series. The show "presents interviews with people who find themselves facing the most terrifying, pulse-pounding moments in their lives—including those behind the camera. . . . Each week highlights over a dozen tales of intriguing true-life experiences ranging from humorous to frightening—but always amazing."[18]

As we watch these people confront these "pulse-pounding" moments—a pilot about to crash his fighter plane at an air show ejects with just seconds to spare—we are allowed not only to view their responses but to speculate about our own. A sense of "it could happen to me" among audience members leads, in turn, to speculation about "What if it really did happen to me?" How would we react if we were put in that same situation? What would we do if we were confronted with the danger faced by those unfortunate individuals caught on videotape? To paraphrase Jack Nicholson's tyrannical Colonel Nathan Jessup in the movie *A Few Good Men,* would we be able to handle the moment of truth?

The same "moment of truth" attraction that applies to *World's Most Amazing Videos* applies to a large number of the medical segments featured on television newsmagazines. These segments often follow individuals as they undergo a new or dangerous medical procedure. Would we also undergo a risky, experimental treatment? How would we handle a life-threatening illness? Will we learn from watching others' actions and model our own behavior on theirs someday if we face a similar predicament?

The Learning Channel's series called *The Operation* fits this voyeuristic, moment-of-truth format. The camera follows individuals and their families as they meet with doctors, undergo surgery and invasive medical procedures, and ultimately recuperate. As we watch these people in their moment of medical crisis, we speculate on how we would react to the traumatic conditions faced by the individuals caught on camera.

Like video vérité voyeurism, the voyeurism of tell-all talk shows also plays to the "moment of truth" attraction. A common technique that embodies this concept is the so-called ambush episode in which one guest surprises and confronts another with a startling revelation or announcement that previously had been kept secret. A woman tells her man that she has been cheating on him. A daughter tells her mother she is working as a prostitute. We get to see how the person who is surprised handles the moment. How will the person react? Calm and collected? Upset and outraged?

A classic example of the ambush technique in which a guest failed to exhibit grace under pressure involved an unaired but now infamous 1995 episode of *The Jenny Jones Show*. On that segment, a thirty-two-year-old gay man named Scott Amedure revealed to Jones and the studio audience his crush on Jonathan Schmitz. Three days after the taping, Schmitz shot and killed Amedure. In May 1999, *The Jenny Jones Show* was held civilly liable to the tune of $25 million for Amedure's death.[19] Schmitz clearly could not handle the made-for-television moment of reckoning.

At a larger level, then, it is a quest for meaning in our mediated lives that is found in the moment of reckoning that attracts us, at least in part, to watch others' real lives unfold on camera. Viktor Frankl, who faced his own moment of truth when he survived three years at Auschwitz and Dachau, wrote that the most basic human need is the need to find and fulfill a meaning in our lives.[20] For Frankl, the most important avenue of finding meaning is "facing a fate we cannot change." In these situations, "we are called upon to make the best of it by rising above ourselves and growing beyond ourselves, in a word, by changing ourselves."[21]

Watching others face the moment in which they find meaning or truth may be one of the appeals of video voyeurism. We consume so much media fare today that we have little opportunity in our own lives to face the type of challenges that give meaning to one's life. We can, however, try to identify with or put ourselves in the place of those who face such challenges on television. We can speculate on what we would do in similar circumstances. We can learn from their reactions what we would or would not want to do. Would we be brave and survive? Would we falter and fail? As voyeurs, we can watch and think about these questions safely, since we are not actually in the same place. For instance, we might wonder how we would survive on a remote island with over a dozen strangers. That may be part of the allure of the CBS program *Survivor,* which debuted in summer 2000 and featured precisely this contrived voyeuristic spectacle. Would we survive the physical and psychological hardships of such a situation?

The Quest for Justice and Reinforcement of Societal Norms

One social force driving mediated voyeurism may be our pursuit to, quite literally, see justice occur in what some perceive to be an unjust society. On *Cops,* the good guys almost always win, and the bad guys almost always lose. The moral order is reinforced and we can sleep safely, knowing that the police are out there, protecting and serving the law-abiding citizens. In a society that fears violence—this despite government data that show many forms of violent crime have decreased steadily since the early 1990s[22]—some people may engage in video voyeurism precisely to achieve the feeling that justice can and does in fact occur.

Research conducted by Mary Beth Oliver of Pennsylvania State University suggests that the concept of authoritarianism is positively related and significantly associated with viewer enjoyment of reality-based television shows, including *Cops, Top Cops,* and *America's Most Wanted*.[23] In brief, the more authoritarian an individual is, the more likely he or she is to enjoy these shows.

Authoritarianism, which is defined in part by social scientists as a person's willingness to submit to authority and to adhere to social conventions, also is associated with greater punitiveness toward criminals and greater admiration of law enforcement officials. In one study, Oliver and a colleague "found that reality-based programs were most enjoyed by viewers who evidenced higher levels of authoritarianism, reported greater punitiveness about crime, and reported higher levels of racial prejudice."[24]

This last finding is most striking and, more important, most disturbing. It suggests that racism, in part, fuels the desire of some people to watch crime-based video voyeurism on television. One experiment that Oliver conducted involved white undergraduate students who watched actual segments from the television show *Cops.* Some students watched a segment in which the suspect was black. Other students watched a segment in which the suspect was white. The study found that authoritarianism was unrelated to enjoyment of the segments featuring white criminal suspects *but* was positively and significantly associated with greater enjoyment of the videos featuring black suspects.

The professors Gray Cavender and Mark Fishman observe that reality-based crime programs "are informed by the conservative ideologies that support current crime policies. Crime is seen as a serious problem, and longer prison sentences, not probation and parole, are offered as the solution."[25] Shows like *Cops,* in turn, suggest that a law-and-order ideology can be reconstructed—by making a spectacle of the criminal and allowing the audience to share the point of view of law enforcement officials.

In a nutshell, one social force driving video voyeurism on shows like *Cops* may be the need some people feel to see that justice is carried out and that laws are enforced. Racism, in turn, may partly fuel this desire.

But race probably does not play a role in all of our efforts to obtain what Norman Denzin calls "video justice."[26] So-called gotcha journalism, in which wrongdoers are captured on tape by hidden camera and then humiliated when confronted with the tape by an intrepid reporter, plays to our quest to see justice accomplished and good triumph over evil. Fox has aired a series of *Busted on the Job* television specials that cater to this interest. We love to see crooked repairpeople busted on tape, since many people feel at some time or another they have been ripped off by a less-than-honest auto mechanic or air-conditioning repairperson. This holds true independent of race. Ultimately, then, part of our fascination with reality-based, mediated voyeurism may be our desire to see the legal and moral order of society reinforced—to see justice prevail.

Ironically, however, some of the mediated voyeurism in which we partake is criticized for changing and redefining social norms rather than reinforcing the status quo. In particular, the voyeurism of the tell-all talk shows is charged with defining down deviance, with bringing beliefs, activities, and behaviors that were once abnormal or aberrant into the realm of social acceptability and the mainstream. The shows represent a very public place where what is normal and what is abnormal is contested and put to debate. As the Yale sociologist Joshua Gamson puts it in *Freaks Talk Back,* there is a certain amount of "normalization through freak show" that occurs on tell-all talk shows.[27]

In summary, some forms of mediated voyeurism—hidden camera footage of newsmagazines and video vérité voyeurism— may appeal to our desire to see justice occur and the norms of society reinforced. Somewhat paradoxically, however, the tell-all talk show variety of voyeurism may actually challenge society's norms about acceptable conduct and beliefs.

Knowledge and the Power of Watching

The cliché has it that knowledge is power. In the so-called information age, the knowledge that is gained from gazing at others' lives may provide us with a sense of power and control in our own lives. It will be recalled from Chapter 1 that Dorothy Kelly, in her analysis of voyeurism in the French novel, notes that the voyeur in literature, such as a lover or suitor, often spies on others to learn about them. This knowledge, in turn, leads to power in the relationship with that person spied on.

That the voyeur holds power over the observed individual should be clear. The voyeur is the taker of information, not the giver. The voyeur is able to learn about others' lives simply by watching them. There is no reciprocal responsibility placed on the voyeur in the watching process. No strings are attached to the receipt of knowledge. The feeling of power that accompanies the voyeur's privileged vantage point may be inherently rewarding. The voyeur knows something important that the individual being watched does not—that the individual is, in fact, being observed.

This type of reward may be the case with watching hidden camera reporting on television newsmagazines like *20/20* that catch people committing acts of fraud, such as repairpersons who do not repair the appliances they are sent to fix or auto mechanics who churn, or generate work for themselves by taking a minor problem and making it into a larger one. We see these duplicitous people but they do not know we are watching. They think they are pulling something over on us, but we know what they are up to. For a videotaped moment, at least, we are put in the privileged, powerful position of watching them.

The knowledge that we glean from watching, in turn, leads to the exposure of their practices and gives us power over their future. The fraudulent repairman, for instance, may be turned in to the police or, in line with the thrill of video justice described in the previous section of this chapter, confronted directly by the reporter with the videotape evidence. Regardless of which option is chosen, our voyeurism ultimately leads to the subordination of these individuals and places us in a position of power above them.

Watching others' lives unfold before us may lead to power in several other ways besides the feeling of power just described that comes from knowledge that, so to speak, puts those being watched in their place. For instance, we may simply learn about other lifestyles or the decisions that other people make. This type of knowledge may give us the power and confidence to adopt those lifestyles ourselves or to reject them. A voyeuristic television newsmagazine report in 1999 on cross-dressing that showed individuals who were comfortable with their decision to cross-dress may have empowered others with latent but similar proclivities to engage in the same behavior. The individuals whose lives were portrayed may have become role models for some in the audience. In other words, people may watch the others on television, know that they are not alone, and then find the courage and power to act in the same way.

Alternatively, these shows may create a sense of power—in particular, a feeling of superiority—in individuals who find the people's lives that they are watching to be beneath them. Indeed, the tell-all talk shows appeal largely to the audience's sense of classism. The people being watched are outsiders or social misfits, and some members of the audience may feel a sense of superiority and power by believing that they are not in the same class or position as these people. Voyeurs in the audience may label the people as sideshow freaks and find feelings of power in being different from them. As Joshua Gamson writes, the tell-all talk shows use the "low-risk strategy of class voyeurism" by selecting guests "from the bottom of the social barrel."[28] The mediated voyeurs in the audience may take power from knowing that they are "normal," whereas those on the talk shows are "abnormal."

In brief, social comparisons through mediated voyeurism may help us understand our own place in society and, in particular, give us a sense of superiority to others. Social psychologists suggest that people often prefer to make what they call "downward comparisons"—favorable comparisons—to enhance or to protect their feelings of self-worth rather than upward comparisons that can lead to feelings of deprivation.[29] Indeed, social comparisons are considered by social psychologists to be "an important source of self-relevant information, and a key determinant of affect and self-esteem."[30] The psychology professors Constantine Sedikides and Michael J. Strube write that downward social comparison increases feelings of psychological adjustment, reduces feelings of being upset, and enhances feelings of self-esteem, particularly in people who are chronically low in self-esteem.[31]

The video voyeurism on *Cops,* in other words, may make us feel superior to those caught by the law. Watching a social outcast or misfit or someone with deep personal problems on *Jerry Springer* may make us feel superior to that person. As Vicki Abt and Leonard Mustazza observe, "trashy television talk programs" can be comforting to middle-class viewers because most of the guests are lower than they are on the social ladder. The middle-class "get to laugh and to feel better about their own class circumstances."[32]

The feeling of superiority or being better off that comes from watching others whom we deem worse off than ourselves may be one of the reasons behind one of the most basic forms of *nonmediated* voyeurism today—rubbernecking at accidents on highways. Nearly everyone these days slows down to gawk at accidents, even if the cars involved have long ago been cleared to the side of the road or highway. Troy Zimmer, a psychologist at California State University at Fullerton, observes, "People know they are vulnerable in life—illness, sickness, accidents or whatever—so when they run across situations like this, there is another unconscious psychological need to see something worse has happened to someone else. In a funny way, it gives us a lift."[33]

Before we leave this section, it must be remembered, of course, that the knowledge we gain from mediated voyeurism may not always be accurate. In the earlier discussion in this chapter about the quest for truth, it was noted that reality-based crime shows like *Cops* may cultivate a distorted picture or message about crime and criminal activity. This faulty knowledge, in turn, may perpetuate and confirm stereotypes about race and other important social concerns. At the same time, it is still possible that people may turn to mediated voyeurism to achieve knowledge and, concomitantly, power.

Being a Player: The Feeling of Action

One social force that may impact mediated voyeurism is the desire of people to feel that they are actively involved in the world around them. Watching and learning about others' real-life problems on a television newsmagazine, for instance, may give us the sense that, in some manner, we are helping them. Knowing about their problems makes us feel involved.

In fact, however, the opposite may be true. Communications researchers have identified a phenomenon that they call the "narcotizing dysfunction" of massive media consumption. The theory suggests that "the result of a flood of communications may be a superficial concern with problems and that this superficiality may cloak mass apathy. The interested and informed individual may know about the problems of society without recognizing that he or she has failed to make decisions and do something about them."[34]

Thus our attraction to mediated voyeurism may, in part, be due to our feeling that it makes us actively involved in the world. In reality, however, it is our voyeurism—our watching—that occurs and, in fact, it may hinder our action. It is much easier to watch, after all, than it is to act.

The Collapse of Conversation and
the Rise of the Image

One social force that drives mediated voyeurism is the displacement of the printed text with the image—in particular, the moving image—as the dominant mode of mass communication. The data bear this out: 98 percent of all households have television sets, and a television is on in the average household for over seven hours each day. In contrast, the number of daily newspapers, as well as newspaper readership and circulation, have declined over several decades, and today so-called Generation Xers are about a third less likely than Baby Boomers to read a newspaper every day.[35] In 1965, for instance, a Gallup poll indicated that in the age group of twenty-one to thirty-five years, 67 percent of those surveyed had read a daily newspaper the day before. In 1998, that percentage had been cut by more than half, down to just 31 percent.[36] Another 1998 Gallup poll revealed that people trust television news more than they do their local newspapers.[37] To paraphrase the tennis star Andre Agassi's one-time pitch for Nikon cameras, images are everything today.

It is a world in which, according to postmodern theorists such as Jean Baudrillard, the image has come to replace the real. It is a world in which the public often is unable to delineate image from reality.[38] Voyeurism, of course, is all about images—watching images of others—and, as mentioned earlier, perhaps a quest for reality and truth.

At the same time the image has risen, our capacity for conversation has fallen. It is a "here we are now, entertain us" world, as the late Kurt Cobain of the grunge rock band Nirvana once sang. We would rather watch and be entertained by communication than actively engage in it ourselves. As the law professors Ronald Collins and Daniel Skover write in *The Death of Discourse*, there is no escaping the fact that electronic visual entertainment is "an essential part of our modern culture of communication"[39] and enjoys "a dominant and almost unchallenged status in our society."[40]

Our quest for visual entertainment drives us toward voyeurism, the essence of image-based pleasure and entertainment that requires no reciprocal communication or feedback to the person observed. As Ellen Hume, executive director of the Democracy Project at the Public Broadcasting Service (PBS), observes, "The private eccentricities of ordinary citizens are revealed on *Oprah* and *PrimeTime Live*, where they become substitutes for real conversation about real problems. Instead of acting like a nation of citizens, we have become a *nation of voyeurs*."[41] In brief, conversation and reading are out; watching and enjoying are in.

Individualism, Hedonism, and Visual Pleasures

In his 1996 book *Slouching Towards Gomorrah*, the conservative legal scholar and onetime nominee for the United States Supreme Court Robert H. Bork launches a massive attack on modern liberalism. Part of that critique centers on what he claims is one of the defining characteristics of modern liberalism—something he calls *radical individualism*, which Bork defines as "the drastic reduction of limits to personal gratification."[42]

If this thesis is correct, then perhaps one of the social forces fueling voyeurism is that we are an increasingly hedonistic, self-absorbed society in which we get our pleasure from watching others' lives without having to interact with them. A sense of community obligation rather than individual gratification might promote active involvement with others rather than passively watching them as spectator sport. Voyeurism is an individual activity—it is personally gratifying to watch others and requires no sense of obligation to interact with them.

Bork makes precisely this point when he describes material—often sexually voyeuristic material—on the Internet: "The more private the viewing becomes, the more likely it is that salacious and perverted tastes will be indulged."[43] Voyeurism is private. We see others but they do not see us. Behind the computer screen, we can engage in visual pleasures and self-gratification without any compulsion for interaction. Much of the sexual voyeurism on the World Wide Web undoubtedly fits the definition of "salacious and perverted" as used by Bork.

There are hidden camera pictures of women as they urinate or sit on toilets. There are pictures looking up women's skirts, taken with video cameras placed in shopping bags at malls or in laundry baskets placed in their own bedrooms by boyfriends or husbands. There are pictures taken of women at the beach as they adjust their swimsuits. All of this is very voyeuristic and designed for the personal pleasure and individual gratification of the viewer.

At the same time, of course, there is very little, if any, concern in this type of voyeurism for the privacy of the person who is the focus on the camera's eye or gaze. The interests of the women captured on videotape for the voyeur's pleasure are ignored. The harms can be severe to the unsuspecting women on discovery of the covert taping.

Robert I. Simon, director of the program in psychiatry and law at the Georgetown University School of Medicine, writes in the *Journal of Forensic Sciences* that the "videotaping of an unsuspecting victim strikes at her core sense of safety and privacy."[44] The victim is usually "horrified, humiliated, mortified, and extremely fearful when discovering she has been covertly videotaped undressing, naked, or engaged in an intimate act."[45]

The victims, Simon adds, suffer harm to their trust of people and fear for their own personal safety and personal humiliation.

Rules of civility and respect for others' space embodied in conceptions of privacy thus are trampled for the individual gratification inherent in voyeurism. A greater sense of community, Bork might argue, would thwart such individual hedonism at the expense of others' privacy. As discussed later in this chapter, changing conceptions of privacy influence voyeurism. When lesser expectations of privacy are coupled with an increased desire for personal pleasure and gratification of the kind Bork describes, it may be that our voyeuristic tendencies are allowed to manifest in mass-mediated content.

Bork also discusses the tell-all television talk shows, and sees them as symptomatic of radical individualism and hedonism. As noted in the Introduction to this book, these tell-all/show-all programs are voyeuristic in nature. We often get to hear and witness sexually titillating, bizarre, or prurient information from others who are often unlike ourselves. And, for which most of us in the audience are quite thankful, we are allowed to eavesdrop on their lives without needing to meet or deal with them. We merely dip into their lives via television.

Bork describes an episode of a tell-all talk show hosted by Montel Williams. In this particular episode, the topic of so-called shore parties was examined. A shore party, as Bork describes it, apparently from watching Williams's show, is one in which "people take vacations, engage in as much random sex as possible, and keep the score on a paper fastened to a refrigerator door."[46] We in the audience are voyeurs—not only do the individuals who engage in shore parties satiate their own hedonistic instincts, but we in the audience take our own individual pleasure in listening to the tawdry details.

The absence of self-restraint on the part of the producers of tell-all talk shows like those hosted by Williams and Jerry Springer also fuels voyeurism. As the professors Vicki Abt and Leonard Mustazza write, "The general lack of restraint and responsibility highlighted on these shows seems matched by that of its producers and syndicators."[47] Viewed from this perspective, the individual self-gratification of the shows' producers—in the form of the profits and ratings that salacious and voyeuristic programming generate—entails a sacrifice of a larger sense of community and responsibility that might restrain the production and distribution of this media content. The economic incentives and forces driving mediated voyeurism are explored in more detail in Chapter 3.

The sense of group responsibility that is replaced by individual gratification finds a perfect outlet in television content. As Abt and Mustazza write, "Why bother with the responsibility of interacting with the real neighbors when you could safely watch them on TV? The activist was largely replaced in our consciousness by the 'couch potato' as national vision gave way to individual voyeurism."[48]

The right-wing individual gratification thesis would also suggest a reason for our acceptance and embracement of voyeuristic tell-all talk shows that often are criticized as trash and freak shows. Our hedonistic tendencies and our desire to be amused and entertained trump all concerns for respect of others and eventually erode standards of taste and morals. All restraint and concern is gone. Bork argues, "In keeping with the progress of liberalism, popular entertainment generally—and the worst of it in particular—celebrates the unconstrained self, and savages those who would constrain."[49]

All of this, of course, is part of the standard rhetoric of the media blame game. The media are constantly bashed for the harm they are alleged to cause to society and our values. It must be remembered, however, as Joshua Gamson keenly observes in his analysis of television talk shows, that one person's trash is another person's gold mine.[50]

In summary, a conservative critique of voyeuristic media content holds that the values of radical individualism and self-gratification that flourished and were embraced in the 1960s now influence our desire to participate in often-tasteless forms of gazing and watching on television and the Internet.

Turning Private into Public

One of the major social forces driving voyeurism is our changing conception of what information should remain closed and private and, concomitantly, what information should be made open and available to the public. As our expectations of privacy decrease, our expectations for receiving more information—our expectations about what is public—increase. Everything becomes fair game for our voyeuristic viewing pleasure. "As the information age enters a new millennium, there is a widespread assumption that nothing is out of bounds," writes Marc Sandalow in a weeklong *San Francisco Chronicle* series on the news media published in 1999.[51]

The President's sex life, for instance, now is fair game for the media, lowering our own expectations of privacy. The sex life of others in Congress, as Larry Flynt initially proved when he bought a full-page advertisement in the *Washington Post* in October 1998 asking for information on the affairs of politicians and then followed up in April 1999 with the publication of *The Flynt Report,* in which he dished up the dirt on right-wing politicos, also is not out of public bounds. As Chapters 3 and 5 suggest, changing journalistic and legal conceptions of what constitutes news—the President's sex life?—necessarily influence what information we as a society consider private. At this point, however, before considering the concepts of news and newsworthiness from a journalistic and legal perspective, it is important to focus on and to define privacy.

Privacy is a social construction—a concept created, maintained, and changed by members of society, including, most notably, journalists and others in the media. Our own definition of what information should be private will vary and change from time to time, pushed along by the media's actions in giving publicity to facts some would deem private. Likewise, conceptions of privacy will vary from place to place—different societies will have different expectations of privacy.

Privacy thus may be evaluated in terms of the power and ability of an individual to control the flow and dissemination of information about himself or herself. Sissela Bok, for instance, defines privacy "as the condition of being protected from unwanted access by others—either physical access, personal information, or attention. Claims to privacy are claims to control access to what one takes—however grandiosely—to be one's personal domain."[52] This is reflected in the sociologist Erving Goffman's concept of *information preserves,* in which people expect to control a set of facts about themselves.[53] In their seminal article on privacy in the *Harvard Law Review* more than 100 years ago, Samuel Warren and Louis Brandeis defined privacy as a personal "right to be let alone."[54] The concept of autonomy, reflected in the ability of an individual to make personal choices that affect his or her life, such as whether to have an abortion, are also reflected in legal conceptions of privacy. Privacy, in brief, involves related concepts of self, control, access, and information.

In our mediated society, we recognize that we have very little control over much information anymore. We know that the private marketers assemble vast data bases about our spending and purchasing habits. Tiny "cookies" are placed on our computers to track our movements on the World Wide Web. We also are well aware that the prying lenses of media cameras are everywhere, waiting to scoop up great visual images to put on the evening news. We know, as well, that surveillance cameras are omnipresent eyes, watching us as we move in clothing stores and as we remove cash at automated-teller bank machines. Surveillance cameras are perched on top of traffic lights in major cities to catch motorists as they blow through yellow lights turning red, and they are buried underground in subway tunnels to deter purse snatchings and muggings. As the communications professors Gary Gumpert and Susan J. Drucker write, "The sanctity of privacy has been eroded by the increasing intrusion of the technology of surveillance."[55]

All of this, of course, influences our expectations of privacy. Our expectations of privacy are reduced. Simultaneously, our expectations about the quantity and type of information that should be made public are raised. This feeds our voyeuristic appetite. We expect to see more. We want to see more. And the media give it to us.

What once were personal and private tragedies now unfold in real time and in public view with nonstop media coverage. In April 1999, cameras captured live the panic and grieving of students who witnessed death face to face at Columbine High School in Littleton, Colorado. Reporters interviewed students immediately after the worst incident of violence in a high school in U.S. history. Church services and vigils—traditionally times of private grieving—turned into public spectacles captured for the camera. Portions of the memorial services for the slain students were televised live on both the Fox News Channel and CNN on May 2, 1999.

It all reeked of mediated voyeurism. KUSA-TV, the Denver NBC affiliate, invited students trapped in the school building to call the station on the telephone and to tell their stories live.[56] Some students did. One student was put on the air before the station retracted its dangerous offer. Let us listen in on death, live, should the student on the phone be found by the shooters. The decision to revoke the offer to go live on the air with students while the shooters still may have been loose apparently reflects the recognition that in this case our opportunity to be voyeurs and listen in on what might be a death as it occurs was outweighed by our desire to protect innocent lives. Indeed, after the initial coverage in Littleton, the Radio-Television News Directors Association sent guidelines to news directors and general managers at over 2,000 stations urging them to cut back on coverage to avoid putting lives at risk.[57]

NBC's Katie Couric spoke with a student who read a farewell letter she wrote to her parents when she thought she would be killed—a private letter made public. If you cannot watch death live or on videotape, listening to others' words as they believe they are about to experience it apparently is the next-best thing.

The next morning on the *Today* show, Couric was at it again. She simultaneously interviewed two people—an African-American man named Michael Shoels, whose son was killed by the so-called Trenchcoat Mafia, and a white student at Columbine High School named Craig Scott who was standing next to Shoels's son when he was shot dead. Scott described the whole incident to Couric and a nation of voyeurs, as Couric held the visibly shaken Shoels's arm and the camera pulled in for a close-up to show her act of compassion and understanding. When Scott told that, in his words, a gun-toting student called Shoels's son "the n-word," the camera zoomed in on Shoels's face to get a reaction shot. To top it all off, the camera also closed in as Shoels and Scott held hands, a black man and a white boy, sharing their grief for the world to see.

And of course, the television newsmagazines and the network anchors were there. *Dateline* aired a two-hour special the night after the shooting. *20/20* and *48 Hours* also did shows on the shooting. The Columbine High story—"Terror in the Rockies" as Fox News's logo dubbed it—kicked the "Conflict in Kosovo" off the television leads and newspaper front pages, if only for a couple of days.

Of course, our voyeurism is fed by individuals such as Shoels, who was interviewed by other networks, and Scott who feel free to tell their stories for the world to hear. As noted in Chapter 1, exhibitionism serves voyeurism. The more willing people are to give up control over information that affects them—the more willing they are, in other words, to give up their privacy— the more mediated voyeurism thrives.

Voyeuristic tell-all talk shows like those hosted by Jerry Springer and Ricki Lake test and push our conception of and beliefs about privacy. Joshua Gamson observes that television talk shows rework what count as legitimate topics for public discussion.[58] "What belongs in private," he writes, "suddenly seems to belong in front of everybody."[59] As Robin Anderson, an associate professor of communications at Fordham University, writes about these shows, "From murder to incest, crime and punishment, almost no boundaries exist between what can and cannot be said in public. No revelation, confession, or disclosure is so personal that it cannot be exposed by a talk show host. In this atmosphere of total exposure, no secrets are allowed."[60]

Our desire to watch—our desire to be voyeurs—ultimately conflicts with our desire to keep private certain aspects of our own lives and to control the dissemination of information about ourselves and our loved ones. This tension was evident when a reality-based television show called *LAPD: Life on the Beat* showed the body of the actor Michael Marich, dead of a drug overdose. Said Marich's mother: "I looked up and thought that apartment looked familiar, and then I saw my dead son's body. The camera circled his body, just like a bunch of vultures, video vultures."[61] She filed suit for invasion of privacy—our interest in watching, she contended, conflicted with her own right to privacy.

The legal balance between voyeurism and privacy interests—between the video vultures, as Marich put it, and our private lives—is explored in Chapter 5, where the legal conceptions of newsworthiness and privacy are examined. At this point, it should be clear that voyeurism thrives on our diminished expectations of privacy and our willingness, at least in some cases, to expose our lives on camera or to tolerate such exposure.

But there may be a somewhat self-serving double standard, at least in some cases of mediated voyeurism, when it comes to privacy expectations and violations. In shows that involve video footage shot during police operations, the individual whose privacy is sacrificed for our viewing enjoyment is portrayed and perceived as a wrongdoer, a criminal suspect. Could it be that broadcasters and the public alike see the privacy rights of suspects and fugitives from the law as somehow less worthy of protection than those of the good, law-abiding citizens in the audience who watch these televisions shows? Shows like *Cops,* in other words, may simply be exposing our belief that it is okay to invade the privacy of those in society whom we look down on. A privacy violation is just a small price to pay for transgressing legal boundaries. The criminal suspect cannot, perhaps we believe but do not like to admit, make a legitimate moral claim to privacy because of his or her nefarious behavior.

Self-Disclosure and
the Desire to Be Seen and Heard

Why are so many people so willing to overshare, as it were, so much about their lives with so many people? Much of the voyeurism on television newsmagazines and tell-all talk shows would not be possible, of course, if individuals were not willing to have the details of their lives publicly exposed. There are many people who fit the mold of television exhibitionists. The question is what social forces motivate the exhibitionists who supply a large amount of the voyeuristic fodder on television.

An important concept here is self-disclosure. The social psychologist Valerian J. Derlega and his colleagues write that self-disclosure may be "loosely defined as what individuals verbally reveal about themselves to others (including thoughts, feelings, and experiences)."[62] The psychology professor Dalmas A. Taylor writes that self-disclosure "deals with the verbal presentation of the self to others."[63] Why do people engage in self-disclosure?

Research and theory from social psychology suggest there are multiple functions served by self-disclosure. These may include (1) *self-clarification,* which occurs when individuals think about and focus attention on themselves in preparation of speaking about themselves to others; (2) *social validation,* in which individuals hope to obtain feedback and advice about the appropriateness or correctness of their beliefs or behaviors from those to whom they open up and reveal themselves; (3) *relationship development,* in which the disclosure of information as a commodity may occur as a form of interpersonal exchange; and (4) *social control,* in which the discloser essentially engages in impression management by selectively and strategically revealing certain pieces of information to influence others' opinions.[64] Any or all of these reasons may play a role in the exhibitionism that fuels much of our mediated voyeurism.

In her examination of talk show participants and tell-all television, the communications scholar Patricia Joyner Priest identifies a number of different motives that people have for agreeing to participate in what she calls *"television disclosure,* the revelation of intimate information broadcast on television."[65] Priest studied thirty-seven persons who appeared on *Donahue* in early 1991, including a woman who claimed to be a sex priestess, a male-to-female transsexual, a man who claimed to be a former homosexual, a gay man suing for a marriage license, a former male prostitute, guests who appeared on an episode of *Donahue* called "Sisters Who Swap Husbands," and a sperm doctor.[66] The bulk of the sample, as Priest observed, was characterized by some feature of lifestyle, personality, or life history that is considered abnormal or deviant by mainstream society. Why do these individuals who speak from what Priest terms an atypical or marginalized position accept invitations to speak?

For some of the individuals Priest studied, the motive was, at least in part, materialistic, such as a free trip to New York City. One person told Priest, "I was as excited to go to the big city, the Big Apple, as I was to be on the show. And they were putting us up in the Drake Hotel, which, you know, I've seen on TV. That was going to be nice, I knew."[67] There were other motives, however, besides the temptation of free lodging and a complimentary airplane ticket.

"The driving motivation expressed by most informants, especially for those who represented severely marginalized groups, was a desire to remedy stereotypes and educate a national audience about discrimination and alternative lifestyles," Priest writes.[68] The desire to inform and to educate suggests an important benefit of tell-all talk shows—despite their seemingly sordid subjects, the shows provide marginalized people with rare access to the means of mass communication to get their message out. As Gamson writes in *Freaks Talk Back*, "Talk shows have offered the most diverse visibility for gay and lesbian and bisexual and transgendered people."[69] Although he notes that media companies "make loads of money" in the exploitive process of providing a forum to these groups, the talk shows are "key places from which to challenge medical and scientific definitions of 'perversion' and to put a 'human face' on sex and gender nonconformity."[70]

The irony is clear, as Priest notes—"The only place available for members of stigmatized groups to confront society's negative conceptions is at the 'freak show.'"[71] Despite this, most guests she studied found that an imperfect forum to reach a mass audience was better than none at all. The dangers of reaching this audience are clear, as the sociologist and sometime–radio talk show host Gini Graham Scott points out in her book on talk shows, *Can We Talk?*—the shows represent a "transmutation of personal problems in to entertainment for the masses" akin to Roman circuses.[72]

In addition to the materialistic and educative motives for appearing on *Donahue*, for a small number of the people Priest studied the primary rationale revolved around the opportunity to fulfill a lifelong dream—to appear on television. She dubs these people "moths," as they are drawn into the light of television. This is not surprising, of course, in a mediated world in which it often seems that people and things are important or real only if they appear on television. We live in a celebrity-driven culture and television provides a chance to be a celebrity.

The chance to feel important—to be in the spotlight—thus has an inherent appeal.

Vicki Abt and Leonard Mustazza contend that this is particularly true among members of the lower class: "They are willing to do anything and say anything since reputation and price are not at risk. Being a television 'star' is worth any social price."[73]

This "celebrity" rationale for exhibitionism obviously applies to more than just the guests on tell-all talk shows. It applies to the thousands of people who try out to be on MTV's program *The Real World*—the young individuals become instant celebrities among teens and twenty-somethings. It holds true for the 6,000-plus individuals who applied to CBS for a chance to be on *Survivor*, as well as for the 1,000 people who applied to be part of that network's *Big Brother* series. It applies to the growing number of college students who volunteer to place computer-attached cameras in their dorm rooms to have their lives shown to the world on web sites such as CollegeWeb.com and on the Real College Life web site.[74] It is a chance, after all, to be well known on campus and beyond. Fame is just a computer-mounted camera away.

More than fame and celebrity, however, may drive mediated exhibitionism. Another motive for talk show revelation for some individuals—individuals Priest dubbed "plaintiffs"—was a chance to make their arguments and to state their "case," as it were, to a surrogate jury—the audience of voyeurs. "Many found that the judicial system had failed them and felt the talk show genre offered another opportunity to court favor or seek redress in the court of public opinion," Priest writes.[75] The shows thus may provide some form of therapy or relief to the people who are willing to tell their stories.

In a nutshell, Priest's research reveals that there may be multiple reasons why people choose to tell their stories or to have them told for them on television. Regardless of the particular motive, the bottom line is clear—exhibitionism services mediated voyeurism.

Cultivating the Demand: The Media's Role

To this point, this chapter has focused on social forces and reasons why we choose to partake in mediated voyeurism. Could it be, however, that media organizations somehow create or at least contribute to our voyeuristic viewing appetite? In any marketplace, after all, merchants drum up support for their products. The media, in brief, may cultivate a demand for mediated voyeurism. Complicity between our own social needs to watch mediated voyeurism and the corporate needs to sell programming would seem quite logical.

At the most obvious and overt level, the broadcast networks and cable channels cultivate demand for mediated voyeurism with commercials and teasers for programs that feature this format. Marketing and advertising of any programming format, voyeuristic or otherwise, are there to develop and retain audience demand. But perhaps the issue is much deeper than this. It may be that the nature of programming itself and the act of media consumption have helped to create the demand for mediated voyeurism.

The media critic Mark Crispin Miller writes in *Boxed In: The Culture of TV* that commercial forces demand our continual consumption of media product.[76] Although there is nothing particularly earth shattering in this observation, Miller's analysis arguably begins to suggest how the media may cultivate our demand for voyeuristic product. He observes that a "largely unacknowledged" fact of American life is "the degradation of experience by technology."[77] This is an important observation. The more we engage in the consumption of the technologies of television and the Internet, the less we experience in the real world through interaction with others.

Mediated voyeurism, however, provides the perfect antidote for this illness. It provides us with programming that gives us the opportunity to vicariously experience, through the observation of others' trials and tribulations, the real world at the same time that we continue to consume media product. We can engage in the "vice" activity of slacking in front of the television set yet receive a sensation, however distant it might be, of real-world experience. When the voyeurism is packaged as "news" on a "newsmagazine" like *Dateline, 20/20,* or *48 Hours,* we can feel even better about our viewing. Not only do we get to watch others' lives and gain a feeling of experience—an experience of "being there," as the Peter Sellers's movie of the same name would have it—but we do so under the auspices of engaging in the socially sanctioned learning activity of news consumption. Mediated voyeurism just might be a decidedly noninteractive form of virtual reality with the goggles and gloves not included.

The genres of programming that came before mediated voyeurism and that still exist today—situation comedies, variety shows, and dramas—may have spawned this need to feel that our television consumption sometimes and somehow gives us the feeling of action, of real-world experience. When everything else on television seems so fake, so contrived, and so "been there, done that," mediated voyeurism arrived in full force in the 1990s to say, "You haven't done this, but it could happen to you." In this way, perhaps, media programming of the past has helped to cultivate, even if unintentionally, a demand for mediated voyeurism.

Another related way in which the media may cultivate our demand for mediated voyeurism is simply by constantly pushing the level of sensationalism to a point where only new, more graphic and real images will satisfy audience demands. A gradual ratcheting up of what we will tolerate and what we will watch occurs, and mediated voyeurism provides the perfect genre for allowing us to test our limits on important issues and concepts of privacy, intrusion, truth, and reality. The nature of television news, with its wall-to-wall and sometimes graphic coverage of tragedies from Columbine to John F. Kennedy Jr., perhaps also cultivates a desire that a portion of our entertainment programming should be similarly as sensational and real. Mediated voyeurism nicely satisfies this desire.

Obviously, the media do not *cause* anyone to watch a particular program or genre of programming. Yet the media may create an environment and climate, not just through advertising and marketing but through programming itself, that *contribute* to our desire to consume mediated voyeurism. Likewise, the constant ratcheting up of sensationalism makes it easier to tolerate mediated voyeurism today.

Summary

There is no single social force that drives mediated voyeurism to the forefront of our culture. Just as there are many varieties of mediated voyeurism today, so are there many social forces at work. This chapter has identified a number of them, from the quest for truth and the desire to see justice done to changing norms and conceptions of privacy and the need to feel superior to others. No one factor by itself is sufficient to "cause" mediated voyeurism. Rather, it is the coalescing of several forces that helps to propel reality-based, mediated voyeurism. As the following chapters suggest, social forces themselves are not the only factors that influence mediated voyeurism. The next chapter suggests that there are economic and political forces at work that are equally as important as social ones in sustaining mediated voyeurism.

3

Priming the Economic and Political Pumps of Mediated Voyeurism

A propitious assortment of economic and political forces converged in the 1990s that expedited the transcendence of mediated voyeurism in our culture. Although none of these variables has directly caused or been the immediate impetus for the rise of mediated voyeurism, each nonetheless has helped to clear its path.

Political and economic concerns about crime and workplace graft led to a rapid escalation at the end of the twentieth century in the use of video surveillance technology as a tool of both law enforcement agencies and private business enterprises. This, in turn, greased the skids for a growing sense of resignation—if not quite willing acceptance—among many people of the fact that their daily activities are constantly subject to recorded visual scrutiny. This assent, however begrudging, is a crucial condition for the growth of mediated voyeurism. It depends in no small part on our embracement of the notion that it is okay for us to watch others' movements and activities, often without their knowledge or consent. The more accepting we are of having our own behavior visually monitored and recorded, the more our comfort level with watching others' activities increases. If we can be watched, in other words, then we certainly should be able to do some watching of our own.

When television newsmagazines use the voyeuristic technique of the hidden camera investigation so popular with audiences, they are essentially acting as pseudo–law enforcement agencies. We accept their secretive technique as a legitimate intrusion on others' lives because we have come to accept the surveillance camera as an omnipresent reality of our own lives, whether we are being watched through a stationary lens at an automated-teller bank machine or by a rotating camera perched on a street pole in an urban metropolis. We may even embrace and extend the process one step further by creating and engaging in our own forms of mediated voyeurism in the confines of our homes and apartments. We borrow the accepted voyeuristic surveillance methods of law enforcement, private business, and the news media when we surreptitiously tape the activities of baby-sitters with our children and cleaning personnel with our possessions. Following the example of the television newsmagazines, we are simply engaging in our own form of private "gotcha" video justice. The political and economic concerns that gave rise to video surveillance in the public street and private workplace have merely been extended to another, more personal domain.

This chapter describes a number of political and economic factors that have facilitated the rise of mediated voyeurism. These include (1) the economic realities of broadcasting and broadcast journalism; (2) the government's predominantly hands-off, marketplace approach to the concept of "public interest" in the realm of broadcasting; and (3) the emergence of politics as a passive, mediated spectator sport. Before addressing this trio of forces, the chapter provides recent examples of the video surveillance described above that is propelled by political and economic concerns about crime and workplace efficiency.

Video Surveillance: The Eyes Have It

Surveillance cameras have long found a home in banks and retail stores. Serving the safety and economic concerns of both de-
terring and capturing would-be thieves as well as monitoring
less-than-honest employees seeking a quick five-fingered dis-
count, cameras are now a pervasive presence in the retail and
banking industries. But increasingly—and disturbingly for
many civil libertarians—the government is now training its own
cameras on the public in the distinctly Orwellian role of Big
Brother (not to be confused, of course, with the voyeuristic program *Big Brother* described earlier in the book).

Cops cannot be everywhere, but cameras can be. So to crack
down on drug dealing and restore a sense of safety in Greenwich Village's famed Washington Square Park, the police department installed a number of not-so-hidden cameras in November 1997. Did the video surveillance campaign work? It all
depends on how "work" is defined. The number of drug complaints and arrests in the park dropped dramatically, from 670
in 1997 to just 99 in 1998.[1] On other hand, some nearby resi-
dents complained the cameras infringed on their privacy. What
is more, there was concern that the electronic eyes merely relo-
cated and displaced criminal activity, pushing it from the park
to other areas of New York City.

Surveillance cameras in the Big Apple are far from unusual
today. A 1998 block-by-block survey conducted by the American Civil Liberties Union (ACLU) estimated that there are
nearly 2,380 surveillance cameras in Manhattan alone trained
on public places.[2] About 2,000 of those cameras were estimated
to be operated by private entities, with the rest belonging to
government agencies. But New York City is far from the only
place today where people are monitored on the street by video
cameras.

Across the country in Everett, Washington, the city council
voted in May 1999 to spend over $200,000 for eight surveil-
lance cameras and accompanying equipment to monitor certain

downtown streets frequented by prostitutes and drug dealers.[3] The cameras were to be mounted on light poles and affixed to business establishments. Everett was following the lead of another Washington state city, Tacoma, in deploying cameras both to deter and to catch criminals. In the mid-1990s, Tacoma, along with Baltimore, Maryland, was among the first major cities to adopt a comprehensive plan to fight crime with cameras.

Although many government-operated cameras monitor activities in public places such as streets, sidewalks, and parks, there is still stiff resistance in some quarters from individuals who claim that privacy interests are being compromised. It will be recalled from Chapter 2 that mediated voyeurism thrives when privacy expectations are diminished. Thus it was that in 1999, Jerry Brown, a former California governor and erstwhile presidential aspirant, refused in his newfound incarnation as the mayor of Oakland to support a plan to put video cameras in some high-crime sections of that East Bay city. "Installing a few or a few dozen surveillance cameras will not make us safe. It should also not be forgotten that the intrusive powers of the state are growing with each passing decade," Brown told the media.[4]

But as the trend continues toward government use of surveillance cameras to monitor everything from crime and vandalism on city buses in Chicago and San Francisco to scofflaws who use the cash-free "E-Z Pass" toll lanes for bridges and tunnels in New York and New Jersey without the proper electronic tags, the inevitable result is that video voyeurism becomes more firmly entrenched. We expect to be watched, and, concomitantly, we expect to be able to watch others. Privacy interests are given short shrift in the process. As one legal commentator put it in a recent law journal article, "Privacy seems to be fighting a losing campaign as more towns turn to surveillance to protect their streets from crime."[5]

And we are learning these lessons about privacy and government-sponsored mediated voyeurism at an early age. In the wake of the tragic shootings at Columbine High School in Littleton, Colorado, for instance, calls for the increased use of cameras in public high schools echoed across the country. Somewhat ironically, many high schools, including Columbine, already had cameras prior to the April 1999 shootings in that school. And so it is today that the same generation that is weaned on watching others' lives unfold on MTV's *The Real World* and *Road Rules* is having its own actions monitored on a near-daily basis by government agents. Students grow up with a diminished sense of privacy that facilitates mediated voyeurism.

But the use of surveillance technology is far from limited to government entities. Businesses use it to crack down on employee practices that may be harming productivity or endangering others. Take the case of hidden cameras found at the Consolidated Freightways terminal in Mira Loma, California, in September 1997. The company had installed the devices several months earlier to track down the suspected use and sale of illegal narcotics by its employees.[6] Keeping drug-addled drivers off public highways and protecting customers' goods on long-haul trips are seemingly noble and legitimate motives that justify a little video voyeurism. So what was the problem?

The cameras were placed behind a mirror in the men's bathroom. The bathroom is perhaps the one place people would least expect to find a surveillance camera and the one place where they most expect to find some privacy. A Consolidated Freightways employee discovered a camera when he tried to fix a bathroom mirror that had come loose. The 600 employees at the Mira Loma site were never warned about the cameras' presence. Although the company emphasized that it never aimed the cameras at the stalls or urinals, some employees were nonetheless outraged. "This is voyeurism," Curry Stephens told the Riverside *Press-Enterprise*.[7] That voyeurism resulted in a raft of civil lawsuits—some of which ultimately were dismissed in 1998—for invasion of privacy, but the local district attorney in Riverside County decided not to file criminal charges against the company under state law.[8] The applicable state law, which also sweeps up vice activities like solicitation of prostitution, prohibits videotaping the interior of a bathroom "with the intent to invade the privacy of a person or persons inside." The district attorney apparently concluded that the intent of Consolidated Freightways was not to invade privacy but to stop the use and sale of illegal drugs behind bathroom doors. A federal law, the Electronic Communications Privacy Act of 1986, was not applicable because it does not cover silent video surveillance but only spoken personal conversations. The case against video voyeurism thus fell through the legal cracks. Other gaps in the law that allow mediated voyeurism to flourish are explored in Chapter 6.

Sometimes workplace surveillance voyeurism comes back to haunt the voyeur-employer. Officials from the Safeway supermarket chain allegedly placed a hidden camera in the office of John C. Phipps, a sales manager in Alaska, to see if he was taking home vendor-supplied alcohol. After learning about the surreptitious tapings and being fired from his job, Phipps sued for invasion of privacy and won. An Alaska superior court judge also ruled in 1999 that Safeway violated an implied covenant of good faith and fair dealing with its employees—specifically, with Phipps—when it taped inside his office without his consent.

Surveillance cameras, of course, can be found today in places other than shop-and-rob convenience stores, banks, freeways, light poles, and workplace bathrooms. To paraphrase the old orange juice industry slogan, they are not just for the government or business enterprises anymore. We have actually brought them into our own homes, allowing them to play a part in our very own productions of mediated voyeurism. Some parents today make use of the so-called nanny cam to capture abusive baby-sitters or to spy on their own children whom they suspect of using illegal drugs. How better to bust the abusive baby-sitter than to confront her or him with a vérité videotape. Home owners and parents, in essence, become the voyeuristic producers of their own investigative newsmagazines.

It should not be surprising, then, that in 2000 a new reality television show debuted that brought real-life video surveillance together with low-brow entertainment. Appropriately dubbed *Cheaters,* the Dallas-based show produced by Goldstein/Habeeb Entertainment actively solicits individuals who believe their spouses or significant others are having affairs. Once contacted, the show's team of investigators goes into motion. First, they monitor the alleged cheater for several weeks to confirm the suspicions. If these are corroborated, the stage is then set for ready-made video drama and the inevitable, emotionally charged confrontation. Camerapersons, accompanied by the show's investigators, swoop in to capture the cheater in the act. The spurned-but-now-vindicated lover, of course, is also present, adding to the heat of the moment. Burly security people from the show are there to make sure that heat does not spark actual violence.

Of course, the cheaters have no one to blame but themselves. Had they been savvy and visited the show's web page at http://www.cheaterstv.com they would have seen the warning: "If you've been cheating on your spouse, better think twice."[9] The page promises that that the show will bring viewers "actual stories of infidelity and marital impropriety as it unfolds."[10] Cheat, in other words, at your own risk.

This is video-surveillance-turned-voyeuristic-entertainment at its finest, or worst, depending on one's perspective. As Jim Henderson of the *Houston Chronicle* wrote in June 1999, the show is set "to test the world's appetite for voyeurism."[11] One of its producers, Tommy Habeeb, made no bones about the entertainment value of *Cheaters* during an August 1999 interview with Bill O'Reilly, host of Fox News Channel's *O'Reilly Factor.* "We're not making *Gone with the Wind* here," he wryly said.

On the show, Habeeb plays a fictitious detective called, in pun-intended fashion, "Tommy Gunn" who nails the not-so-fictitious philanderers.

How does the show attempt to avoid legal problems? "You'd be surprised what people will do to be on television and for a dollar," Habeeb told O'Reilly, explaining that even the exposed cheaters eventually sign releases—the show's producers pay them to sign—allowing the use of their images. The show's other producer, Bobby Goldstein, also knows something about the law. Not surprising, he was a divorce attorney before one of his ex-clients sued him and was awarded $100 million.[12]

Cheaters was not the first voyeuristic television program to combine entertainment with video surveillance techniques. Fox television's *Busted on the Job* took care of that. What is *Busted on the Job*? Consider an episode that aired in September 1999. It was packed with actual workplace surveillance videotape featuring everything from employees of a business stealing company goods to baggage handlers at an airport rifling through travelers' suitcases on the tarmac. Individuals claiming on-the-job injuries and collecting worker's compensation were caught on videotape lifting heavy items and moving furniture. There was even what might be called a "voyeur within voyeur" segment in which a male employee of an unnamed company was captured on videotape peering under the door of a women's locker room. The voyeur-employee was caught, in other words, by the voyeur-employer. *Busted on the Job* proves a new maxim for the surveillance society—"One person's surveillance is another person's amusement."

In summary, the ubiquitous presence of surveillance cameras helps to promote an atmosphere ripe for voyeurism. We become accustomed to being the focus of a camera's gaze, and we simultaneously believe, in somewhat quid pro quo fashion, that we should be able to do some of our own gazing at others. It is a culture in which being watched is becoming increasingly a part of our daily lives.

The Economics of Mediated Voyeurism

Broadcasting in the United States is, with a few rare exceptions such as the Corporation for Public Broadcasting, a for-profit enterprise. This is an obvious and inescapable fact, yet it is an incredibly important one with which to begin this section. Bottom-line economic concerns are omnipresent. They influence the media content, including voyeuristic content, that we watch.

A number of economic factors have come together today, each of which in its own way and in the aggregate facilitates the rise of voyeuristic media content. Economic deregulation of broadcast ownership, coupled with an ever-increasing focus on bottom-line concerns in broadcast journalism, creates an atmosphere in which the media often will give us whatever it is that we, as a nation of voyeurs, want to watch. Voyeuristic mediated content thrives in this profit-intensive atmosphere—there is little to stop it other than low ratings or excessive costs. As the next section suggests, the cost for producing mediated voyeurism is far from excessive.

Low Costs, High Profits

The economic reality of reality television shows like *Cops,* as well as television newsmagazines like *Dateline* and *48 Hours,* is that they are much cheaper to produce than situation comedies like *Friends* with high-paid ensemble casts. No temperamental, high-priced Hollywood "stars" are necessary for an interesting episode of *Cops*—the police and the suspects are the pro bono stars. The police will work for good publicity. All it really takes, then, before editing is a cameraperson and sound specialist riding along with the officers as they patrol the streets. As Richard Campbell, a journalism professor at Middle Tennessee State University, writes, shows such as *Cops* "are cheap to produce, with low overhead and a big return on a minimum investment."[13] The shows are sometimes called clip shows because the consist primarily of video clips.

These shows also have a long shelf life and can be repeatedly recycled. Mark Fishman, a sociology professor at Brooklyn College, writes that programs such as *Cops* and the now out-of-production *Real Stories of the Highway Patrol* "are filmed without dates or other temporal references that might age the programs. Episodes can be reshown. If a show lasts at least two seasons, there are enough episodes to repackage and sell as reruns in syndication to independent stations or cable networks."[14] Like pornographic photographs, in other words, the images on reality television are "evergreen"—their appeal is not diminished by the passage of time.

Thus it was in 1999 that the show *LAPD: Life of the Beat* ceased new production after four successful seasons but continued to run in syndication in markets across the country. At the same time, *Cops* was starting its twelfth season on Fox, followed on the network's Saturday night schedule by another reality-based show, *America's Most Wanted*.[15] While new episodes of *Cops* were airing on Fox in 1999, a cable network with its own voyeuristic programming, Court TV, acquired the rerun rights that same year to the four-time Emmy-nominated show and began airing them weeknights in a prime-time slot.[16] Court TV even featured a *Cops* "Marathon" in September 1999. The seminal reality television show, in brief, was alive and well as the new millennium was ushered in. What is more, Fox ordered new episodes of several other video vérité voyeurism shows in 1999, including a dozen new episodes each of *World's Wildest Police Videos* and *Guinness World Records*.[17] NBC ordered thirteen new episodes in 1999 of its own hour-long voyeuristic shock monster, *World's Most Amazing Videos*.

Voyeuristic tell-all talk shows are also relatively inexpensive to produce, requiring only one high salary for the host.[18] The old cliché is correct—talk really is cheap. Gini Graham Scott writes in *Can We Talk?* that talk shows began to flourish in the 1980s in large part because

> they were much less expensive than the dramatic shows, which re-
> quired scripting, paid actors, and rehearsal time. Instead, the talk
> shows just required one or two hosts who could quickly respond to
> the day's guest list, along with a booker or producer (or staff of
> bookers and producers as these shows grew) to line up guests—an
> average cost of $25,000–$50,000 per half hour. Such shows could
> quickly be put together and taped for national distribution in a day
> or two.[19]

The television newsmagazines that bring us voyeuristically into others' lives are not only relatively inexpensive to produce but they also continue to appeal to the audience in large-enough numbers to attract high ratings and big advertising dollars. The simple fact is that "reality sells." That is what Susan Zirinsky, executive producer of CBS's *48 Hours* newsmagazine, told me during a June 1999 conversation in her West 57th Street office in Manhattan. Not only are newsmagazines "much cheaper to put on," Zirinsky stated, but they help to satisfy what she calls "an insatiable thirst for real human drama." That thirst was such in 1999 that she believed television was "not yet satu-rated" with newsmagazines despite their presence on the major networks' prime-time schedules nearly every night of the week.

A secondary market for television newsmagazines—overseas distribution—further enhances their economic value. News-magazines produced in the United States are increasingly being used to satiate a global demand for programming and the mag-azine genre is proving to be very popular.[20] What makes the overseas market particularly interesting and unusual is that the major U.S. networks can sell not only entire episodes or hours of newsmagazines abroad but they can also peddle individual segments or stories from within an episode. It is a matter of slic-ing and dicing, in other words. How does this work?

In brief, overseas buyers are sent story lists from which they can pick and choose segments that have the most appeal to their audiences. The segments themselves are generally delivered in a raw format that includes natural sound but eliminates graphics, voice-overs, and bumpers with the U.S. newsmagazine hosts.[21] The end result may be that an international client chooses segments from competing U.S. newsmagazines such as ABC's *20/20* and CBS's *60 Minutes* and then repackages them, back to back, in the same show. The same thirst for human drama that Susan Zirinsky described in the United States apparently applies overseas.

To quench that thirst on the home front, Zirinsky strives to select topics that have substantial editorial merit from a journalistic perspective as well as audience appeal sufficient to keep *48 Hours* economically viable amid prime-time competition. She noted that some topics are selected because of what she calls a "relatability" factor—can the audience relate to the subject matter or the individual featured? Other topics have a "glad that's not me aspect" of appeal, she told me when I interviewed her. And she acknowledged the voyeuristic characteristics of some episodes of *48 Hours,* calling it "shocking" at times how much some of the individuals featured on the program allow their activities to be recorded by the show's camera crews. Ultimately, however, whatever the audience appeal of a particular segment may be, Zirinsky works hard to select only those subjects on which she feels she can perform her journalist's duty.

Infotainment

Although Susan Zirinsky attempts to maintain journalistic integrity on a show that she acknowledges faces the economic pressures of competing in a prime-time slot against entertainment programming, she may be fighting a lonely and losing battle. Other journalists seem to succumb too easily today to the bottom-line concerns of their corporate owners. Broadcast news often becomes infotainment, a bastardized hybrid of news and entertainment that panders to viewers' wants rather than attempting to meet their needs.

Doris Graber, a professor of political science at the University of Illinois at Chicago, summarizes in a recent issue of the *Harvard International Journal of Press/Politics* the confluence of economic factors that produce infotainment:

> The media's dilemma lies in the structure of the media system in the United States. It is predominantly a private business that receives its financial support largely from advertisers or audience fees. To stay lucrative, the general audience media must maximize the number of viewers. This often results in news formats geared to publics that are not well versed in political issues and not particularly interested in them. Generally, media organizations have responded to this challenge with more brevity, simplicity, and, if possible, entertaining angles to news stories. When they operate in this spirit of these guidelines, they often produce shallow infotainment.[22]

Into the realm of infotainment, in turn, falls much of the video voyeurism that flourishes on reality-based shows like *Cops,* television newsmagazines like *Dateline,* and even on broadcast news shows that thrive on sensationalistic videos of real-life fires, rescues, and disasters. Vicki Abt and Leonard Mustazza write, "Reality-based television makes us dissatisfied with the traditional separation between information and entertainment or between fact and fiction. We now demand a new and more potent mix called 'infotainment.'"[23] This blurring of boundaries impacts our current beliefs of what constitutes news and what constitutes entertainment.

Whether the video vérité voyeurism of the media ride-along technique—camera-toting members of the media literally ride along with law enforcement agents on patrol—is news or entertainment is ambiguous. Steve Cohen, news director at KCOP in

Los Angeles, acknowledged in *Daily Variety* in 1999 that some journalists have come to believe that ride-alongs are really "voyeurism and not journalism."[24] Eroding standards of news in broadcast journalism—an erosion largely fueled by concerns for profits—allow infotainment and voyeurism to thrive. The difficulty in defining news itself contributes to this process.

How does one define news? Arriving at an agreeable definition is an elusive, if not impossible, task for both ivory tower academics and streetwise journalists. Yet local television newscasts often admonish viewers, "If you see news, call us." This exhortation assumes, of course, that we know news when we see it, much as the former United States Supreme Court Justice Potter Stewart once famously proclaimed to know pornography when he saw it.

Because defining news is so problematic, we often resort to simply identifying it by distinguishing characteristics. Traditional news characteristics include such things as timeliness, proximity, prominence, oddity, and consequence. Journalists also tend to think of news as something external to themselves, something that they reflect rather than construct.[25] In fact, as Carlin Romano writes, "the old fashioned view that 'news' is simply a mirror placed before reality still lives."[26]

Today, however, it is recognized by many scholars that news is not something that simply exists "out there," independent of the journalist, waiting to be discovered. News, instead, is something that journalists and editors make, that they construct, that they produce.[27] News is a story, in other words, that journalists tell—that they shape and create with the words they choose, the facts they select, and the sources they choose to contact.

Unfortunately, the news stories that journalists tell today often are derided. This is especially true in the realm of television, a medium that allows us to watch and satiate our voyeuristic appetites. The political scientist Dean Alger observes in the *Harvard International Journal of Press/Politics* that in recent years "there has been much concern expressed about the increasing 'tabloidization' of the news media and the media's role in the general degradation of the dialogue of democracy."[28] He is not alone in this observation.

Richard M. Cohen, a former senior producer of the *CBS Evening News,* writes in *Conglomerates and the Media,* "In television, journalism is no longer a calling. It's a big deal job with a fat paycheck. Objectives have changed. We are audience-driven now. We are not mission-driven: propelled by our responsibility to inform. We're just here to entertain, to soothe. We're here to sell our wares."[29]

The quest for corporate profit is all-consuming and it impacts what constitutes news, Cohen argues. He writes that "TV's only ax to grind is its demand to try to earn large profits" and that "corporate ownership of the networks and local stations is destroying the integrity of news."[30] An extensive 1998 report conducted by the *Columbia Journalism Review* supports this cynical position. The journal found that today "more so than at any other moment in journalism's history" news is "hurt by a heightened, unseemly lust at many companies for ever greater profits."[31]

Broadcast journalism, however, is not just money driven. It is also picture and video driven. After all, we like to watch, and, in particular, we like to watch something other than a news anchor reading directly to us from the morning newspaper at which we already looked. Stories that are visually appealing—stories that have great pictures, laden with emotion or blood—inevitably get more play on the typical twenty-two minutes of a thirty-minute newscast that are devoted to something other than commercial advertisements or the station's own promotional announcements. These stories, in turn, squeeze out other potential news stories altogether from the twenty-two-minute news window—stories that might have been more important for an informed electorate but that lacked good videotape.

The pictures, especially on local television news, often are of crime and violence. The political science professor Franklin D.

Gilliam Jr. and his colleagues at UCLA observed in a recent study, "Television's insatiable demand for 'good pictures' and riveting stories means that the most gruesome or notorious episodes of crime receive extensive attention while other forms of crime are virtually ignored."[32] These pictures of violence and crime, as noted above, drive out other stories from newscasts. The simple fact often is, as the University of Pennsylvania professor of communications Phyllis Kaniss observed in the *American Journalism Review,* "If it doesn't bleed—or choke with emotion—it doesn't air."[33]

Per the voyeurism value, then, local television news is propelled by what the journalist Jamie Malanowski once dubbed as a "fetish for video."[34] Pictures are essential for storytelling in broadcast journalism, and, Malanowski argues, images of murder, scandal, greed, and sex travel.[35] The end product? Local news, writes the Pulitzer Prize–winning television critic Howard Rosenberg, often amounts to little more than "an extension of the entertainment programs that surround it."[36]

Despite this pandering to violence and videotape, we love—in line, once again, with the voyeurism value—to watch sensationalistic local newscasts. Lawrence K. Grossman, former president of NBC News and PBS, observed recently in the *Columbia Journalism Review* that local newscasts are the public's number one source of news and that people rank them higher in quality and credibility than the network news or any other news source.[37] A 1998 study conducted on behalf of *Broadcasting & Cable* magazine bears this out, despite the fact that 32 percent of those surveyed believe that local television news is sensationalized.[38]

Local newscasts, of course, are not the only news criticized. Network television news is accused of dumbing down our standards of news. NBC News, for instance, was accused in the late 1990s of offering "news lite" on its evening newscast, featuring supposedly lighter, softer news stories.[39] Coverage of the incidents surrounding the death of Princess Diana, according to some journalists and press analysts, "reflect[s] how entertainment values have replaced traditional news values in many U.S. newsrooms."[40] Poorly-sourced and gossip-laden television news coverage of the Monica Lewinsky and President Clinton sex scandal was attacked as a sign of declining news values.[41] Wall-to-wall coverage on the cable news channels for a solid week after the death of John F. Kennedy Jr. in 1999 illustrated the spectacle that celebrity death has become as infotainment. As Don Henley once cogently sang about the nature of broadcast news, "It's interesting when people die, give us dirty laundry."[42]

Rick Kushman, the television columnist for the *Sacramento Bee*, echoes the erstwhile Eagle's disturbing sentiment in a column written shortly after the media's excessive coverage of the events surrounding Kennedy's death: "Too soon, it will be another tragedy or scandal or death that will fire up television news engines and inundate America with unedited, unrestrained images and chatter, and once again the power of that uber-coverage will swamp all of us in mini-hysteria."[43] In 2000, that next story turned out to be the saga of Elian Gonzalez. Coverage of his removal from a Miami home was unedited and unrestrained on the cable news channels. It did indeed, to use Kushman's terms, "swamp us in mini-hysteria."

The *Bee* columnist points out that along with wall-to-wall live news coverage of genuine news stories such as war in Iraq in December 1998, we get more voyeuristic fare, including videotape of "freeway chases, house fires or air show crashes in Europe with near equal enthusiasm, particularly if they happen at air time. What we do not get is a true perspective on the events, or even someone explaining the power of that constant television coverage."[44] It is this lack of restraint on the part of journalists when it comes to treating minor and unimportant events with the same massive coverage as meaningful ones that leads Kushman to a conclusion that is troubling but reflects the nature of the news business today: "The message it all conveys, along with the empty local news teases and the network anchors promoting cheesy stories on prime-time newsmagazines, is that TV news people are in it for ratings, profit and glory, not journalism."[45]

Howard Kurtz, the always-astute media reporter and columnist for the *Washington Post,* observed in 1998 that broadcast news is suffering from a "a crisis of tabloidism. The business has channel-surfed lately, from Marv Albert to Diana to the nanny trial to O.J. and back again. We are complicit, in varying degrees, in the paparazzi phenomenon."[46] The paparazzi, of course, are the long-lens voyeurs who often capture celebrities in states of surprise or otherwise-candid moments when they least expect it. Tom Rosenstiel, director of the Project for Excellence in Journalism, echoes Kurtz's sentiments. He observes a "philosophical collapse in the belief and purpose of journalism and the meaning of news."[47] Television news ultimately becomes, as Neil Postman of New York University and the television journalist Steve Powers write in their book *How to Watch TV News,* "only a commodity that is used to gather an audience which will be sold to advertisers," and, what is more, it is a commodity "delivered as a form of entertainment."[48]

Deregulation of ownership in the broadcast industry will only exacerbate the economic pressures that now affect news. In particular, the Telecommunications Act of 1996 eliminated a numerical cap of twelve on the number of television stations that a single entity could own. The result? Further concentration of ownership. In 1998, just two years after the Telecommunications Act was signed into law, the nation's top twenty-five television station groups owned or controlled a whopping 36 percent of the nation's commercial television stations. In 1996, they owned 25 percent. That is a 49 percent increase in control. In real numbers, the top twenty-five groups owned 432 television stations in 1998 compared with 290 in 1996. The desire for profit will surely be ratcheted up as competition is reduced and corporate oligopolies prevail.

Mediated voyeurism thrives in an atmosphere in which news standards erode and profits accrete. *Dateline,* for instance, may be called a "news" magazine by many, but how much of that program really constitutes news? Are the voyeuristic features that dip into other people's lives—their medical traumas, their family misfortunes—really news? Or are these segments merely something we call infotainment? The 1998 *Columbia Journalism Review* report noted earlier concluded, "The 'tabloidization' of TV news magazines is strictly geared to ratings and profits."[49]

In summary, what broadcast journalists think of as news today often has very little to do with truth seeking or promoting democratic self-governance. Instead, it has much to do with using videotape that panders to our voyeuristic proclivities and, at the same time, produces a profit for the stations and networks. News amounts to little more than whatever it is we want to watch.

Letting Marketplace Forces Determine the Public Interest

One of the most important, controversial, and contested political and legal concepts in broadcast television today is *public interest*. The Federal Communications Commission (FCC), the federal administrative agency charged with regulating the broadcast industry, is mandated to ensure that broadcasters serve the "public interest, convenience and necessity."[50] The key part of this phrase, originally borrowed from an 1887 Illinois railroad statute, is public interest.

At its most basic, primitive level, the dispute over the meaning of this crucial concept can be reduced to a dialectic: Is the public interest whatever the public is interested in watching, as determined by economic marketplace forces such as audience size and demographics, or is the public interest whatever the public needs to watch, as determined by government agencies and politicians? Even more simply, the dispute boils down to a wants versus needs contest: Is the public interest measured by what the public *wants* to watch or by what the public *needs* to watch?

Unless children are the primary audience or there is a concern that programming somehow will harm children—a three-hour-per-week educational programming requirement for U.S. broadcasters and the current television ratings system for violent content now embody these child-centric concerns—the FCC largely embraces a distinctly hands-off, marketplace competition conception of the public interest. The public interest, at least where adults are concerned, is measured by what the public is interested in watching.

This reflects a broader political ideology that leaves questions of media accountability up to economic forces. It is the same laissez faire ideology that eliminated the cap on the number of television stations a corporation could own. Whether a program genre such as mediated voyeurism is good or bad—whether it serves the public interest—is not for the government to determine. It is left to audience members, who "vote" with their remote control wands. If enough people of the age, gender, race, and income profile desired by potential advertisers use their remote controls to tune in to mediated voyeurism, then it will flourish. The government will not step in to halt its success, despite some of the alleged problems—invasions of privacy, exploiting racial stereotypes, rampant sensationalism—discussed with certain varieties of mediated voyeurism in Chapter 2.

The United States Supreme Court in 1981 made clear that the FCC's reliance on market forces rather than government intervention to satisfy the entertainment preferences of the audience and program diversity does not violate the First Amendment. That case, *FCC v. WNCN Listeners Guild,*[51] focused on the topic of format changes proposed by radio stations seeking license renewals or transfers. A format is a consistent theme of programming that dominates air play at a radio station. Music formats, for example, include country, classical, oldies, alternative, and adult contemporary, among others.

If a company purchases a radio station and decides to change its programming format from classical music to adult contemporary because it is more profitable, should the FCC review that decision to determine whether it is in the public interest? What if there are no more classical music stations left in the market after that format change? Should the FCC then step in to deny the sale or transfer of the license of the classical station?

The Supreme Court concluded that the FCC's policy to rely on marketplace forces to determine what programming flourished and perished was constitutionally sound. The fact that the FCC would not step in to preserve a rare, dying, or unprofitable format was permissible. The public interest, in other words, was better served by letting economic forces—audience size, demographics, and advertising revenue—determine radio stations' formats than by permitting government agencies such as the FCC to meddle and tinker with the formats. If no classical stations are left in a market that features a glut of economically successful alternative rock stations, then that means the public interest is being served. The FCC, in other words, is the dictator of neither programming formats nor, more important, the public interest.

That deference to economic forces is one of the reasons that the public interest concept provides little relief to organizations such as the National Association for the Advancement of Colored People (NAACP) that lament the dearth of color, quite literally, on major network television. In 1999, the NAACP attacked the complete absence of minority lead characters on the twenty-six prime-time television shows that the Big Four networks—ABC, CBS, NBC, and Fox—were slated to debut for the fall 1999 schedule.[52] If the market does not support African-American lead characters on the four major networks, however, that is simply the nature of the public interest. If the WB and UPN networks become known euphemistically as "black" networks—three of the top four shows among African Americans by the end of 1998 were on the upstart WB network—then that type of de facto segregation apparently serves the public interest.

Programming obligations under the public interest standard that catered to adults' *needs*, as compared to adults' *wants*, have dried up. The controversial Fairness Doctrine, which imposed content obligations on broadcasters to serve up issues of public concern, "is now officially moribund."[53] In its place are rules such as the aforementioned Telecommunications Act of 1996 that deregulate ownership of the media and that "have fueled a consolidation so profound that even insiders are surprised by its magnitude."[54] These conglomerates ultimately are interested in the bottom line, which means that they must give the public what it wants and, in turn, give shareholders what they want. And today, the public often wants voyeuristic content in its many varieties. If the marketplace demands video voyeurism, then that *is* the public interest and there is little if anything the FCC can do to prevent it. Such content will proliferate until it is no longer popular and economic forces reduce its prevalence, in accord with the usual invention-imitation-decline life cycle for successful programming formats.

A recent, high-profile license renewal dispute involving four Denver, Colorado, television stations illustrates that the FCC will not use its public interest power to stop the erosion of news content into a quagmire of sensationalistic and voyeuristic videotape infotainment. In April 1998, the FCC's Mass Media Bureau rejected a petition filed by a public interest group, Rocky Mountain Media Watch, to deny the license renewal applications of the four stations, including network affiliates for ABC, CBS, NBC, and the WB.[55]

Who or what is Rocky Mountain Media Watch? According to its home page on the World Wide Web, the group was founded in 1994 "by media activists with media and research skills to challenge the unbalanced and unhealthy diet of information presented by the media corporations."[56] The group, led by Paul Klite, conducted content analyses of local newscasts. It measured things such as the amount of time spent on stories about crime, disasters, government, schools, and other topics. One of these studies was even published in the prestigious *Harvard International Journal of Press/Politics*.[57]

Based on its content analyses, Rocky Mountain Media Watch contended that local newscasts on the Denver stations in question contained (1) excessive violence and mayhem; (2) inadequate coverage of local politics and social issues such as education, poverty, and AIDS; and (3) inappropriately high levels of soft news, chitchat between anchors, and celebrity-driven stories. The watchdog organization cleverly dubbed the end product of this mixture *toxic television news*. Rocky Mountain Media Watch claimed that this mixture of allegedly excessive and exploitive violence, deficient news coverage, racial and gender stereotyping, and excessive commercialization and triviality was "harming the citizens of Colorado."[58] What was the harm?

Rocky Mountain Media Watch, at times citing the research of other scholars, alleged among other things that (1) media violence negatively influences children's learning, aggression, and empathy; and (2) distorted TV news causes viewer alienation, cynicism, violent behavior, ignorance, racial polarization, and disempowerment.[59] In other words, the group made a causal attribution argument about the nature of media effects: *Message X* (local television news in Denver) causes *Harms Y* (aggression, cynicism, ignorance, etc.).

The harms that the four stations' local newscasts were allegedly causing to Colorado's citizens meant, according to Rocky Mountain Media Watch, that the stations were not serving the public interest obligations imposed by the FCC on commercial broadcasters. Rocky Mountain Media Watch offered four ideas "for remedy as conditions for re-licensure" for the stations. These included (1) compelled broadcasting of Public Service Announcements (PSAs) designed to alert Denver citizens to "TV news' unbalanced and unhealthy diet of information and its potentially harmful side-effects"; (2) compelled daily broadcasting of so-called media literacy shows on prime-time television to teach children and adults how to decode advertising messages and understand topics such as the effects of media violence and media ownership; (3) mandatory education programs for each stations' employees regarding media violence effects; and (4) mandatory development by each station of a plan to improve news coverage of local elections.

The FCC did not buy Rocky Mountain Media Watch's public interest argument, however well intended or misguided it might have been. In rejecting Rocky Mountain Media Watch's claim that the public interest requirement required sanctions be imposed on the stations, the FCC wrote, "Although we believe that Media Watch's views regarding violence in news programming are legitimate matters for discussion within the Denver community, the alleged predominance of violence in the stations' local evening newscasts does not present a basis for intervention by the Commission in connection with a license renewal application."[60] The FCC added that under the First Amendment, "editorial judgments regarding news programs are committed to a broadcaster's good faith discretion."[61]

The only time, in fact, the FCC *will* scrutinize the news judgment of broadcasters as part of the license renewal process occurs when there is extrinsic evidence that a station has deliberately distorted or staged news events.[62] A recent example of a staged news event is a now-infamous 1992 *Dateline* story in which NBC employees used "sparking devices" to trigger an explosion in a General Motors pickup truck to illustrate a story about an alleged design defect.[63]

In articulating its policy against deliberate distortions and staging, the FCC stated,

Rigging or slanting the news is a most heinous act against the public interest—indeed, there is no act more harmful to the public's ability to handle its affairs. In all cases where we may appropriately do so, we shall act to protect the public interest in this important respect. But in this democracy, no government agency can authenticate the news, or should try to do so.[64]

To constitute a deliberate distortion of news, two conditions must be met. First, "the distortion or staging [must] be deliberately intended to slant or mislead."[65] Second, "the distortion must involve a significant event and not merely a minor or incidental aspect of the news report."[66] The allegation of deliberate distortion must be supported by extrinsic evidence, meaning "evidence other than the broadcast itself, such as written or oral instructions from station management, outtakes, or evidence of bribery."[67]

The deliberate distortion or staging exception, of course, will never serve as the entree, or point of attack, for groups like Rocky Mountain Media Watch that are concerned with excessive real-life violence on the news, unless the violence is somehow staged or manipulated. There was no allegation that the Denver television stations created or staged the crimes about which they reported. They did not manipulate the events themselves. What is more, this exception will not thwart the growth and development of vérité voyeurism. If hidden camera videotape presented as news is neither staged nor manipulated, it cannot be regulated by the FCC. Packaging voyeuristic videotape as news on a newsmagazine or newscast thus largely exempts it from FCC control.

One of the few possible instances in which the FCC would step in to regulate mediated voyeurism would occur if the voyeurism were of the sexually prurient variety described in the Introduction and Chapter 1. Obscene speech is not protected by the First Amendment, and the FCC has the power to zone, or "channel," nonobscene but otherwise indecent speech into time periods of the day when children are not likely to be in the audience. Thus it is that sexual fetish voyeurism does not proliferate on broadcast television but instead propagates on the much more loosely regulated World Wide Web.

In summary, the FCC's current interpretation and application of the public interest standard allows mediated voyeurism to flourish on television, unfettered by government forces. The fact that some brands of mediated voyeurism may, as Chapter 2 suggests, involve sensationalistic content that jeopardizes privacy concerns or capitalizes on racial prejudices and stereotypes makes no difference. If the public wants to watch that content in sufficient numbers to sustain its economic viability, then the FCC is satisfied that the public interest is being served.

Politics as Spectator Sport

Before leaving the economic and political forces that allow the voyeurism value to flourish, we must recognize that today politics itself often is served up on television as a voyeuristic spectator sport. There are three primary ways in which television represents and promotes politics as voyeurism: (1) news coverage that often focuses on the private, titillating, or prurient aspects of politicians' lives; (2) political talk shows in which dialogue is denigrated and spectacle is celebrated; and (3) horse-race coverage of campaigns that suggests politics is something to be passively watched rather than actively joined. Taken together, these three factors suggest that politics, like voyeurism, is all about watching others and, in particular, watching them as a form of entertainment.

Television networks, in particular the twenty-four-hour-a-day cable news channels, seem to be obsessed with exposing the private lives of politicians. Besides the obvious voyeuristic appeal of President Clinton's "not appropriate" relationship with

Monica Lewinsky, other political stories fit the voyeurism mold. The allegations of then Texas governor George W. Bush's past cocaine use that erupted in August 1999 provided journalists with yet another opportunity to ponder the point at which a public individual's right to privacy ends and the audience's right to be voyeurs begins.[68] Digging deep into almost anyone's past will surely bring up a few titillating and salacious details that may make for interesting viewing but do very little for promoting democracy.

But television embraces politics as voyeurism in ways far beyond dishing out titillating, private, or prurient facts about politicians. In particular, many of the political talk shows of the late 1990s foster and promote politics as a sensationalistic and voyeuristic spectacle. How do the shows do this?

First, many political talk shows devalue discourse, much as voyeurism does not involve discourse but merely watching. It is ironic, of course, that these programs are called "talk" shows, since they, like voyeurism, often have very little to do with well-reasoned discussion or discourse. More often, they involve guests—combatants, really—shouting over one another, resulting in what the late philosopher-educator and First Amendment theorist Alexander Meiklejohn might have called a "dialectical free-for-all."[69] The shows embrace what the journalist Alicia C. Shepard calls "television's shout culture."[70] The arguments that occur, as she points out in a recent edition of the *American Journalism Review,* often are insult driven and the guests most likely to be invited back are "vociferous shouters who are at home in a circus-like atmosphere."[71]

Almost everything on shows such as *Crossfire, Hardball,* and the *Capital Gang* is reduced to what Georgetown University's Deborah Tannen calls in *Brill's Content* a "left-right fight":[72]

> The very structure of these shows is based on underlying metaphors of war and sports: Two sides duke it out; one wins, the other loses. But it's all a game: See the warring parties jocularly sparring at the

end of the show, as the camera pulls away? Those who take part in these pseudo-debates know that there is a display aspect to it.[73]

Both the circuslike atmosphere and the display aspect of these shows that Shepard and Tannen respectively describe suggest that politics is something in which discussion, as is true with the practice of voyeurism, is superfluous. James Fallows, former editor of *U.S. News & World Report,* emphasized precisely this point in his 1996 critique of the media and politics, *Breaking the News:* "The pressure to keep things lively means that squabbling replaces dialogue."[74] And what are the ramifications of this cacophony according to Fallows? "The discussion shows that are supposed to add to public understanding may actually reduce it, by hammering home the message that 'issues' don't matter except as items for politicians to squabble about."[75]

Fallows's last point is critical as it pertains to the relationship between politics and mediated voyeurism. Political issues are *not* something in which the public is to become actively involved, the talk shows subtly suggest. Instead, the issues serve only as props for entertainment, providing the mechanism for conflict that leads to the shouting that ultimately leads to spectatorship. The shows fit neatly under the category of infotainment, described earlier in this chapter. Marvin Kalb, a veteran journalist and now director of the Joan Shorenstein Center on the Press, Politics, and Public Policy at Harvard University, remarked in the *American Journalism Review,* "If you enjoy infotainment and the veneer of news and the essence of gossip, the 24-hour-a-day cable shows are God's gift."[76] Politics, then, is all about spectatorship, precisely as voyeurism also is all about watching. When we watch these shows, we may feel as if we are participating in politics. In fact, however, we really are mere spectators gawking at a highly contrived, political cock fight. As voyeurs, we do not need to actually participate in politics—watching the spectacle, these shows subtly insinuate, is enough.

What is more, the hosts and guests on these shows often rise to celebrity status in our mediated culture. They frequently overshadow the subject matter with their outrageous remarks and outsized egos. Just as the late John F. Kennedy Jr.'s magazine *George* cleverly blurred the lines between politics and entertainment, so too do many of the political talk shows. It is as if we are voyeurs watching a well-scripted, conflict-driven Hollywood production: The thrill and enjoyment comes in watching, not participating.

Beyond the frenetic political talk shows, another aspect of media coverage of politics is directly connected to the voyeurism value. It is horse-race journalism. Horse-race coverage of political campaigns, as the name implies, emphasizes who is winning, who is gaining, and who is fading fast, all at the expense of serious discourse and discussion about the substantive issues. Near-daily polls before elections—increasingly the polls occur *long* before elections, as the 2000 presidential campaign made clear—show viewers who is ahead and who is behind in the various "races" for office. Journalists often focus not on the substantive issues facing the politicians but rather on their strategies for staying at the top of the pack or, alternatively, for making a move to come up on the rest of the field.

In the summer of 1999, for instance, journalists obsessed not on the substance or lack thereof of the Republican George W. Bush's politics but instead on whether he could maintain his "front-runner" status despite allegations of cocaine use. How should Bush handle the allegations and questions? What strategy, in other words, would work best for Bush? Should he keep his mouth shut? Should he attack the press as violating his right to privacy? Should he tell all as quickly as possible so as to reduce damage later? All was strategy, with no substance.

The role of the journalist and the talk show pundit is to prognosticate incessantly about such questions of strategy. As Bartholomew H. Sparrows, associate professor of government at the University of Texas at Austin, writes in his 1999 book

Uncertain Guardians, "Journalists are the expert handicappers; the voters the passive spectators on the sidelines of a 'game.'"[77]

The strategy focus that dominates horse-race journalism may contribute to the politics-as-voyeurism phenomenon in another important way: It may alienate potential voters from active participation in the political process through its constant emphasis on the candidates' motives and self-interests. Joseph N. Cappella and Kathleen Hall Jamieson of the Annenberg School of Communication at the University of Pennsylvania suggest in their 1997 book *Spiral of Cynicism,* "Excessive strategy coverage may activate cynicism in the electorate. Cynicism may result from the spectatorship that the strategy format engenders."[78] This, in turn, may estrange individuals from the political process.

Cappella and Jamieson's rigorous studies suggest, in fact, that "a single strategically framed news story can activate cynical attributions. Large doses are not necessary."[79] The strategic news stories then prompt the audience's own political stories, "which are themselves cynical and loaded with strategic language."[80] Ultimately, their research indicates that the price paid for the reinforcement of the cynical beliefs of potential voters by journalists' strategic framing of stories is "public disengagement both from the political process and from the press."[81] Much as the voyeur does not participate or actively engage with the object of his gaze, the potential voter may not participate or engage with the political process due in part to the media's own voyeuristic coverage of politics.

The bottom line today is that politics often is portrayed by journalists as a spectator sport, be it a horse race between politicians or a wrestling match between commentators. Dialogue is out, replaced by snappy yet substance-free sound bites and the pointless pontification of pundits, and watching is in.

Now that we have covered some of the historical, social, economic, and political forces that facilitated the rise of mediated voyeurism in the 1990s, the next chapter turns to a different subject. It addresses the technological forces—the cameras, the equipment—that make much of mediated voyeurism possible.

Don't Look Now, but Somebody's Watching You

Mediated voyeurism never has been as easy to produce as it is today. That is attributable in no small part to some very small parts. In particular, credit belongs to amazing advancements in recording technology that allow everyone from the journalist working for a megamedia conglomerate to the quiet, nice-guy next door working for himself to capture unguarded moments from the lives of others on videotape.

The lightweight portable video camera—either handheld or shoulder-mounted—makes possible much of the video on a program such as the reality-producer Paul Stojanovich's *World's Wildest Police Videos*. The show, which debuted in 1998 and falls into the video vérité category of mediated voyeurism defined in the Introduction, relies almost exclusively on video recorders used by law enforcement agencies, news bureaus, and other sources to supply its raw material. The cameras required for this type of mediated voyeurism need not be miniature or hidden to effectively bring viewers an action-packed hour of highway car chases and surface street shoot-outs. The cameras that capture footage for this show instead may be held by a person flying in a police or news helicopter or they may be mounted on the dashboards of highway patrol cruisers.[1]

A Case When Size Does Matter

Although it is not always the case with reality television shows like *World's Wildest Police Videos* or *Cops,* when it comes to some other forms of mediated voyeurism, the maxim that "size matters" indeed holds true. And this time around, the rule of thumb is quite simple: the smaller the better.

Developments in miniature, covert recording devices have especially facilitated two forms of mediated voyeurism—the hidden camera investigative journalism popularized on show-all television newsmagazines and the sexual voyeurism that is rampant on both amateur and commercial sites on the World Wide Web. Tiny cameras, concealed in a person's clothing, cloaked in a seemingly innocuous object such as a smoke detector or pen, or hidden behind a stray nail hole in a wall, allow both the intrepid reporter and the pornographic voyeur to thrive in the new millennium. The mediated voyeurs in the audience, watching behind television and computer screens, reap the benefits.

Consider first the case of investigative journalism. A number of the legal cases from the late 1990s involving mediated voyeurism that are analyzed in Chapter 5 center around the use of miniature cameras and microphones by journalists. For instance, the dispute in a case called *Sanders v. American Broadcasting Companies*[2] centered on an ABC investigative report in which a reporter wore a small video camera hidden in her hat. The device—dubbed appropriately enough a "hat cam"—allowed the reporter Stacy Lescht to covertly videotape the actions of telepsychics employed by the Psychic Marketing Group in its Los Angeles offices. Lescht also wore a microphone attached to her brassiere to pick up conversations.

In another California case, *Shulman v. Group W Productions*,[3] a television producer outfitted an air ambulance nurse with a small wireless microphone that picked up her conversations with a woman rendered paraplegic in a car accident. The microphone caught the suffering woman pleading to die. And then there is the infamous *Food Lion v. Capital Cities/ABC*.[4] It involved ABC employees working for the now-canceled newsmagazine *PrimeTime Live*. They obtained jobs at Food Lion and then went to work wearing tiny cameras secreted in their wigs and clothing to record footage about alleged food-mishandling practices at the supermarket chain. Although a federal appellate court in October 1999 reduced the damages awarded to Food Lion to the nominal sum of two dollars,[5] this case did not resolve the controversies—legal or ethical—regarding the use of hidden cameras by journalists.

These recording devices enable the mediated voyeurism of investigative journalism to occur with greater ease and frequency. As will be recalled from the Introduction, mediated voyeurism is defined as the consumption of revealing images of and information about others' apparently real and unguarded lives, often yet not always for purposes of entertainment but frequently at the expense of privacy and discourse, through the means of the mass media and Internet. In each of the cases described above, it was the development of new technology that allowed investigative journalists to bring us revealing images of and information about things such as the work of telepsychics, paramedics, and supermarket employees. The size of the cameras and microphones allowed them to be hidden such that these individuals could be recorded in moments that appeared real and unguarded. The unobtrusive nature of the recording device is essential, in other words, for noninterference with the action. It puts the "vérité" in voyeurism.

But investigative journalism is not the only form of mediated voyeurism facilitated by new recording technology. Over 100

sites on the World Wide Web are filled with images of unsuspecting men and women showering, undressing, and even engaging in sexual activities with their partners.[6] These pictures
are sometimes taken with hidden cameras placed in gym bags in
locker rooms or with cameras concealed behind mirrors. In
these voyeurism sites are further levels of sexual, voyeuristic
fetish images that are made possible by new covert recording
technologies. There are images of unsuspecting women taken
while they sit on a toilet, pictures euphemistically known as
"upskirts" of women's underwear shot from underneath their
skirts while they walk through shopping malls or stand in lines,
and cleavage photographs called "downblouses" taken, as the
name suggests, from above to peer down women's blouses.[7] A
man recently was arrested for using a video camera concealed
in a gym bag to shoot up the skirts of ten women at Jacobs
Field, home of the Cleveland Indians baseball team. He allegedly placed the bag near their feet while the women stood in
line at a concession stand.[8] Sometimes the victim knows the
voyeur—a devious boyfriend or husband may use a hidden
camera to capture images of an unsuspecting significant other
while she showers or uses the bathroom.

Advancements in video technology make all of this possible.
Indeed, these advancements help to transform ordinary instances of Peeping Tom voyeurism—the physical act of peering
into bedroom windows, for instance, without the aid of recording technology—into *mediated* voyeurism. Today voyeurs need
not even be physically present when the image is captured. They
merely install the right equipment and then sit back and watch
the revealing images from the safety and seclusion of their own
home and perhaps later post them on the World Wide Web for
everyone else to watch as many times as they would like. As the
attorney Ellen Alderman and Caroline Kennedy observe in *The
Right to Privacy,* "Video cameras can secretly record the most
private of activities, ensuring that the violation can be repeated
over and over for new viewers."[9]

No Lights, Small Cameras, Lots of Action

Miniature video technology today is both inexpensive and readily available to anyone seeking to produce a little mediated voyeurism. It is no longer just for James Bond. A simple search of the World Wide Web in October 1999 turned up a growing number of businesses that specialize in selling the type of high-tech recording gadgets that would make even 007 envious. The names of the companies give a clear idea of what they are all about: Hidden Camera Solutions,[10] Spy Company,[11] Gadgets By Design,[12] Eyetek Surveillance,[13] See-it Surveillance Company,[14] and ISIS Surveillance Systems & Equipment Company.[15] The much-vaunted "e-commerce," it seems, might better be dubbed "see-commerce."

Consideration of some of the products offered by these companies will make anyone who fears mediated voyeurism shudder. For instance, Hidden Camera Solutions offers covert video cameras that are hidden in a wide range of everyday household items. Its on-line catalogue boasts wireless cameras concealed in clock radios, boom boxes, stuffed animals, and smoke detectors.[16] Other "wired" cameras are hidden in lipstick containers as well as both wall and desk clocks. The prices for these items? Some are well within reach of many people. The black-and-white wireless clock radio camera, for instance, was specially priced at $379 in October 1999, and the stuffed animal camera—described on-line as "a perfect nanny cam"—was marked at $495.

Hidden Camera Solutions never suggests that these tools be used for prurient sexual voyeurism. Instead, its on-line literature suggests the products are designed "to insure peace of mind and the safety of your family and business. Prevent employee, housekeeper or roommate theft by using concealed video surveillance cameras."[17] Some of these "private" law enforcement uses of video technology were described in Chapter 3. We borrow the accepted voyeuristic surveillance methods of law enforcement, private business, and the news media when we surreptitiously tape the activities of baby-sitters with our children and cleaning personnel with our possessions. Following the lead of the television newsmagazines, we are engaging in our own rather primitive forms of private "gotcha" video justice. We may not be George Holliday capturing the beating of Rodney King by members of the Los Angeles Police Department, but we are catching something a little closer to our own lives. The camera thus gives us a sense of power and control that can be used to accomplish justice or, alternatively, as suggested in this chapter, to accomplish the prurient. Like all technologies, video recording devices can be used for good or evil.

A company called Gadgets By Design features a product that carries the distinct potential for use in the kind of upskirt voyeurism described earlier. This company sells a "wireless backpack camera and transmitter system."[18] The company boasts the system is "mobile and will not draw any attention," due to a lining that "fully conceals the camera and makes the system totally undetectable."[19] The cost? At $580, it is certainly more than your average backpack, but apparently it is worth the price for those seeking to produce a little mediated voyeurism.

Such backpacks and bags are the precise kind of tool employed by many so-called upskirt voyeurs. They drop a backpack near the feet of a woman standing in line and then hope that the covert camera, buried within but with its lens unobstructed and pointing upward, gets a crisp shot of the woman's underwear or lack thereof. Harold Duquette, a police detective in Alexandria, Virginia, told a reporter for the *Washington Post* in 1998 that the most popular method of upskirt video peepers is precisely that—concealing a small video camera in a shoulder bag, with the lens directed out of the top, and then dangling the bag under a woman's skirt or placing it on the ground next to her.[20]

Such a devious use of its camera backpack, of course, is not described on the Gadget By Design web pages. The company simply states that it designs and builds "complete surveillance systems for your special applications."[21] It is, of course, the special *misapplications* that could cause the most trouble in the realm of mediated voyeurism.

The hidden camera need not come disguised in the form of a household object or a backpack. It may simply be placed behind a nail hole in a wall. Consider, for instance, Spy Company's DH2000 MKIII-IR pinhole video camera.[22] It is touted as "the world's smallest high resolution pinhole chip camera."[23] All that is necessary for its use is a hole in the wall the size of one-sixteenth of an inch. It can even operate in low-light conditions.

The dangers of such pinhole cameras are clear. These technologies allow mediated voyeurism to flourish. The mirror may really have two faces if you count the camera behind it, and the walls may really have eyes if you purchase the "covert wall picture" from ASA Systems Inc.[24] You simply plug the "picture" into the wall and transmission begins immediately. The potential for abuse is clear. Lauren Weinstein, a technology professional and moderator of the on-line Privacy Forum, contends that "what you have going on all over the place now is people who are just kind of planting cameras everywhere they can find places that are at least theoretically in public and then using them however they want."[25] It is the "using them however they want" part that is most frightening to those who do not want to be the focus of the voyeur's gaze.

And what about tools that could be used by journalists for hidden camera investigations? ISIS Surveillance Systems & Equipment Company offers "a wide variety of body worn cameras."[26] The company peddled cameras in 1999 that came on or in ties, shirts, glasses, jackets, and baseball caps. And then there is a company called Spy Centre and Private Eye Enterprises, Inc., which offers its own line of body-worn cameras.[27] It sells an eyeglass case video camera that according to its on-line literature, "obtains great body worn video. The Eyeglass Case Camera fits in your front shirt pocket and the video cable plugs into a body worn video recorder."[28] The same company offers a wristwatch video camera that it claims "provides unmatched directional capability for the user to acquire the perfect covert video shot of any subject without drawing unwanted attention simply by moving the forearm position or angle of wrist."[29]

In a truly great irony, the tool on which most mediated voyeurism described in this book is consumed—the television set—can also be a common tool for recording voyeuristic images. Louis R. Mizell Jr., a former special agent and intelligence officer for the U.S. Department of State, writes in his recent book *Invasion of Privacy*,

> Sometimes you watch television and sometimes the television watches you. At least three companies make television sets that conceal video cameras. The camera will work if the television is on or off and can be triggered to begin taping by movement or sound. Some companies have installed these television cameras in lunch rooms. Interestingly, the same companies that made the TV camera also advertise a Video Camera Detector.[30]

With all of this video gadgetry, it is easy to see how mediated voyeurism may be produced by virtually anyone with about $500 to spare and lots of free time and ingenuity. A well-placed camera can capture almost anything. As the next section reveals, that is precisely the problem.

Abusing the Nanny Cam: Hot for Sitter

Tiny cameras can serve many valid purposes. They allow journalists to expose the problems of abuse in nursing homes and the practices of devious repairpersons in our homes. They also allow private individuals to check up on the nanny. Unfortunately, products like those described above can be used for more than just catching a mischievous baby-sitter mistreating a toddler or an errant employee tapping the till. Baby-sitters and young girls, it seems, are the frequent target of video voyeurs.

Consider first the case of thirty-one-year-old Daniel LaBelle of Weymouth, Massachusetts. He pleaded innocent in May 1999 to charges of allegedly filming two teenage baby-sitters with a hidden camera in his home's bathroom.[31] The specific charges were posing or displaying a child for pornography.[32] In July 1999, a grand jury indicted LaBelle on eleven counts, including three of possession of child pornography and three of posing a child in a state of nudity.[33]

How did the Weymouth police catch on to LaBelle's alleged voyeuristic activities? Quite by accident. A thirteen-year-old girl who was baby-sitting for the suspect allegedly found a tape marked with the name of a popular movie, *My Best Friend's Wedding*. She proceeded to pop it into the VCR.[34] What to her wondrous eyes did appear but images not of that hit movie's stars but instead of her very own fifteen-year-old sister who previously had sat for LaBelle. The older girl was shown getting out of the shower. The younger girl then went to the bathroom and allegedly discovered LaBelle's concealed weapon of choice—a video camera hidden in a cabinet.[35]

And then there was the case against Walter R. Conte Jr. He allegedly had a similar fetish for young girls and hidden cameras. Conte, then the principal at Brush High School in the South Euclid-Lyndhust School District in Ohio, allegedly used a video camera in his bathroom at home to videotape cheerleaders as they changed for a beach party.[36] Police reportedly confiscated thirty-eight videotapes from Conte's home, one of which showed partially dressed cheerleaders, all of whom were younger than eighteen years.[37]

In April 1997, Conte pleaded no contest to one count of interception of oral communication, one count of possession of a criminal tool, and six counts of voyeurism.[38] In May of that year, he was sentenced to six months in the Lake County jail and ordered to perform 200 hours of community service.[39] And then in June 1997, Conte was fired as principal of Brush High School.[40] His penchant for video cameras and nubile teens had cost him an $80,000-a-year job.

Conte's problems did not end there. Several of the girls filed civil lawsuits against him. One cheerleader eventually settled her suit in 1998 for an undisclosed amount of cash.[41]

These are the types of voyeuristic images that often find their way to the World Wide Web. Sites with names like Upskirt Heaven, which boasts "The finest in upskirt, panty, & voyeur images available,"[42] and Upskirt Pictures, which bills itself as "A site for the real voyeur,"[43] abound in cyberspace. Many locations, such as The VoyeurWeb,[44] feature amateur "contributor" or "private shots" sections that allow voyeurs to send in their own hidden camera work of neighbors, relatives, and significant others.[45] A quick peek at the Online Voyeur site gives a sample of hidden camera photographs available to customers.[46] Although some images on some these sites appear to be of more-than-willing participants—exhibitionists, really, as described in Chapter 1—others involve unsuspecting and unwilling women who likely would be outraged to know their bodies were being displayed for the viewing pleasure of others.

David Bernstein, vice president of an adult industry publication, proclaimed in 1999, "Voyeur sites are the biggest thing on the Internet right now."[47] Why are the sites so hot? Bernstein thinks he knows. "Traditional porn is no longer enough. People are always looking for something different, and hidden cameras are the next big thing."[48]

Technology today makes the hidden cameras about which Bernstein speaks possible. There is, then, a clear link between technological developments and the proliferation of mediated voyeurism. New technologies make possible everything from the "hat cam" investigations of journalists to the "upskirt" intrusions of video voyeurs. And what does this mean for those of us who do not want to be the target of mediated voyeurism? As Alderman and Kennedy write, "You will likely think twice the next time you enter a public rest room or try on clothes in a dressing room, and you may even start checking your own mirrors."[49]

5

Free Press, Free Voyeurs?

"Congress shall make no law ... abridging the freedom of speech, or of the press," reads the First Amendment to the United States Constitution. Ratified in 1791, the First Amendment was drafted by James Madison long before the advent of the sophisticated electronic technology described in Chapter 4 that makes mediated voyeurism possible. Today, that amendment increasingly safeguards, or at least is called on to safeguard, mediated voyeurism—our right to peer and to gaze into places typically forbidden to average citizens and to facilitate our ability to see and to hear the innermost details of others' lives without fear of legal repercussion. Why? The increase in the offering of reality television programs and newsmagazines has resulted in a surge of lawsuits filed by persons featured on those shows.[1] The First Amendment, in turn, is trotted out by the media as a defense against those suits.

Whether the First Amendment protects mediated voyeurism ultimately is left to the courts that interpret its meaning and, in particular, to the United States Supreme Court. The nine justices who sit on the nation's high court are the final arbiters of its meaning. Their word determines the scope of freedom of expression in the United States. To the extent that the First

Amendment press freedom is construed expansively by the judiciary, our right to be voyeurs is enhanced. To the extent that it is narrowly interpreted, our ability to watch others' lives unfold voyeuristically is limited.

If press freedom is viewed broadly to serve mediated voyeurism, then several propositions must be supported by courts construing the First Amendment. First, they must provide journalists, photographers, and camerapeople with enhanced protection in both their ability to *gather* voyeuristic images—to enter buildings, use telephoto lenses and hidden cameras, and lie if necessary to procure information—and to *disseminate* private but titillating and embarrassing true facts about others. The media must, in other words, receive special protection that other people would not normally possess to go places, see things, and tell stories if the voyeurism value is to carry the day in First Amendment jurisprudence.

Second, the public's so-called right to know—a right that is not explicitly mentioned in the First Amendment, or anywhere else in the Constitution for that matter—must be the official, judicially accepted battle cry to defend voyeuristic media practices. Journalists already heartily embrace the right-to-know mantra. As Christopher Meyers, a philosophy professor at California State University, Bakersfield, writes, "An appeal to the public's right to know serves as the core element of the journalism ethos."[2] Courts too must adopt the right-to-know claim if the voyeurism value is to be privileged under the First Amendment. Why? If the public has a right to know, then the public has a right to watch so that it can know. Concomitantly, if the public has a right to know, then the press must have a right to gather the same images the public has a right to watch.

The media themselves also must push the envelope of the First Amendment to guard their ability both to gather the visuals and videotape we like to watch and then to publicize and broadcast those images. Put more bluntly and perhaps cynically, the First Amendment must be pushed by large media conglomerates and corporations to protect the kinds of high profits and ratings that often are generated by relatively low budget voyeuristic techniques such as hidden camera reportage and ride-along journalism. Not only, then, does the voyeur benefit from an expansive reading of the First Amendment, but so do the corporate entities that feed us voyeurism. They reap the monetary rewards of large audiences, which translate into hefty advertising revenue.

But this is still not enough if the voyeurism value is to be privileged by the First Amendment. The audience's right to receive speech—a right, in particular, to receive voyeuristic video images and others' personal information—must triumph over individuals' ability to control the flow of information about themselves. In other words, the rights of one person—the person who is the object or focus of the voyeur's gaze—must be sacrificed to privilege the rights of another person—the voyeur. The right to watch must trump the right not to be watched. It is an essential trade-off of rights if the voyeurism value is to prevail in the new millennium.

For example, the right of the audience of a television newsmagazine such as *PrimeTime Live* to watch hidden camera footage of employees at Food Lion supermarkets allegedly repackaging spoiled meat—a real case discussed in more detail elsewhere in the book—must trump the right of the unsuspecting employees caught on tape either to suppress or to punish its dissemination. Likewise, the right of the audience to watch police officers raid a home during the execution of a search warrant must take precedence over the right of the home owner to keep journalists and media cameras out of his or her home when the police enter. Two cases very similar to this scenario—*Wilson v. Layne* and *Hanlon v. Berger*—are described later in Chapter 6.

If, alternatively, press freedom is viewed narrowly under the First Amendment, then the access of the press to both the places and the information that make for mediated voyeurism will be curtailed. The press would be granted no special immunity from laws such as trespass and fraud that would otherwise hinder its news-gathering (read, *image*-gathering) ability. As a general rule, in fact, the United States Supreme Court has held that journalists receive no greater protection than other citizens when it comes to violating general laws that apply to all people, such as trespass and general principles of contract law.

For instance, the Court ruled in 1991 that when a reporter breaches a promise of confidentiality to a source—in essence, violates a contract not to reveal the source's name—the reporter can be held liable to the source for damages incurred by the violation.[3] In the particular dispute, the source lost his job as a result of two newspapers breaking their promises to protect his identity. Justice Byron White wrote for the majority of the Court in that case, *Cohen v. Cowles Media,* that "enforcement of such general laws against the press is not subject to stricter scrutiny than would be applied to enforcement against other persons or organizations."[4] The First Amendment does not, in other words, exempt the press from liability for breaking promises.

Despite its language in a 1972 decision that "without some protection for seeking out the news, freedom of the press could be eviscerated,"[5] the United States Supreme Court has not been willing to provide extensive First Amendment protection for the press to gather images. As the communications law scholar Matthew D. Bunker and his colleagues observed in a 1999 law review article, "First Amendment protection for newsgathering has remained largely inchoate."[6] Courts and juries today, in fact, are more willing to punish the press for how it gathers information than for how it reports information. A country that privileges interests such as an individual's concern for privacy— a concept described in Chapter 2 and again later in this chapter—over an audience's voyeuristic proclivities clearly will pull in the reins on mediated voyeurism by imposing legal liability for both intrusive news gathering and invasive news reporting.

Of course, the situation is not as black and white as this description would have it. It seldom is with the law, a fact that is just as frustrating for the general public as it is aggravating for first-year law students. The Supreme Court does not provide blanket support to voyeurs' rights to watch others under the First Amendment, just as it does not give absolute protection to the privacy interests of celebrities and others who are the frequent subjects of mediated voyeurism. More often than not, courts engage in the time-honored tradition of balancing interests, weighing the merits of one right or claim against another to reach a solution. In the case of mediated voyeurism, they must balance First Amendment interests in free speech and press—interests that directly serve the audience's right to receive voyeuristic speech and images—against concerns such as the privacy of the individual whose property is trespassed to acquire voyeuristic images or whose personal information is disclosed to titillate the audience. The legal issues that affect voyeurism often are couched in such terms of balancing.

For instance, in its 1998 decision in *Shulman v. Group W Productions*[7]—a case described later in this chapter—the California Supreme Court faced a question involving the voyeuristic dissemination of a videotape showing a woman rendered paraplegic by a car accident begging to die. As the high court of California framed the overriding issue in *Shulman,*

> At what point does the publishing or broadcasting of otherwise private words, expressions and emotions cease to be protected by the press's constitutional and common law privilege—its right to report on matters of legitimate public interest—and become an unjustified, actionable invasion of the subject's private life?[8]

How courts resolve the tension between the audience's interest in voyeurism and an individual's interest in privacy is a key issue that is explored in this chapter. Initially, the chapter suggests three ways in which courts protect the audience's voyeuristic First Amendment interests. First, courts tend to adopt an expansive definition of "newsworthiness." This is extremely important because newsworthiness is a complete defense to an invasion of privacy lawsuit that would otherwise punish the media for the dissemination of truthful, private, and embarrassing facts about an individual.

Second, and closely related to the first point, courts are wary of second-guessing the editorial control and discretion of journalists, providing them instead with wide latitude to bring us voyeurism masquerading as news. Courts are extremely deferential to journalists' choices about content, having repeatedly held that under the terms of the First Amendment, editing should be left to editors. This breathing room allows profitable voyeuristic content to flourish.

Third, a perhaps more subtle legal force leading to the propagation of mediated voyeurism is the United States Supreme Court's well-established decision to give large, megamedia corporations the same First Amendment rights as individuals. As will be suggested later, these corporations simultaneously use the First Amendment as a sword to make money and deploy it as a shield to protect their voyeuristic practices.

Building on this chapter's discussion of this trio of legal forces that facilitate the growth of the voyeurism value, the next chapter examines a current legal backlash that could stunt the media's voyeuristic proclivities. It is suggested that a 1999 United States Supreme Court decision restricting media ride-alongs with law enforcement, when considered along with a new wave of state and federal anti-paparazzi legislation that cropped up in the wake of Princess Diana's August 1997 death and a growing number of state laws that restrict videotape voyeurism of the sexually prurient variety, signals that the voyeur's rights under the First Amendment are far from absolute.

Privacy Laws and Voyeurism

Chapter 2 suggested that the concepts of voyeurism and privacy are related. As our expectations of what is or should remain private *decrease,* our expectations about what information is fair game for public consumption and mediated voyeurism *increase.* In the terms often used by social scientists, this is known as an "inverse," or "negative," relationship. An inverse relationship exists when one item—in this case, voyeurism—increases or goes up while another item—here, privacy—decreases or goes down.

The legal system today protects privacy in its many forms. For instance, a woman's right to choose to have an abortion is protected, the United States Supreme Court held in 1973's still-controversial *Roe v. Wade* decision,[9] by an unenumerated, or implied, right to privacy found in the United States Constitution. Privacy is this sense refers to the ability to make one's own autonomous choice, free from government control or interference.

Privacy can also take the form of statutory protection of information designed to prevent others from voyeuristically peeping at our lives. For instance, after Robert Bork was nominated in the 1980s by former President Ronald Reagan to the United States Supreme Court and during his ill-fated confirmation hearings, a Washington, D.C., weekly paper published a list of 146 videos Bork allegedly had recently rented. Although Bork's cinematic tastes came up clean—he primarily rented Westerns and family films—the threat to privacy was clear. Shortly after this transpired, Congress quickly passed—perhaps for the sake of some of its own members' more carnal tastes—a piece of federal legislation restricting access to movie rental information known as the Video Privacy Protection Act of 1988.[10]

Protection against mediated voyeurism can also take the form of civil remedies that allow one person to sue another under various privacy "torts" or theories of legal relief. One privacy tort, known as *public disclosure of private facts,* is particularly relevant here. Under this theory, a reporter or media entity may be held legally liable for giving publicity to truthful but otherwise private and embarrassing information about an individual if the publication of that information would be highly offensive to a reasonable person.

This theory is significant in terms of mediated voyeurism because it suggests that there are some images and information that society believes should remain private, sheltered from the prying eyes and ears of a voyeuristic nation. Publicizing an embarrassing fact that an individual has kept secret deserves punishment, according to this theory. As the law professor Robert C. Post of the University of California–Berkeley observes, this privacy tort recognizes and embodies civility rules that suggest there are "information preserves" that are integral to individuals and that deserve respect.[11] Courts too acknowledge this important interest. The Supreme Court of the state of Washington observed in a 1998 case that "every individual has some phases of his life and his activities and some facts about himself that he does not expose to the public eye, but keeps entirely to himself or at most reveals only to his family or to close personal friends."[12]

But there is a critical caveat, or exception, to the public disclosure of private facts tort that allows us to play the role of voyeur and to discover the facts that others want to keep secret. It is a defense that the media often raise when sued for publicly disseminating private and embarrassing information about a person. The defense is *newsworthiness* and it is described below.

Newsworthiness:
The Voyeur's Legal Defense

One critical legal standard with a direct bearing on the voyeurism value is newsworthiness. Newsworthiness, as noted above, is a defense to the invasion of privacy theory known as public disclosure of private facts. If published information or images are considered by a court to be newsworthy—courts often use the phrase "of legitimate public concern" interchangeably with newsworthiness—there can be no liability for the media.

Newsworthiness also is a defense for a legal theory called appropriation. Appropriation occurs when a person or corporation uses the name or likeness or image of another person—usually a celebrity—for commercial gain without the consent of the person. For instance, if a cereal company places an image of the golfer Tiger Woods on its boxes without Woods's permission, Woods can claim appropriation. If the photograph or name is used in connection with a newsworthy story, however, there is no liability, even if the person did not consent to the use of the photograph or name. Thus a newspaper that uses a picture of Woods to accompany a story about the golfer winning a tournament would be protected from liability.

As Chapter 3 made clear, journalists often have trouble defining news. Many times it amounts to whatever the public is interested in watching or reading and whatever will boost advertising revenues. The definitional problem is exacerbated when courts—not journalists—are asked to provide a definition of what is newsworthy.

Courts, unfortunately for the targets and victims of mediated voyeurism, often defer to journalistic judgment—the same ratings-grabbing, videotape-driven judgment described in Chapter 3—when deciding whether a particular story is newsworthy.[13] They generally adopt what the law professor Diane Zimmerman aptly describes as the Leave-It-to-the-Press Model for defining news.[14] In other words, journalists often are awarded, by judicial default, the power to provide the legal definition of news. As Zimmerman observes, "The vast majority of cases seem to hold that what is printed is by definition of legitimate public concern."[15] Courts, in turn, have "gradually increased the scope of the newsworthy defense since its initial formulation in 1890."[16] As the veteran legal scholar Donald M. Gillmor and his colleagues wrote in 1996, "The news media have for the most part been able to persuade the courts to accept their standards of what is newsworthy."[17]

This legal definition promotes and serves the voyeurism value. How? Many broadcast journalists, as described earlier in the book, are increasingly driven by economic and entertainment concerns—not concerns over whether they are serving some abstract public good or democracy with a product they call news. They are, in turn, driven to provide sensationalistic videotape that captures and holds the attention of a large audience. In other words, broadcasters are compelled to provide videotape that the public *wants* to watch, not necessarily what it *needs* to watch to engage in wise and informed decisionmaking. If the public wants to watch something, news shows will keep serving it up to the audience on behalf of the advertisers who want to reach that audience with their commercials. As Kathleen Hall Jamieson, dean of the Annenberg School for Communication at the University of Pennsylvania, writes, "The primary function of the mass media is to attract and hold large audiences for advertisers."[18]

It should be clear by now, then, that both the legal and journalistic definitions of news ultimately are shaped by economic marketplace forces. Broadcast news programs and television newsmagazines will keep feeding us whatever it is that we *want* to watch. The legal scholar and law professor C. Edwin Baker writes, "Market-based incentives will lead media producers to provide audiences with what they want."[19]

Most courts, in turn, will continue to trust the news judgment of broadcasters in determining what is newsworthy. The courts will protect what we want to watch if it is chosen by journalists who know that we want to watch it. The power of the media to define newsworthiness for the courts thus protects their ability to pander to our desires to voyeuristically watch others, provided the videotape and facts are packaged as news. The deep bow that courts give to journalistic judgment in defining what is newsworthy is topped by the even deeper bow that members of the media, in turn, give to public tastes and preferences in determining newsworthiness.

It is critical to note that when courts actually do attempt to define newsworthiness, they often do so with nebulous and expansive concepts such as "matters of public interest"[20] and "legitimate public interest."[21] Almost anything can be said to be of public interest, of course, if the public is interested in it. In turn, broadcast journalists will produce whatever it is that the public is most interested in at the time—whatever it is, in other words, that we want to watch.

The judicial admonition to consider "community mores"[22] in determining whether something is newsworthy does little to stop a community that likes to watch from watching. In other words, as we become a nation of mediated voyeurs, and more and more people watch reality TV shows and become accustomed to hidden camera investigative news shows, the community standards issue is rendered moot. If the community wants to watch, then that is the community's value and norm.

It is this kind of logic that allowed a federal court in California in 1997 to hold, in the context of a cause of action for appropriation, that "the scope of newsworthiness is extremely broad" and includes photographs of "sexual touchings" between the erstwhile couple Pamela Anderson Lee of *Baywatch* fame and Motley Crüe bad-boy drummer Tommy Lee.[23] A year later, in a 1998 case involving another videotape of the overexposed Anderson Lee having sex (this time with a different man), the same federal court observed that California courts "have consistently held that newsworthiness is not limited to high minded discussion of politics and public affairs" and instead have established "that the romantic connections of celebrities are newsworthy."[24] This time, the newsworthiness defense precluded Anderson Lee from recovering for both an action for appropriation and one for public disclosure of private facts. This same type of logic also extends the newsworthiness defense outside of the area of newscasts, newsmagazine, and reality television shows like *Cops* to talk shows that cater to voyeuristic audiences that crave the public revelations of embarrassing facts such as *The Sally Jessy Raphael Show*[25] and *Donahue*.[26]

Beyond these cases, however, a 1998 decision handed down by the Supreme Court of California involving a reality television show illustrates the broad scope of the newsworthiness defense to the public disclosure of private facts tort. That case—*Shulman v. Group W Productions*[27]—is described in the next section.

"I Just Want to Die"

"I just want to die," forty-seven-year-old Ruth Shulman told a nurse, Laura Carnahan, as she was being hoisted on a stretcher into an air ambulance helicopter. Shulman had just been riding in a car driven by her daughter on Interstate 10 in smoggy Riverside County, California. She was returning home to Palos Verdes from the desert resort town of Palm Springs along with her husband, son, and daughter, when the car suddenly spun off the side of the highway. It landed upside down in a drainage ditch. Emergency personnel were forced to use the jaws-of-life rescue machine to pry Shulman free.

Carnahan tried to reassure Shulman. She told her that she was "going to do real well." But Shulman sensed she was not going to do real well—she would, in fact, be rendered paraplegic by the accident—and she repeated her death wish to Carnahan. "I just want to die. I don't want to go through this."

Unfortunately for Shulman, she had no idea that those words, uttered during moments of intense pain, suffering, and confusion, would be broadcast three months later to all of greater Los Angeles on a reality-based television show called *On Scene: Emergency Response*. Shulman had no idea that at the accident scene and in the air ambulance, the consoling and beneficent Nurse Carnahan was wearing a tiny wireless microphone that picked up and recorded their conversations. What is more, Shulman did not know that Joel Cooke, a cameraman for the company that produced *On Scene*, was recording the events inside and outside of the helicopter. Of course, even had Shulman somehow realized that her words and image were being recorded, she was in no mental condition to consent in an informed manner to the tapings. At one stage, in fact, she asked Nurse Carnahan whether she was dreaming.

Shulman would not learn about the media voyeurism until the program aired. She was still in her hospital room and received a call from her son, Wayne, who told her to turn on the television set. "Channel 4 is showing our accident," Wayne told her. Ruth Shulman was shocked and angered. As she would later tell a reporter for the *Los Angeles Times*, "They took one of the most tragic moments of my life and made it entertainment for the nation."[28]

Rather than sit back and be a passive victim of mediated voyeurism, Shulman filed a lawsuit against Group W Productions, the producers of *On Scene*. Like many disputes against the media, it would prove to be lengthy, protracted litigation. In fact, it took nearly eight years from the date of the accident—June 24, 1990—before the California Supreme Court issued its critical ruling in the case on June 1, 1998.

One of Ruth Shulman's legal theories against Group W Productions was based on public disclosure of private facts, an invasion of privacy theory described earlier in this chapter. Shulman argued that the broadcast of her appearance and words while she was riding in the rescue helicopter constituted the disclosure of private and embarrassing facts that would be highly offensive to a reasonable person. The facts certainly were private, given that the inside of the helicopter was equivalent to a private hospital room, and they definitely were embarrassing based on her state of confusion, physical distress, and mental anguish.

But the case would ultimately hinge on something else—whether the facts were newsworthy. As the California Supreme Court wrote, "The element critical to this case is the presence or absence of legitimate public interest, i.e., newsworthiness in the facts disclosed."[29] How the court would resolve that issue—its reasoning and analysis—tells us much about the legal forces that allow voyeurism to propagate with the law's consent.

The California Supreme Court began by attempting to define newsworthiness. It initially acknowledged that the concept is difficult to explicate and that there is "considerable variation in judicial descriptions of the newsworthiness concept."[30] In an opinion written by Justice Kathryn Mickle Werdegar, the court noted that if every piece of information or image that found its way into a newspaper or newscast was considered newsworthy—"if all coverage that sells papers or boosts ratings is deemed newsworthy" as the court put it—then the newsworthiness defense would essentially "swallow the publication of private facts torts."[31] In other words, the newsworthiness defense would always apply, the defendants would always succeed and the plaintiffs would always lose. Mediated voyeurism thus would prevail and the public disclosure of private facts tort would be rendered a meaningless remedy.

On the other hand, the court wrote, "If newsworthiness is viewed as a purely normative concept, the courts could become to an unacceptable degree editors of the news and self-appointed guardians of public taste."[32] Such a purely normative definition would raise serious First Amendment questions about whether courts were usurping press freedom from the media. The court thus attempted to seek a middle ground between the extremes of the hands-off, leave-it-to-the-press model of newsworthiness described earlier and what might be called the hands-on, judge-as-editor model.

In its endeavor to locate a point in between the two poles, the California Supreme Court came down much closer to the leave-it-to-the-press model of newsworthiness. It made it clear that judges and justices should not act as editors looking over the shoulder of journalists. "The courts do not, and constitutionally could not, sit as superior editors of the press," Justice

Werdegar wrote for the court, adding that "in general, it is not for a court or jury to say how a particular story is best covered."[33] Werdegar's reference to the Constitution illustrates a clear example of how the First Amendment rises to the defense of mediated voyeurism.

Whether a publication, then, is newsworthy is not governed by "the tastes or limited interests of an individual judge or juror." A publication is newsworthy instead, the court wrote, if "*some* reasonable members of the community *could* entertain a legitimate interest in it."[34] The words "some" and "could" are emphasized here because they provide critical space for mediated voyeurism to breathe and to masquerade as news. Majoritarian tastes, in other words, do not control what is news. If *some* person out there *could* find voyeuristic videotape newsworthy, then it must be protected.

The court did not stop there, however, in showing deference to the press. It expressly emphasized that newsworthiness is "not limited to 'news' in the narrow sense of reports of current events" but must include the "use of names, likenesses or facts in giving information to the public for purposes of education, *amusement* or enlightenment, when the public may reasonably be expected to have a legitimate interest in what is published."[35] Quoting an earlier California case, the court added, "The constitutional guarantees of freedom of expression apply with equal force to the publication whether it be a news report or an entertainment feature." With those statements, the court made it clear that the lines between amusement, entertainment, and news are slippery, if not nonexistent, and that the newsworthiness is not destroyed by amusing or entertaining features of a story or broadcast.

But the court did not fully adopt a leave-it-to-the-press model of newsworthiness or abandon the concern for privacy. It recognized a line previously acknowledged by other courts between newsworthiness and information that constitutes "a morbid and sensational prying into private lives for its own sake." The court quoted an earlier decision that suggested that voyeurism was the opposite of newsworthiness. It noted that private facts were not newsworthy "when the community has no interest in them beyond the voyeuristic thrill of penetrating the wall of privacy that surrounds a stranger."[36] Finally, the Supreme Court of California articulated a number of factors that determine whether information is newsworthy, including its social value, the degree of the intrusion into the privacy interest of the plaintiff, and the extent to which the plaintiff voluntarily brought attention to himself or herself.

With those principles in mind, the court proceeded to analyze whether the newsworthiness defense would protect Group W Productions from liability for its broadcast of Ruth Shulman's image and words. To resolve this question, the court engaged in a two-step process.

First, it considered whether the subject matter itself—the rescue and medical treatment of auto accident victims and the work of emergency rescue personnel—was newsworthy. It quickly concluded that the subject was indeed newsworthy, noting that "automobile accidents are by their nature of interest to the great portion of the public that travels frequently by automobile." It added that videotape of the rescue and medical treatment of car crash victims such as Ruth Shulman also was newsworthy because it demonstrated "a critical service that any member of the public may someday need."[37]

But the court recognized that just because a particular *event* may be newsworthy does not necessarily mean that the identification of the plaintiff as the *person* involved in that event is also newsworthy. The court thus turned to the second and more difficult part of its inquiry: deciding whether Ruth Shulman's own words and appearance were newsworthy.

Attorneys for Shulman argued that her image and words were "not *necessary* to enable the public to understand the significance of the accident or the rescue as a public event."[38] It might have been possible, for instance, to screen out or block out Shulman's face and to omit the audio portion that contained her voice. The Supreme Court of California, however, squarely rejected this argument. It reasoned that the fact that "the broadcast *could* have been edited to exclude some of Ruth's words and images and still excite a minimum degree of viewer interest is not determinative." That decision was one of editing, one better left to Group W Productions than to the judicial system, the court reasoned. Indeed, the court remarked that "it is difficult to see how the subject broadcast could have been edited to avoid completely any possible identification [of Ruth Shulman] without severely undercutting its legitimate descriptive and narrative impact." Shulman's words and images were vital, the court reasoned, because they helped to demonstrate the importance of Nurse Carnahan's work. The court thus concluded that images and audio of Shulman were substantially relevant to the show's newsworthy subject matter—the rescue of accident victims and work of medical personnel. Shulman's lawsuit for public disclosure of private facts was thrown out.

The decision marks a victory for voyeurism. What the television show did was to give the entire nation—not just drivers on that particular stretch of Interstate 10 in Riverside County, California—the chance to rubberneck at Ruth Shulman's grave medical conditions. *New technologies, operating in the name of newsworthiness and corporate profits, extend our voyeurism, giving us the right to watch a grown woman's life nearly end.* The fact that Shulman was not a public figure was not enough in this case to render her images and words non-newsworthy. The fact that she was rendered paraplegic made no difference as well. It was just "too bad, so sad" for Shulman. It just happened to be her turn that day—her tragic dumb luck—to be the unfortunate and unwitting victim of mediated voyeurism. She was newsworthy under the law.

Editing Is for Editors

A second force beyond newsworthiness that allows mediated voyeurism to thrive in contexts other than privacy claims was hinted at in the California Supreme Court's decision in Ruth Shulman's case—the vast deference given under the First Amendment to journalists' decisions. In particular, the United States Supreme Court has made it clear that editing is best left to editors.

This journalistic independence, of course, is essential if the press is to be an independent watchdog on the government rather than a government lapdog. If the government controlled editorial judgment and told journalists what images to broadcast and what information to print, the press no longer would be able to serve as the unofficial fourth branch of government that checks abuses of power by the legislative, executive, and judicial branches. A state-controlled media would operate merely as a public relations organ, only providing the official and favorable government view. The public, in turn, would be left to itself to ferret out government corruption.

But an obvious yet important side effect, or cost, of this deep deference to journalistic freedom is its abuse in the name of corporate profit. As Chapter 3 made clear, economic forces determine much of what passes for "news" these days, and there is much indeed that passes for news that seemingly has very little to do with wise and informed decisionmaking in a self-governing democracy, education, or other matters that affect the collective well-being of society. When the economic realities of the media are coupled with the judicial deference granted to the press, the low-cost videotape voyeurism format will flourish while the watchdog role of the press, which could generate expensive and time-consuming lawsuits, will dissipate. Ironically, of course, the video vérité voyeurism that is so cheap to create has produced a rash of expensive and time-consuming lawsuits like Ruth Shulman's and others described.

The University of Michigan president Lee Bollinger's "fortress model" of freedom of expression is useful in understanding how abuse of journalistic freedom occurs.[39] This model suggests that one way to prevent government intrusion on speech or the press is "to secure the boundary of protected speech at some considerable distance from the speech activity we truly prize."[40]

Using this fortress model, we might consider news that affects self-governance or politics as a speech activity that we truly prize. But to protect this type of core speech, the United States Supreme Court has placed the boundary of protected speech, as Bollinger might put it, some considerable distance away from that core speech. To take Bollinger's metaphor a step further, the wall of the fort is placed far from the building that we want to protect within it. Voyeurism falls in the protected gap between the wall and core political speech. How is this reflected in First Amendment jurisprudence?

Historically, the United States Supreme Court has recognized a broad definition of the press, not confining it to newspapers and periodicals but instead letting it sweep up "every sort of publication which affords a vehicle of information to the public."[41] In other words, the protection granted to the press extends far beyond hard news shows to include other programs that blur distinctions between news and entertainment. The Court made it clear as well in a 1972 decision "that liberty of the press is the right of the lonely pamphleteer who uses carbon paper or a mimeograph just as much as of the large metropolitan publisher who utilizes the latest photocomposition methods.[42]

The United States Supreme Court also has refused to engage in drawing sketchy lines between inherently ambiguous concepts like "good" and "bad" journalism. In refusing to create such a false dichotomy, the Court has suggested that even shoddy journalism merits First Amendment protection. The Court made this clear in its 1931 decision in the case of *Near v.*

Minnesota.[43] Jay Near's newspaper, *The Saturday Press,* had printed articles that, the Court observed, "charged, in substance, that Jewish gangsters were in control of gambling, bootlegging, and racketeering in Minneapolis, and that law enforcing officers and agencies were not energetically performing their duties."[44] The local district attorney had attempted to permanently enjoin publication of the newspaper as a nuisance and was successful. Near eventually appealed to the United States Supreme Court, which by a narrow majority—the nine justices split five to four—reversed in his favor. Chief Justice Hughes observed in writing the majority opinion,

> Some degree of abuse is inseparable from the proper use of everything, and in no instance is this more true than in that of the press. It has accordingly been decided by the practice of the States that it is better to leave a few of its noxious branches to their luxuriant growth, than, by pruning them away, to injure the vigor of those yielding the proper fruits.[45]

What is most striking about this language is not the rather flowery, Shakespearian prose but rather that the Court is willing to tolerate an irresponsible press in order to protect a meritorious one. The majority was not willing to mandate or protect only responsible journalists or a responsible press. As it said later in its opinion, "The fact that the liberty of the press may be abused by miscreant purveyors of scandal does not make any the less necessary the immunity of the press from previous restraint in dealing with official misconduct."[46] The Court's language in *Near* would be echoed decades later in *Miami Herald Publishing Co. v. Tornillo.*[47]

In *Tornillo,* the United States Supreme Court considered whether a state right-of-reply statute granting a political candidate free access to newspaper space to reply to criticism and attacks on his character and record by a newspaper violated that newspaper's First Amendment right of freedom of the press.[48] In holding that the statute was unconstitutional, the Supreme Court discussed the role and responsibility of journalists in a self-governing democracy.[49] The Court, in an opinion authored by Chief Justice Warren Burger, observed that "a responsible press is an undoubtedly desirable goal, but press responsibility cannot be mandated by the Constitution and like many other virtues it cannot be legislated."[50]

The Court has extended this sentiment of journalistic deference beyond the print medium to the realm of broadcasting. In *Columbia Broadcasting System v. Democratic National Committee*,[51] for instance, the Court observed,

> For better or worse, editing is what editors are for; and editing is selection and choice of material. That editors—newspaper or broadcast—can and do abuse this power is beyond doubt, but that is no reason to deny the discretion Congress provided. Calculated risks of abuse are taken in order to preserve higher values. The presence of these risks is nothing new; the authors of the Bill of Rights accepted the reality that these risks were evils for which there was no acceptable remedy other than a spirit of moderation and a sense of responsibility—and civility—on the part of those who exercise the guaranteed freedoms of expression.[52]

In addition to the United States Supreme Court, the Federal Communications Commission has recognized a broad definition of news.[53] It has held, for instance, that the syndicated nightly tabloid program, *Hard Copy,* is a bona fide newscast and that the daytime talk show, *The Sally Jessy Raphael Show,* involves bona fide news interviews.[54]

The bottom line is that although the broad deference that courts extend to the media and journalistic judgment may be necessary for an independent press to play a watchdog role, today the profit-driven concerns of media companies may trump the desire to perform that important function. The breathing space given to the press for that role may be abused to disseminate sensationalistic mediated voyeurism.

The Corporate Media and the First Amendment Shield

"Trusts with the capacity for overbearing power are being merged and acquired into existence as if there were nothing at stake but stock values. Today's deals may weigh on the culture for decades."[55] So writes Todd Gitlin, a professor of sociology at New York University, describing what he perceives as a relentless conglomeration juggernaut in the communications and media industries.

The speech and images propagated by the conglomerates about which Gitlin writes are protected by the First Amendment. Corporations are protected by the Constitution as if they were people rather than the legally created entities that they are. This is not too surprising at first glance, of course, given that the First Amendment specifically calls for protection of "the press." As C. Edwin Baker, a professor at the University of Pennsylvania Law School writes, "The 'press' is the only business to receive explicit constitutional protection," a decision premised largely on the assumption that "the press should provide the public with information and opinion uncensored by government."[56]

More than 200 years after the First Amendment was ratified, however, it is clear that many of the corporate entities that engage in speech activities are controlled, directly or indirectly, by other corporate entities that may be engaged in distinctly *non–press*-oriented activities. General Electric owns NBC. Disney owns ABC. What is more, newspaper chains such as Gannett and Knight-Ridder that own large numbers of papers across the United States must attempt to walk a fine line between the often-conflicting goals of generating corporate profit and providing the public with information and speech that enlightens and serves the public interest. As Chapter 3 revealed, the politics of ownership deregulation embodied in the Telecommunications Act of 1996 has increased concentration of ownership in the broadcast industry and has facilitated the growth of the "trusts" about which Gitlin writes.

It is in this atmosphere that the low-cost, high-profit mediated voyeurism format of the television newsmagazine and reality-based program businesses flourishes. The First Amendment can be used as a shield, in turn, by corporate entities to ward off attempts to dictate or control this content. The First Amendment might be employed, for instance, to blunt any attack on shows that pander to our sensationalistic and voyeuristic thirst for vérité video. If these shows are criticized as trash and in need of some government supervision, then the First Amendment provides a ready response. Media-related corporations would simply argue that their autonomy as speakers in the metaphorical marketplace of ideas—their ability to freely choose and to decide for themselves what images are worthy of being viewed—would be violated by government intervention.

Those same corporations, of course, have a loud and increasingly dominant voice in the marketplace of ideas. Put simply, they control access to the avenues of communication production and information distribution that nonlegal entities—read, *real people*—do not possess. Although a growing number of us may have a page on the World Wide Web, most of us do not own newspapers. Family newspapers are a dying breed. But corporations—newspaper chains or groups, in particular—own newspapers. Many newspapers. In 1986, for instance, about 63 percent of daily newspapers in the United States were owned by chains. By 1998, that figure had reached 80 percent.[57]

The premise of providing individuals with the autonomy necessary to choose their own speech, free from government intervention, writes the Yale Law School professor Owen Fiss, is that this "will lead to rich public debate."[58] The danger, however, as Fiss points out, is that when profit-driven corporations are the speakers in question, the exercise of autonomy "might not enrich, but rather impoverish, public debate."[59] Although there are examples of well-intended public debate on the mainstream media today—so-called town hall meetings conducted from time to time by the major networks, for instance, on shows such as *Nightline*—it seems evident that much of what we watch today does not enrich public debate. Speech often is viewed by corporations more as a salable commodity than as a public or social good.

The hands-off corporate-speech doctrine, nurtured and protected by the First Amendment, largely presumes that any government intervention must be feared and is evil. But as many scholars today argue, perhaps we have almost as much to fear from corporate entities that control the means of production and transmission of speech and images as we do from the government. If it is true, as the late communications professor Herbert Schiller wrote, that "the bulk of cultural work provided to the American public is organized and controlled by a handful of giant business,"[60] then perhaps it is time for some of what Kathleen Sullivan, dean of the Stanford Law School, calls "cultural trustbusting."[61] Perhaps, in other words, it is time to roll back some First Amendment protection for corporate entities that engage in the speech-and-image businesses in order to promote deliberative democratic discourse and improve the quality of information flow.

The standard argument for reduced First Amendment protections for corporate speech usually proceeds along the following lines. If media-related corporations are merely legally created entities as compared to real people, if their First Amendment press protection is premised on serving the collective needs of all citizens in a democracy as opposed to generating profits for the private wants of a few shareholders, if access to the marketplace of ideas is radically skewed in favor of wealthy corporations as opposed to private individuals, and if the airwaves on which much mediated voyeurism appears are held in public trust rather than privately owned, then the door is open for increased government intervention and regulation of the corporate media.

Such intervention, of course, would potentially jeopardize the freedom of the press to serve as a watchdog on the government. If the government is telling the press what to do, how can it possibly expose government abuse? That is the standard defense against such intrusion on corporate speech rights. One thing is clear, however. In the absence of such intervention, there is little to stop the proliferation of sensationalistic mediated voyeurism. The First Amendment provides a shield behind which corporate-produced mediated voyeurism may seek protection. With this in mind, let us turn to some recent examples in which the government—at the federal and state levels—has taken steps to curb mediated voyeurism, including that disseminated by media corporations.

Legal Backlash Against Mediated Voyeurism

For those of us in the television audience to play the role of voyeur, there necessarily must be something to watch. We cannot, after all, be voyeurs without receiving any videotape, photographs, or other forms of the reality-based visual images that we like to consume. This means, in turn, that videotape and photographs must be gathered for us by the media.

A host of different laws now exist in most states, however, that place limits on the ability of the media to gather photographs and videotape of the sights and sounds that make up mediated voyeurism. Some of these laws are age-old remedies that have evolved over time with the common law and can be applied, with varying degrees of difficulty, to the modern image-gathering methods of the media. Others can be found in statutes created by state legislative bodies. Three common-law remedies against the tactics of mediated voyeurism—trespass, intrusion into seclusion, and fraud—are discussed below. As will become clear, they are not always successful in precluding or punishing mediated voyeurism.

Trespass: Forgive Not the Press for Its Trespasses

The common law of *trespass* can be used to punish individuals, including journalists, who intentionally enter the property of another person without his or her consent or permission. If a journalist thus runs across the property of a celebrity to take his or her picture and the celebrity has not consented to the entry, then a trespass has likely occurred and a remedy to voyeuristic news gathering has been put into play. The United States Supreme Court, as noted earlier in this chapter, has held that the press receives no special First Amendment protection when it violates generally applicable laws—laws that apply to everyone and do not single out or target journalists or other members of the media—such as trespass. As one federal appellate court wrote in 1995, "There is no journalists' privilege to trespass."[62]

But the trespass tort does not always provide an absolute remedy against undercover, hidden camera media voyeurism. The case of *Desnick v. American Broadcasting Companies, Inc.,*[63] involving a 1993 *PrimeTime Live* report on an eye care facility that allegedly performed unnecessary cataract surgeries to collect Medicare reimbursements, makes this clear. As part of its segment on the Desnick Eye Center—a business that at the time had twenty-five offices in four states and performed more than 10,000 cataracts operations each year—ABC rounded up seven "test patients." The test patients, wearing hidden cameras on behalf of ABC, secretly videotaped their visits to Desnick offices in Wisconsin and Indiana.

At the offices, each of the ABC confederates requested an eye examination. The results? The two test patients who were *un-*

der sixty-five and thus ineligible for Medicare reimbursement were told they did not need cataract surgery, whereas four of the five patients who were *over* sixty-five were told they needed the procedure. Suffice it to say, the *PrimeTime Live* report, narrated by the irascible Sam Donaldson, did not paint the Desnick Eye Center in a flattering light.

Desnick sued for trespass. The contention? That ABC committed a trespass by insinuating the test patients, equipped with the hidden cameras, into the Wisconsin and Indiana offices. Desnick's argument was relatively straightforward—it never would have consented to the entry by ABC's test patients into its offices had it been aware in the first place that their real purpose was to gather voyeuristic and secretive videotape to expose the center's alleged problems. In a stunning victory for voyeurism, however, Judge Richard A. Posner of the U.S. Court of Appeals for the Seventh Circuit rejected Desnick's argument and kicked out the trespass lawsuit.

How did Posner and the other members of the appellate court reach the conclusion that trespass had not occurred? Bending over backward to protect the hidden camera reporting, Posner began by looking at the original intent and purpose of the law of trespass—to protect "the inviolability of the person's property."[64] In plain English, the purpose of trespass law is to prevent others from interfering with one's ownership or use of his or her own property. With that in mind, Posner wrote,

> There was no invasion in the present case of any of the specific interests that the tort of trespass seeks to protect. The test patients entered offices that were open to anyone expressing a desire for ophthalmic services and videotaped physicians engaged in professional, not personal, communications with strangers (the testers themselves). The activities of the office were not disrupted.[65]

Business went on as usual, in other words, at the eye care center. There was no interference with Desnick's property by the camera-equipped patients. Whether other courts will follow this logic is unclear. As Jonathan D. Avila, litigation counsel for CBS Broadcasting in Los Angeles, emphasized in a 1999 law review article, "The laws of the various states are not in accord as to whether an undisclosed intent to conduct hidden-camera taping may give rise to a claim for trespass, where the landowner has consented to the physical presence of the camera person."[66] Trespass, however, is not the only legal theory that may be used against mediated voyeurism. The next section discusses one privacy theory that may provide a remedy in some, but not all, cases of video vérité voyeurism.

Intrusion into Seclusion: The Current Battleground for Hidden Cameras

Another legal remedy against mediated voyeurism is a privacy theory commonly known as *intrusion into seclusion.* Designed to protect an individual's "zone of privacy," this remedy holds that an individual such as a journalist who intrudes, physically or otherwise, on the solitude or seclusion of another person is liable for damages to that other person if the intrusion would be highly offensive to a reasonable person. To succeed in an intrusion lawsuit, the person filing the claim must possess a *reasonable* expectation of privacy in the place, location, or information in question. In general, there is no reasonable expectation of privacy if one either is in a public place or, if on private property, can be seen from a public place. For instance, if a celebrity is sunbathing in his or her front yard, and the yard and celebrity are plainly visible from the public sidewalk or street running in front of the house, there is no reasonable expectation of privacy and taking a photograph would not constitute an intrusion. If, however, there is a ten-foot tall solid stone wall surrounding the front yard, then the celebrity is more likely to possess a reasonable expectation of privacy. A photographer who decided to scale the wall to capture a picture would intrude on the celebrity's seclusion. If the photographer repeated the actions, he or she might also be charged under stalking and harassment statutes that exist in many states.

There has been, in line with the rise of the voyeurism value and the development of sophisticated recording devices, a dramatic increase in recent years in the number of lawsuits based on intrusion into seclusion. As the media attorney Victor Kovner and his colleagues write, this increase "derives principally from advances in surveillance technology, as the equipment becomes more compact and more powerful. Today, hardly a news cycle passes without word of some intrusion claim or potential claim."[67]

Intrusion into seclusion lawsuits, however, will not stop the deceptive and voyeuristic use of hidden cameras if those cameras are recording events that occur in a public place. This principle recently saved NBC and its newsmagazine *Dateline* from liability for hidden camera reportage in a 1999 decision handed down by a California appellate court. In *Wilkins v. NBC*,[68] producers from *Dateline* were investigating the practice of some companies—often adult entertainment or so-called dial-a-porn businesses—of charging for services on supposedly toll-free "800" telephone numbers. The "800" numbers, in fact, would provide access to pay-per-call "900" numbers.

A company called SimTel Communications leased and programmed "800" number and "900" number phone lines and then sold the leases to investors. After SimTel placed an ad for its services in *USA Today*, producers from *Dateline* arranged for a meeting with representatives from the company at a Malibu, California, restaurant. The *Dateline* producers did not reveal their affiliation with the newsmagazine. They also did not reveal that they were wearing hidden cameras that would capture images of the lunchtime encounter, some of which would later be broadcast by *Dateline* on a report called "Hardcore Hustle" and would spark a lawsuit by the SimTel employees for intrusion into seclusion.

The lunch, along with the surreptitious taping, took place at an outside table. The table was located in the middle of a crowded patio, close to other tables. One of the SimTel employees spoke freely about the business and its services while waiters were standing next to the table. Given the public setting—the appellate court noted that the SimTel employees "were not seated in a private dining room of a restaurant"[69]—the employees did not possess a reasonable expectation of privacy. The appellate court thus held that they could not maintain a lawsuit based on intrusion into seclusion. There simply was no "seclusion" into which to intrude on the outdoor patio. The use of hidden cameras in this case was protected.

But what about a slightly different situation? What if the hidden camera videotaping by the news media takes place *inside* the business establishment that is under investigation? Does the intrusion into seclusion tort provide a remedy in this situation? Unfortunately, the law of hidden cameras is unsettled today, and the answer appears to be either "sometimes yes, sometimes no" or "it depends on the facts of the case."

Courts have made it clear, however, that expectations of privacy are substantially lower inside a business establishment than they are inside a person's private home or residence. Busting businesses with hidden camera videotape, of course, is favorite fodder for television newsmagazines. A December 1998 decision handed down by a federal court in Arizona called *Medical Laboratory Management Consultants v. American Broadcasting Companies, Inc.*[70] illustrates how the intrusion theory may provide little relief against such business-place mediated voyeurism.

That case involved a report by ABC's now-defunct newsmagazine *PrimeTime Live* (it was essentially rolled into *20/20* along with coanchors Diane Sawyer and Sam Donaldson) called "Rush to Read" on allegedly faulty pap smear testing. Medical Laboratory Management Consultants performed pap smear testing in Phoenix, Arizona. An ABC employee named Robbie Gordon contacted one of the owners of the facility, John Devaraj. Rather than reveal her true identity, however, Gordon lied. She said she was a medical laboratory technologist who wanted to find out more details about the costs of running such a laboratory herself. In fact, as the federal court would later observe, Gordon's "only interest in Medical Lab was as a possible source of information for an upcoming episode of *PrimeTime Live*."[71]

When the owner agreed to meet with Gordon at the business in March 1994, Gordon brought along Jeff Cooke. Cooke, an undercover camera specialist, wore a camera hidden in his wig. Like Gordon, Cooke also lied to the owner of the laboratory. He claimed to be a computer expert. Cooke captured the entire two-hour visit to the laboratory on videotape.

The group primarily talked in a conference room that had windowed French doors and was visible to a nearby accounting clerk. Devaraj also took Gordon and Cooke on a tour of the facility. As the court described it, "The conversation and office tour took place in a laboratory that was at least partially open to the public and was accessible to employees."[72] In fact, other employees were present for portions of the conversations during the tour. The discussion itself focused on the pap smear testing industry as a whole as well as the general practices at Devaraj's business. There was no effort made to ensure that the conversations were confidential.

After the negative *PrimeTime Live* report aired—Devaraj was not named in the report but his face was shown during the broadcast—the owner sued for intrusion into seclusion. He claimed that his privacy was invaded by the use of false pretenses to secure entrance to the laboratory and by the secret videotaping of the conversations. Unfortunately for Devaraj—fortunately, however, for ABC and mediated voyeurs everywhere—the federal court concluded that there had been no intrusion. Why?

First, the court observed what it called a "diminished expectation of privacy in the workplace." Citing prior case law, it emphasized that "when courts have considered claims in the workplace, they have generally found for the plaintiffs *only* if the challenged intrusions involved information or activities of an intimate nature."[73] The court gave an example of an actual case involving such "intimate" information. It involved an employer who had searched through and read an employee's personal medical records that were sitting on that employee's desk. But where "the intrusions have merely involved unwanted access to data or activities *related to the workplace,* claims of intrusion have failed." Applying these principles to the facts given above, the court concluded that Devaraj "can claim no reasonable expectation of privacy in the location or contents of the conversation." As in the *Wilkins* case, then, there was no solitude or seclusion that was intruded on, despite the fact that this time around the hidden camera taping took place *inside* the plaintiff's place of business instead of *outside* at a public restaurant.

But the court in the *Medical Laboratory* case did not stop its analysis there. It gave a second, independent reason to deny Devaraj's claim for intrusion into seclusion. The conduct by the ABC employees simply was not highly offensive to a reasonable person. As noted earlier, a person who files a lawsuit for intrusion must prove both that there was a reasonable expectation of privacy in the place or thing intruded on *and* that the intrusive conduct would be highly offensive to a reasonable person. How could the court reach the conclusion that lying in order to use hidden cameras to secretly videotape conversations inside someone else's business was not highly offensive? The court simply pulled out another shield that sometimes protects mediated voyeurism—the alleged motive for the intrusion. Under the law in most states, the question of offensiveness is determined, in part, by the intruder's motive or reason for engaging in the intrusive conduct.

In this case, the media claimed a noble motive for its lying and use of hidden cameras. ABC was reporting on an important health issue that could impact millions of women. As the court stated, "The information was clearly in the public interest." In contrast, the court noted that it is only when the intrusion is "gratuitous, threatens the safety of anyone involved, or unnecessarily intrudes on a target of the news in his private capacity"[74] that it is likely to be considered highly offensive. Because the intrusion by ABC was not gratuitous but instead was done to tell an important story, and because no one got hurt during the taping and Devaraj was acting in his business capacity, the factors that would indicate "highly offensive" conduct simply were not present. ABC's conduct thus was protected and the intrusion claim was tossed out.

But as mentioned earlier, the law of hidden cameras is extremely volatile today. Different courts may reach very different conclusions depending on the unique factual situation in question. A much-anticipated decision handed down by the Supreme Court of California in June 1999 in a case called *Sanders v. American Broadcasting Companies, Inc.*[75] makes this clear. That opinion appears, at least on the question of privacy expectations in the workplace, to contradict the *Medical Laboratory* ruling. Unlike the federal court in Arizona in the *Medical Laboratory* case, which threw out a claim for intrusion based on the media's use of a hidden camera in the workplace, the high court of California allowed a plaintiff to proceed with a lawsuit for intrusion that also featured hidden camera taping inside a business establishment under media investigation. The *Sanders* decision, if followed by courts in other states, could deal a serious, but probably nonfatal, blow to mediated voyeurism and, in particular, to hidden camera voyeurism in the workplace.

The *Sanders* case grew out of a 1992 *PrimeTime Live* investigation of the telepsychic industry. Chances are that if you are an insomniac or night owl, you have probably seen so-called infomercials—thirty-minute commercials thinly masquerading as television shows—for telepsychic hot lines. You have probably also questioned whether the people at the other end of the telephone line were "real" psychics. ABC too apparently had its doubts about the industry and it decided to investigate.

An ABC employee named Stacy Lescht obtained employment for a few days as a telepsychic in the Los Angeles office of a company known as the Psychic Marketing Group (PMG). While working for PMG, Lescht sat at one of about 100 cubicles in a large room taking phone calls and giving psychic readings. Each cubicle had three sides, and each side was five feet high. Access to the room in which the telepsychics worked was generally restricted to employees only. When she was not on the phone, Lescht talked with the other psychics. She could easily overhear their conversations in the surrounding cubicles.

Unknown to her fellow employees, however, Lescht wore a small hidden camera in her hat—a "hat cam" as the California Supreme Court fittingly put it—and an audio microphone attached to her brassiere. She taped the conversations that she had with her unsuspecting fellow employees. One of those other telepsychics was a man named Mark Sanders. In one taped conversation with Sanders, Sanders was standing in the aisle just outside Lescht's cubicle. Two other employees also joined in that conversation, which, according to the court, was conducted in "moderate tones of voice."[76] A second taped conversation occurred in Sanders's cubicle. Both Lescht and Sanders were seated in the cubicle while they discussed Sanders's personal aspirations in what the court described as "relatively soft voices." Portions of the second conversation aired on the *PrimeTime Live* broadcast. Sanders ultimately sued Lescht for intrusion into seclusion based on her secretive video and audio recordings made in the PMG offices.

By the time the case reached the Supreme Court of California, it faced a very narrow but important issue—"whether a person who lacks a reasonable expectation of *complete* privacy in a conversation because it could be seen and heard by coworkers (but *not* the general public) may nevertheless have a claim for invasion of privacy by intrusion based on a television reporter's covert videotaping of that conversation."[77] The court would ultimately answer that query in the affirmative—a person such as Mark Sanders could still maintain a claim for intrusion in this situation. It would reject ABC's argument that because other employees could hear the conversations there was no expectation of privacy.

To reach this conclusion, the unanimous court rejected the notion that there must be "absolute or complete privacy" to successfully pursue a cause of action for intrusion into seclusion. "Mass media videotaping may constitute an intrusion even when the events and communications recorded were visible and audible to some limited set of observers," Justice Kathryn Mickle Werdegar wrote for the court. Werdegar, it will be recalled, wrote the majority opinion in Ruth Shulman's case.

In allowing a claim for intrusion based on covert media taping to proceed in a place of business, the court observed that privacy "is not a binary, all-or-nothing characteristic. There are degrees and nuances to societal recognition of our expectations of privacy."[78] In this case, the circumstances that suggested there *was* a reasonable expectation of privacy included (1) the fact that the room in which the recordings were made was not regularly open to observation by the press or public but instead was generally limited to employees only; (2) the fact that the conversations recorded were not between a proprietor and a customer but rather between one employee and a member of the media posing as an employee but who "acted solely as an agent of ABC when she talked with and secretly recorded the other psychics";[79] and (3) the fact that the only other people who could overhear the taped conversations were fellow coemployees. As the court emphasized, "There was no evidence the public was invited into the PMG Los Angeles office, or that the office was visited by the press or public observers on a routine basis or was ordinarily subject to videotaped surveillance by the mass media."[80] The court thus concluded that Sanders indeed possessed a reasonable expectation of privacy against being videotaped by an "ABC employee planted to collect videotape for use in a national television broadcast."[81]

The *Sanders* decision clearly is a blow to hidden camera voyeurism conducted by the media inside workplace or business settings. But the Supreme Court of California was careful *not* to create an absolute, or "per se," rule that there *always* is an expectation of privacy in the workplace. "We hold *only* that the possibility of being overheard by coworkers does not, as a matter of law, render unreasonable an employee's expectation that his or her interactions within a nonpublic workplace will not be videotaped in secret by a journalist," the court wrote.[82]

The Supreme Court of California also made it clear that it was not ruling on whether the intrusion by Lescht was or was not highly offensive. It will be recalled from the *Medical Laboratory* case that the person bringing a lawsuit for intrusion must show not only that there was a reasonable expectation of privacy but also that the intrusion would be considered highly offensive to a reasonable person. Offensiveness, in turn, is determined in part by the intruder's motive. The California Supreme Court wrote in *Sanders,* "Nothing we say here prevents a media defendant from attempting to show, in order to negate the offensiveness element of the intrusion tort, that the claimed intrusion, even if it infringed on a reasonable expectation of privacy, was justified by the legitimate motive of gathering news."[83] In other words, ABC could still make a claim that Mark Sanders's intrusion case should be thrown out because ABC had a legitimate motive—showing and telling the public about the practices of the for-profit telepsychic industry—for using a hidden microphone and cloaked camera.

It should be clear from this brief review of current case law that intrusion into seclusion claims may be used to punish mediated voyeurism but they are far from a complete remedy. In fact, as the *Wilkins* and *Medical Laboratory* cases suggest, intrusion often fails to provide a remedy for hidden camera voyeurism, even when the media lie or fail to reveal their true identities or purposes. The *Sanders* decision, in contrast, may cast a chilling effect over video vérité voyeurism captured by undercover media operatives in the workplace. The key issues are the reasonableness of one's expectation of privacy in the location or information captured by cameras and microphones and the offensiveness of the conduct engaged in by the media. The unique set of facts in each case will prove critical in resolving these questions. Two things are clear, however, as of the writing of this book: The law of hidden cameras is far from settled, and the extent to which intrusion claims will prevent or hinder mediated voyeurism remains to be seen.

Fraud: Food Lion Roars Back, Then Goes Out with a Whimper

The law of *fraud* can be invoked—sometimes successfully, sometimes not—when the media use deceptive news-gathering techniques to obtain voyeuristic videotape. Fraud generally occurs when an individual knowingly makes a false statement about an important fact to another person who, in turn, relies on that statement and is harmed by it. In addition, the person who makes the false statement must do so with the intent to deceive or induce the reliance by the unsuspecting individual.

The law of fraud most often applies in distinctly *non*–media-related cases. For instance, consider the used car dealer who represents to a potential customer that a particular vehicle has never been in an accident. In fact, the car has been in a major collision that affects its steering and the dealer knows this. If the customer relies on the false information and the car later breaks down because of the earlier accident, the duped buyer may have an action for fraud. As the case described below suggests, the law of fraud can be stretched from this typical scenario to apply to fraudulent conduct by members of the media seeking voyeuristic videotape.

The ABC television newsmagazine *PrimeTime Live*—it should be clear from this and some of the earlier examples that the law of hidden cameras might just as well be called the law of *PrimeTime Live* investigations—conducted a voyeuristic hidden camera report in the early 1990s to expose alleged food-mishandling practices at the then fast-growing Food Lion grocery store chain. Its producers deliberately lied on résumés to gain access to the store as employees. The producers submitted false references, false employment histories, and false reasons for wanting to work in a Food Lion store. For instance, one ABC employee wrote on her Food Lion job application, "I love meat wrapping. I would like to make a career with the company."[84]

Relying on these misrepresentations, Food Lion hired one of the producers. Once on the inside, the ABC employee proceeded to shoot some hidden camera footage and tape some audio behind the food counters and in the butcher shop. The network eventually broadcast a very negative report by Diane Sawyer about Food Lion's allegedly unsanitary food-handling practices on November 5, 1992. After the report aired, the supermarket chain's market value and profits plummeted, and it was forced to close eighty-eight stores. Food Lion blamed this disastrous turn of events on the *PrimeTime Live* report. It sued Capital Cities/ABC[85] under several legal theories based on how the network gathered its information, including fraud and trespass.

In December 1996, just over four years after the report first aired, a federal jury in North Carolina found that ABC's deception amounted to fraud and trespass. It later ordered ABC to pay nearly $5.5 million in damages. The verdict sent shock waves through the journalism world, with a Chicken Little "the sky is falling" type of outrage. It was the end of voyeuristic journalism as we knew it. The public's right to watch hidden camera footage would be irreparably harmed.

But the supermarket chain's victory would not last too long and as always seems to happen despite the doomsayers' prognostications, the sky did not come crashing down on journalism. Instead, the multimillion-dollar damage award was reduced significantly by the trial judge to $315,000. But the cutting did not stop there. On appeal in October 1999, the sum was pared down again, this time to a paltry nominal damages award of two dollars.[86]

The Fourth Circuit Court of Appeals, in a split two-to-one decision in favor of ABC, concluded that the fraud verdict could not stand because it was "an end-run" around the First Amendment protection of the press.[87] Although the majority acknowledged that ABC employees had used deceptive practices to obtain its voyeuristic videotape, it concluded that this deception "did not harm the consuming public" and that ABC's intent, in fact, was "to benefit the consuming public by letting it know about Food Lion's food handling practices."[88] All that was left for the supermarket chain to collect was one dollar to compensate it for ABC's trespass and one dollar for the breach of loyalty owed by the ABC-turned-Food-Lion employees to their deceived employer, Food Lion. Not a bad cost-of-doing-business price for ABC to collect the materials of mediated voyeurism.

It should be noted that it was not the hidden cameras per se that got ABC in trouble with the jury but rather the trespass, deception, and fraud. Although the fraud did not stand up on appeal, the split decision from one federal appellate circuit court does not resolve the issue in other appellate courts. The Fourth Circuit did *not* conclude that fraud could never be used in a similar case as means of attacking news-gathering practices. The viability of a fraud cause of action to attack deceptive news gathering thus remains unsettled without a decision from the United States Supreme Court.

There are, then, a number of potential legal avenues available to victims of mediated voyeurism, such as trespass, intrusion into seclusion, and fraud. But today, apparently, those remedies are not always enough to check mediated voyeurism. The confluence of three recent developments in the law suggests there may be a stepped-up movement against mediated voyeurism. These developments include (1) a 1999 United States Supreme Court decision that limits the media's ability to capture voyeuristic videotape during so-called police ride-alongs; (2) a wave of anti-paparazzi legislation that cropped up after the 1997 death of Princess Diana; and (3) a small but growing number of states passing laws that make videotape voyeurism a criminal offense. This trio of legal happenings is discussed in the next chapter. The common thread that unites them, as will become clear, is an interest in and concern for privacy and the control of information flow that contradicts mediated voyeurism.

Check Your Camera at the Castle Door

Two Modern Castles

Nearly 400 years ago in England in 1604, the King's Bench handed down a decision in a dispute known as *Semayne's Case*. In it, the court famously resolved that "the house of every one is to him as his castle and fortress, as well as for his defense against injury and violence, as for his repose."[1]

In 1993, the castle of then seventy-one-year-old Paul W. Berger, in poor health and on oxygen and medication, and his wife, Erma, sat on 75,000 acres of rugged ranch land located near Jordan, Montana. In 1992, some 2,000 miles away from Montana in the Washington, D.C., suburb of Rockville, Maryland, was the castle of Charles H. Wilson, a then forty-seven-year-old grandfather, and his wife, Geraldine.

Unfortunately for both the Bergers and Wilsons, their castles proved at the time to be little defense against injury done not only by the government but by the media. Ultimately, however, the intrusions into their homes by members of both the government and the media would lead to the establishment of an important United States Supreme Court precedent in 1999. That precedent would deal a serious blow to one of the most intrusive and invasive forms of mediated voyeurism—the entry, without consent, into one's home by the media, with microphones recording sound and cameras capturing pictures, during the execution of arrest and search warrants by government officials.

Despite the differences in their circumstances, the stories of the Bergers and the Wilsons tell a single cautionary tale about the dangers of mediated voyeurism and lead to one conclusion—there *are* limits to our rights to be voyeurs, especially when the public's so-called right to know butts heads with the Fourth Amendment. The Fourth Amendment protects the privacy of an individual in his or her home, person, property, and possessions. Ratified by three-fourths of the states in December 1791 and unchanged over the past 200-plus years, the Fourth Amendment reads:

> The right of the people to be secure in their persons, houses, papers, and effects, against unreasonable searches and seizures, shall not be violated, and no warrants shall issue, but upon probable cause, supported by oath or affirmation, and particularly describing the place to be searched, and the persons or things to be seized.

In the cases of both the Bergers and the Wilsons, the law enforcement officials who searched their property did possess warrants. Those warrants, however, made no reference to the media microphones, cameras, and personnel that would tag along with the government officials who entered their respective castles. The Supreme Court, in a unanimous opinion authored by Chief Justice William Rehnquist, eventually would conclude "that it is a violation of the Fourth Amendment for police to bring members of the media or other third parties into a home during the execution of a warrant when the presence of the third parties in the home was not in aid of the execution of the warrant."[2] The facts in the companion cases of *Hanlon v.*

Berger and *Wilson v. Layne* that would lead to this conclusion, as well as the Supreme Court's justification for its decision, are set forth below.

Hanlon v. Berger

In the earlier morning hours of March 23, 1993, Paul Berger awoke to find a convoy of vehicles coming down the country road leading to his remote Montana ranch. Berger, who had been in and out of the hospital during the previous five months and was released just ten days before after treatment of pneumonia and high blood pressure, got into his pickup truck and met the phalanx of twenty-one government agents as they approached. His eighty-one-year-old wife, Erma, also in ill health, stayed behind in the house.

It was there on the country road that Berger encountered Joel Scrafford. Scrafford was a special agent for the U.S. Fish and Wildlife Service (USFWS). The USFWS, it seemed, had been told by former employees of Berger that they had seen him poison or shoot government-protected golden and bald eagles a few years earlier. According to legal documents filed by attorneys for the Bergers, Scrafford told the elderly rancher that a search warrant was about to be executed for his ranch. Berger would be "run . . . down to the lockup in Billings" if he failed to cooperate. "We've been ordered by the court to search every building that you have here—and check your pastures for poison," Scrafford continued.[3]

In fact, however, the Bergers' residence was *excluded* from the scope of the search authorized by a warrant issued five days before by a federal magistrate. Berger was never given a copy of the warrant that would have revealed this important fact.

Scrafford asked Berger if he could hitch a ride back to the ranch in Berger's truck, ostensibly so that he could tell Berger more about the search. Berger, who by this time was shaken and very upset, agreed. When they reached Berger's residence, the old man consented to Scrafford's entry into his residence and they walked into the house together. It was there that Berger was interrogated by Scrafford, who was later joined inside the house by a second USFWS special agent named Richard C. Branzell. According to briefs filed by the Bergers' attorney, the rancher was bombarded with leading questions about his alleged use of illegal poisons and killing of eagles. Berger was never advised, however, of any of his rights, including his right to remain silent.

More disturbing, perhaps, Berger was never advised of some other very important facts—facts that would have revealed the atmosphere of mediated voyeurism that engulfed the entire search. Berger was never informed, for instance, that Scrafford was wired with a hidden microphone. What is more, he was never informed that the microphone was the property of CNN and that it was continuously transmitting live audio to a CNN technical crew. As the attorneys for the Bergers wrote in a brief filed with the United States Supreme Court, "Agent Scrafford was the Media's human 'boom mike' as he wore the hidden Media microphone which allowed the Media to secretly monitor and record everything said solely for the Media's benefit."[4] CNN also had mounted a small camera on the hood of one of the government vehicles.

The Bergers would later learn that the conspiracy between the government and media was deeper than just a hidden microphone and the presence of CNN personnel. In fact, about two weeks before the search of the Berger ranch, the assistant U.S. Attorney in charge of the Berger investigation entered into a written agreement with Jack Hamann, a correspondent from CNN's environmental unit. Hamann was interested in using taped footage and audio of the upcoming search for two of its television shows, *Earth Matters* and *Network Earth*. The agreement provided in relevant part,

> The United States Attorney's Office for the District of Montana
> agrees to allow CNN to accompany USFWS Agents as they attempt

to execute a criminal search warrant near Jordan, Montana, some time during the week of March 22, 1993 . . . CNN shall have complete editorial control over any footage it shoots; it shall not be obliged to use the footage; and does not waive any rights or privileges it may have with respect to the footage.[5]

The federal magistrate who would later issue the warrant was never informed about this agreement. The magistrate, in fact, had no knowledge of the media's planned participation during the search, much less any knowledge about the videotaping of the search for commercial broadcast purposes. There was no mention of the teaming of the police power of the government with the publicity power of the press.

CNN ultimately would capture more than eight hours of tape at the Berger ranch that day in March 1993. It would later broadcast portions of both the video footage at the ranch and the sound recordings made inside the Bergers' house. Paul Berger, in turn, ultimately would be acquitted by a federal jury on all three felony counts involving the killing of wildlife and convicted of only one misdemeanor—using a registered pesticide known as Furadan in a manner inconsistent with its label's instructions.

But the outcome of the criminal prosecution against Paul Berger far from closed the chapter on the Berger ranch invasion. The Bergers decided to sue both the government and CNN. They and their attorneys attacked the efforts to capture sensationalistic and voyeuristic audiotape and videotape during the raid. In particular, the Bergers alleged that the government violated their Fourth Amendment right of privacy and protection against unreasonable searches and seizures when it allowed a CNN hidden microphone to be placed on the body of USFWS Special Agent Scrafford when he entered the Berger home.

The Bergers did not stop there. They went on to contend that CNN itself had worked so closely with government law enforcement personnel in coordinating the use of microphones and video recorders that the CNN journalists on the scene were themselves transformed into government officials. Because the reporters were akin to government agents—"state actors" in legal parlance—the Bergers alleged that they too had violated the Bergers' Fourth Amendment rights when the CNN microphone entered their house without their consent. The case would ultimately reach the United States Supreme Court on both issues.

Before reaching the Supreme Court, however, the Ninth Circuit U.S. Court of Appeals would hear the case. The circuit courts of appeals are intermediate appellate courts in the federal judicial system. The Ninth Circuit's jurisdiction sweeps up many of the states in the Western part of the United States, including Montana. It is also considered to be one of the most important—if not one of the most left leaning—intermediate appellate courts through which cases pass before they reach the Supreme Court.

In this case, the Ninth Circuit agreed with the Bergers that *both* the government *and* the media had violated their Fourth Amendment rights. The media, in essence, were acting as one with the USFWS agents who executed the search warrant on the Berger ranch. The press, which normally plays a so-called Fourth Estate, or watchdog, role in checking for and exposing government abuses of power, was now one and the same with the very entity it usually protects the public against. In this case, there was collusion between the government and press in the form of a written agreement and the use of a media microphone on a government agent. It was not simply, then, that the government had violated the Fourth Amendment rights of the Bergers; the media had done so as well. The search was unreasonable.

The appellate court emphasized that it was voyeuristic entertainment interests—not valid law enforcement goals—that ultimately determined much about how the execution of the warrant was carried out. The Ninth Circuit wrote,

> The record in this case suggests that the government officers planned and executed the search in a manner designed to enhance its enter-

tainment, rather than its law enforcement value, by engaging in, for example, conversations with Mr. Berger for the purpose of providing interesting soundbites, and to portray themselves as tough yet caring investigators, rather than to further their own investigation.[6]

The search, the Ninth Circuit added, was ultimately for "the mutual benefit of the private interests of the media and the government official's interest in publicity."[7] In other words, CNN's commercial imperative of turning a profit with the use of voyeuristic audio- and videotape, as well as the USFWS's own interest in looking and sounding good to a nationwide television audience, largely drove the manner in which the search was carried out. As the Ninth Circuit Court of Appeals noted, "This search stands out as one that at all times was intended to serve a major purpose other than law enforcement."[8]

The Ninth Circuit also ruled that the Bergers could proceed to trial against CNN on two claims in addition to the Fourth Amendment violation. Both claims directly relate to the voyeuristic news-gathering efforts of CNN. First, the appellate court held that the Bergers could state a common-law claim of trespass against CNN. Trespass, as described earlier in this chapter, is an intentional and unauthorized entry on the property possessed by another. The Bergers did not authorize or consent to the CNN personnel entering their property. What is more, the Ninth Circuit observed that "although Mr. Berger consented to Agent Scrafford's initial entry into the home, he never consented to the entry of the media-owned microphone that Agent Scrafford wore."[9] The age-old law of trespass thus was reinvigorated and reinforced as another weapon against modern-day reality-based voyeurism.

The other claim that the Ninth Circuit ruled should proceed to trial was for something called *intentional infliction of emotional distress*—in attorney-speak, a claim for IIED. To state a legal claim for IIED, plaintiffs such as the Bergers must generally show that the defendant—in this case, CNN—engaged in extreme and outrageous conduct with either the intention of causing, or with the reckless disregard of causing, severe emotional distress in the plaintiff. In this case, the intentional intrusion by the media into the Berger home with a hidden microphone concealed on a government agent would constitute the extreme and outrageous conduct.

Both the government and CNN appealed separate parts of the Ninth Circuit's decision to the United States Supreme Court. The government, in particular, argued that it did not violate the Fourth Amendment rights of the Bergers when it allowed Scrafford to wear a media microphone into their home without their consent. CNN did not attack the trespass or intentional infliction of emotional distress rulings by the Ninth Circuit, but instead challenged its conclusion that CNN personnel had worked so closely with the USFWS agents that they too had become government entities and, concomitantly, also violated the Fourth Amendment rights of the Bergers. The Supreme Court's decisions on these two issues are set forth later in this chapter. Before analyzing those decisions, however, we will consider the facts of the companion case to the Bergers' involving mediated voyeurism that the Supreme Court ruled on in May 1999.

Wilson v. Layne

Much as the Bergers' brush with mediated voyeurism began in the early morning hours, so did the even more frightening and intimidating experience of Charles H. and Geraldine Wilson. The Wilsons were lying in bed in their suburban Rockville, Maryland, home on the morning of April 16, 1992. Their nine-year-old granddaughter was also there. Little did they know that at about 6:45 A.M. their peace and tranquillity would come to a loud and violent end.

Outside their house were members of both the U.S. Marshals Service and the Montgomery County, Maryland, Sheriff's Office. They were there with a warrant for the arrest of Dominic Jerome Wilson, the Wilsons' twenty-seven-year-old son. The younger Wilson was wanted for violating his parole on previous felony charges of robbery, theft, and assault with intent to rob. His parents' house was the address that police had for Dominic, but he did not live there and he was not in the house on the morning of April 16. The marshals and officers who assembled, however, did not know that. They were there as part of something called "Operation Gunsmoke," a national fugitive apprehension program designed to track down individuals such as Dominic Wilson whom law enforcement officials considered to be dangerous criminals.

Charles and Geraldine Wilson heard a loud knocking at their front door. The Wilsons then heard their granddaughter, Valencia, going to the door. They called out to her to see what was going on. When the young girl did not respond—she had, in fact, gone outside at the officers' request and they had moved her to a safe location away from the house—and the knocking continued, Charles Wilson climbed out of bed to investigate. He was wearing only his underpants.

When he reached the living room, he was confronted by three government agents, all of whom had their guns drawn. According to documents filed by the Wilsons' ACLU attorneys with the United States Supreme Court, Wilson raised his hands in the air and "was ordered in foul and abusive language to get down on the floor." He was "forcibly detained, belly-down on his living room floor with [an officer's] knee in his back and gun to his head," according to the Wilsons' brief.[10] At that time, Geraldine Wilson came into the living room wearing only a sheer nightgown.

After the law enforcement personnel made a protective sweep of the premises and searched the house for Dominic and finally were convinced that the older Wilson was not his son, they left. But that fruitless search did not end matters. As it would turn out, two other people were also in the house with the U.S. marshals and the Montgomery County sheriffs—a male reporter and a female photographer from the *Washington Post*. The photographer took numerous pictures and the reporter snooped around the house. They were not there to assist the law enforcement personnel, but instead were present only to gather information and voyeuristic images for a newspaper story. The Wilsons never consented to the presence of the *Post* employees in their private residence. The warrant executed by the marshals, like the warrant in the Berger case, made no reference to involvement by members of the media.

Also like the Bergers, Charles and Geraldine Wilson decided to file a lawsuit against the mediated voyeurism that transpired in the sanctity of their home that morning. They contended that the police-led media invasion of their residence violated their Fourth Amendment right to be secure against unreasonable searches and seizures. They argued in a brief filed with the United States Supreme Court that

> given the media's power to disseminate information and images far and wide, without any government restraints, bringing them into a private home is particularly destructive of privacy and runs counter to basic notions of what privacy ultimately entails—the ability to control when and how and to what extent information about oneself is disclosed to others.[11]

In addition to arguing that the Wilsons' Fourth Amendment right to privacy trumped the public's implicit First Amendment right to know about what went on during the search, the Wilsons' attorneys emphasized that the reporter and photographer were there for only one reason—to gather information to sell newspapers, not to help in the execution of the warrant or to apprehend Dominic Wilson. The media "were engaged in an entirely different search—a search for information and photographic images for the benefit of their employer, *The Washington Post*—a search that was not authorized by the warrant."[12] The law enforcement officials, in turn, simply hoped to get some good press by having the media tag along. As with the case of the Bergers, the reality-based mediated voyeurism in the Wilsons' situation was intended partly to help the commercial imperatives of the media (selling newspapers) while generating favorable publicity for the difficult and dangerous work of law enforcement.

Law enforcement officials countered the Wilsons' arguments. They contended that several important functions and goals were served by allowing the media into a private home to watch and photograph the execution of a valid arrest warrant. In a brief filed with the United States Supreme Court on behalf of the U.S. marshals involved in the search, attorneys argued that "over many years officers have permitted third-party members of the news media to accompany them and to observe and record their entry on private premises, for purposes such as to facilitate accurate news coverage or to deter criminals by publicizing their crimefighting efforts."[13] The attorneys also argued that the press could serve a watchdog function during the execution of search warrants. They could monitor the situation and thus deter police abuses of power and protect the rights of suspects. In other words, the *Post* reporter and photographer were there not to invade the Wilsons' privacy or to take pictures but actually to protect them from the marshals. It is highly doubtful, of course, that the Wilsons were aware that *Post* employees doubled as pseudo–guardian angels while they worked for one the country's most prestigious newspapers. Alternatively, the government asserted, the media's presence could also protect the safety of the officers, presumably from the Wilsons.

The Wilsons' lawsuit ultimately would be heard by the Supreme Court as a companion case with the Bergers' lawsuit. Before reaching the nation's highest court, however, the Wilsons' case was heard by the Fourth Circuit U.S. Court of Appeals. Like the Ninth Circuit, the Fourth Circuit is a federal appellate court, but its jurisdiction covers a number of Middle Atlantic states, including Maryland.

The Fourth Circuit ruled against the Wilsons and in favor of the law enforcement officials. It did so on the grounds that the officers were entitled to something that is known as a "qualified immunity" for their actions. The qualified immunity doctrine provides that government officials do *not* violate an individual's civil rights if their conduct does not breach a "clearly established" statutory or constitutional right of which a reasonable person should have known. The Fourth Circuit ruled that at the time the search of the Wilsons' residence transpired in April 1992, it was not clearly established by prior case law that bringing members of the media into a house during the execution of a warrant to observe and take photographs violated the Fourth Amendment. The officers thus were immune from legal liability.

The Supreme Court Weighs In

The United States Supreme Court issued its decision in the companion cases of *Wilson v. Layne* and *Hanlon v. Berger* on May 24, 1999.[14] The Court faced two very narrow questions: (1) Do law enforcement officials violate the Fourth Amendment rights of individuals when they allow the media into a private residence to observe and record the execution of a warrant? and (2) If law enforcement officials do indeed violate the Fourth Amendment rights of individuals when they allow the media into a private residence during the execution of a warrant, was this rule clearly established at the time of the searches involving the Wilson and Berger homes? To answer these questions, the Court focused heavily on the facts in the case involving the Wilsons' Rockville, Maryland, residence.

Writing for a unanimous Court on the first question, Chief Justice William Rehnquist stressed the "centuries-old principle of respect for the privacy of the home" that is embodied in the Fourth Amendment's protection against unreasonable searches and seizures. Rehnquist added that just because officers might have obtained an arrest or search warrant as required by the Fourth Amendment, "it does not necessarily follow that they were entitled to bring a newspaper reporter and a photographer with them."[15] In the case of the search through the Wilson home, the Chief Justice emphasized that it was obvious the reporters "were not present for any reason related to the justification for police entry into the home—the apprehension of Dominic Wilson."

The Supreme Court then attacked and squarely rejected law enforcement arguments in support of the mediated voyeurism that transpired in the Wilson residence. In a stern rebuke to mediated prying and voyeurism, Rehnquist wrote,

> Surely the possibility of good public relations for the police is simply not enough, standing alone, to justify the ride-along intrusion into a private home. And even the need for accurate reporting on police issues in general bears no direct relation to the constitutional justification for the police intrusion into a home in order to execute a felony arrest warrant.[16]

The Chief Justice emphasized that the media were there for "private purposes," not to check potential police abuses or to protect suspects or the occupants of the house: "*The Washington Post* reporters in the Wilsons' home were working on a story for their own purposes. They were not present for the purpose of protecting the officers, much less the Wilsons. A private photographer was acting for private purposes, as evidenced in part by the fact that the newspaper and not the police retained the photographs."[17]

The Court thus concluded that the benefits of mediated voyeurism inside a private home during the execution of a warrant were clearly outweighed by the constitutional protection of the Fourth Amendment. "We hold that it is a violation of the Fourth Amendment for police to bring members of the media or other third parties into a home during the execution of a warrant when the presence of the third parties was not in aid of execution of the warrant."[18] The Court then turned to the second issue—whether this principle was clearly established at the time the searches of the Wilson and Berger residences transpired, in 1992 and 1993, respectively. As noted above, the officers could escape liability under the qualified immunity doctrine if it was not established that they were violating a constitutional right.

Unfortunately for the victims of mediated voyeurism in the two cases, the Court ruled that it was *not* clearly established at the relevant times that law enforcement officials violate the Fourth Amendment when they bring members of the media into a home during the execution of a warrant. Citing the "undeveloped state of the law"[19] on this question in 1992 and 1993, the Supreme Court held that the officers were entitled to the qualified immunity defense. On this second question, Justice John Paul Stevens broke from the other eight members of Court. He believed that it was well established back in the early 1990s that the actions of the officers violated the Fourth Amendment.

On June 1, 1999, just one week after the initial decisions were handed down, the United States Supreme Court issued another important ruling. It left standing the conclusion by the Ninth Circuit Court of Appeals in *Hanlon v. Berger* that CNN journalists had become the equivalent of law enforcement officials when they joined members of the USFWS in the raid on the Bergers' Montana ranch. Although the government officials themselves had wiggled off the hook under the qualified immunity doctrine just a week before, now the United States Supreme Court was, in essence, telling CNN that the network would have to defend itself at trial. The reaction from the Berger camp was joyous.

"We're still celebrating," Henry Rossbacher attorney for the Bergers, told the Associated Press after news of the June 1 ruling. "We anticipate this case soon will go to trial."

Ramifications for Mediated Voyeurism

The practical impact on reality-based, mediated voyeurism of the *Wilson v. Layne* and *Hanlon v. Berger* cases seems clear. Because it is now official and clearly established that the police violate the Fourth Amendment when they bring the media into a private residence to capture audio, photographs, or video during the execution of a warrant, police are much less likely to allow such practices to continue. In turn, the audience of voyeurs is less likely to see what occurs in the privacy of another person's home during the execution of a warrant. We will be less privy to how the suspects live, see what they wear, and know what their moments of disgrace and capture look like from inside the confines of their own homes.

On the other hand, the Supreme Court's decision will far from end the video vérité voyeurism of the police ride-along. The Court did *not* prohibit the media from riding with the police. What is more, it did not prohibit the media from taking pictures or videotape from a public place, such as a street or sidewalk *outside* a person's home while a warrant is executed. The only real limits suggested in the Court's opinion relate to bringing journalists *inside* private residences.

Ultimately, the Supreme Court's decision suggests that there are constitutional limitations—limitations that reside in the Fourth Amendment's protection against unreasonable searches and seizures—that constrain the extent and scope of reality-based mediated voyeurism. The Fourth Amendment protects the privacy interests of an individual's home, and it was there—at the front door of everyperson's proverbial castle—that the Court drew the line on mediated voyeurism in the cases of Paul and Erma Berger and Charles and Geraldine Wilson in 1999. The media are still welcome to ride along and shoot video from the streets and sidewalks and from the inside of police cars, but they put the police at risk of liability when they enter a home without the owner's consent.

Before leaving the cases of *Hanlon v. Berger* and *Wilson v. Layne*, I will emphasize two serious dangers of ride-along voyeurism that will *not* be limited by the Supreme Court's decision. The first is the collaboration of press and government.

This pairing jeopardizes journalistic independence. The press cannot play a watchdog role on the government when it teams up with the government and cuts deals with the government. The joining together of the police power of the state with the First Amendment powers of the press is an awesome and dangerous combination. The Supreme Court's decision does nothing to prevent such a teaming up of forces.

The second danger of ride-along voyeurism that will continue is even more serious—the loss of human life. Amanda Smailes paid the ultimate price in the media's search for sensationalistic and voyeuristic videotape on November 24, 1996.[20] Her story is a frightening encounter—one that ended in death—with mediated voyeurism run amok.

The twenty-one-year-old college student was driving home around 1 A.M. along a winding and hilly stretch of U.S. Route 11 in Darkesville, West Virginia. She had just finished working the late shift at the Wal-Mart in nearby Martinsburg. Smailes had no idea of the danger that was fast approaching behind her on that two-lane highway.

Robert Lee Sparkman Jr. was drunk and he was driving like a maniac. He was being chased, sometimes at speeds of over 100 miles per hour, by Trooper Kevin Plumer of the West Virginia State Police. The chase had gone on for about ten minutes when Sparkman rounded a blind curve and quickly came up behind Smailes's Ford Escort. The drunk attempted to pass the Escort but instead plowed it into a nearby utility pole, killing Smailes instantly.

At first it seemed just another tragic tale of a drunk driver killing an innocent victim. But there was more to this story. Riding along with Trooper Plumer was a cameraperson and an audio person working on behalf of a since-canceled reality television program called *Real Stories of the Highway Patrol.*

As Lawrence Schultz, the Martinsburg attorney for the Smailes family, would ultimately find out after watching and listening to the tapes many times, the audio person riding in the backseat, Peter Schmidt, was far more than just a passive observer. Schultz detected Schmidt's voice egging Trooper Plumer on in the dangerous pursuit.

"Go get him," Schmidt is heard to say at one point. "Stay on his tail, Kevin," he encourages the trooper at another time. Were the media now encouraging—aiding and abetting in legal terminology—in what many would consider to be reckless police conduct that ultimately would lead to a death?

Schultz thought so. He decided to file what is known as a wrongful death lawsuit on behalf of Amanda Smailes's mother, Cynthia, as the administrator of her estate. Schultz sued Schmidt as well as the cameraperson, James Allen Porter; Leap Off Productions, the producer of *Real Stories of the Highway Patrol;* and New World/Genesis Entertainment, the company that distributed the show. Schultz argued that the media defendants were liable because they encouraged Trooper Plumer to continue on with a course of conduct they knew or should have known was reckless—a nighttime, high-speed chase of an intoxicated driver on a winding two-lane road. Schultz also sued the West Virginia State Police; Trooper Plumer, the driver of the vehicle; and the bar that served Sparkman alcohol.

The West Virginia State Police settled with Schultz and the Smailes family in the wrongful death action for a whopping $775,000 in March 1998. But the matter did not end there. The media defendants—dubbed the "entertainment defendants" by the attorney, Schultz, in the lawsuit—were represented by attorneys for Fox, which according to Schultz had purchased the stock of Leap Off Productions around the time of the accident. In September 1998, they too decided to settle with the Smailes rather than take the risk of going to trial and facing a potentially hostile jury composed of local West Virginians. Under the terms of the settlement agreement, Schultz cannot reveal the money that the media coughed up to get out of the matter. Smailes's parents, however, told the Associated Press that it was a "very substantial" sum.

Schultz argues that the producers of *Real Stories* knew the activity that allegedly caused Amanda Smailes's death was dangerous but nonetheless actively sought it out. He bases this in part on the fact that the host of *Real Stories* was Maury Hannigan, the former head of the California Highway Patrol (CHP). The CHP, in turn, enforces a very specific and restrictive policy for situations like that which occurred in the case of Amanda Smailes. General Order 100.42 of the California Highway Patrol provides in relevant part:

> If an officer who is assigned a ride-along participant is directed or required to respond to an extremely hazardous situation, he/she shall ensure that the immediate supervisor is aware that a ride-along participant is present. *In extremely hazardous situations, it may be advisable to leave the ride-along participant at a safe location and return for the individual after the incident has been concluded.*[21]

Schultz argues that this language suggests that Hannigan and the producers of *Real Stories* knew the danger of allowing the media to be present during situations like that in the case of Amanda Smailes. Yet the show went to a state, West Virginia, that did not have a policy like that of the CHP so that it could capture exciting footage. Although there are many reasons to settle a case, that argument probably had some merit, because the media defendants ultimately settled with Schultz before the case could go to trial.

And what is the lesson to be learned from the tragic impact of mediated voyeurism in the *Real Stories* incident? The attorney Lawrence Schultz has an answer: "The news media, especially television, have enormous power to modify and provoke behavior. With that power comes responsibility. The responsibility is to be sure that the camera crew is simply recording events, not driving them. Where a camera crew encourages dangerous behavior, and the situation turns deadly, employers should expect to be haled into court."[22] The United States Supreme Court decisions in *Hanlon v. Berger* and *Wilson v. Layne* obviously cannot prevent the kind of extreme situation that killed Amanda Smailes. Those cases have nothing to do with car chases and clearly do not prohibit camera crews from riding along with the police. But the two cases do mark an initial step designed to curb the excessive mediated voyeurism propagated by ride-along entertainment.

As the next section suggests, it is not just the United States Supreme Court that is erecting barriers to prevent reality-based mediated voyeurism. In the wake of the tragic car crash in August 1997 that killed Diana, Princess of Wales, in a tunnel in France as she allegedly was being chased by photographers, both federal and state legislative bodies in the United States have gotten into the act of crafting statutes to restrict the voyeuristic, telephoto efforts of the paparazzi. Indeed, the true legacy of Princess Diana's death may prove to be more than just a weepy, record-selling reworking by Elton John and Bernie Taupin of *Candle in the Wind*; it may be a web of legislation restricting the ability of the media to take the kind of voyeuristic photographs and videotape that are the fodder of both the print and television tabloids.

Paparazzi Bashing 101

For years we have spotted photographers around the edges of our personal property and trailing us in the streets and parks with high-powered lenses, taking pictures of private moments and of our children who have no concept of what it means to be a "public figure." It is difficult to explain to a youngster why we must interrupt what we are doing and go inside to wait for our pursuers to leave, which sometimes doesn't happen.[23]

The actor Michael J. Fox of television's *Family Ties* and *Spin City* fame was telling Henry J. Hyde and the other members of

House Committee on the Judiciary in May 1998 about the horrors of the so-called paparazzi and encouraging them to support pending federal legislation designed to curb their actions. He was joined in testimony by the comedian Paul Reiser of the now-canceled situation comedy *Mad About You.* Reiser related similar horror stories, including one about how overzealous photographers and journalists tried to obtain pictures of his son, born several weeks prematurely, at a hospital. "The reason these people were trying to get a picture of my son—or more likely, a picture of me emotionally distraught over the bed of my hospitalized son—is not because they care one way or the other about either of us," Reiser said, "but simply and obviously because there is a market for this. They stand to be paid for these invasions of privacy. And the more invasive and intimate, the more valuable their trophy."[24]

The parade of horrors went on that day. Adding to the fray was the actor Richard Masur, then president of the powerful Screen Actors Guild, which has nearly 100,000 members across the United States. He emphasized that "personal privacy has always been highly treasured" in the United States and that "no one, no matter how their notoriety came about, should be seen as consenting to reckless endangerment or trespass."[25]

The star-studded panel was assembled, along with a collection of legal scholars, to speak out on behalf of two bills that were pending at the time before the 105th Congress. One, originally proposed by the late Sonny Bono, a congressman from California, less than one month after Princess Diana's death in Paris, which many blamed on a reckless pursuit by motorcycle-riding paparazzi, was dubbed the "Protection from Personal Intrusion Act" (H.R. 2448). The legislation would make it a crime to persistently physically follow or chase a victim "in circumstances where the victim has a reasonable expectation of privacy . . . for the purpose of capturing by camera or sound recording instrument of any type a visual image, sound recording, or other physical impression of the victim for profit."[26] In other words, it applied only to commercial photographers, not to the average fan out to capture a photograph for his or her own scrapbook or living room.

The other piece of proposed legislation, known as the "Privacy Protection Act of 1998" (H.R. 3224), was introduced in the House by Elton Gallegly along with a similar version in the U.S. Senate by Dianne Feinstein and Orrin Hatch. Like Bono's bill, it too made it a crime to persistently follow or chase an individual for purposes of obtaining a photograph or visual image for commercial purposes if the individual had a reasonable fear that death or bodily injury might result from the chase. Gallegly's bill, however, used existing federal law and sentencing guidelines to permit the prosecution of wrongdoers if death or serious bodily injury in fact resulted from being chased.

Bono, Gallegly, and Feinstein, not coincidentally, are all from California, the home of Hollywood and its powerful lobbying forces, including the Screen Actors Guild. Actors, of course, make their living out of being watched by the public on the silver screen or television. But when it comes to being watched in real life—when it comes to being the subjects of reality-based mediated voyeurism, in other words—they claim their privacy interests must trump certain press practices that they view as egregious and atrocious. Thus the introduction of the bills designed to satisfy their interests over that of a nation of voyeurs.

Although the bills never made it into law before the 105th Congress ended, two other congressmen, John Conyers and Bill McCollum, picked up the fight again in 1999 for more legislation designed to restrict the press's ability to gather voyeuristic images of celebrities. They introduced a very similar piece of legislation in the 106th Congress titled the "Personal Privacy Protection Act" (H.R. 97). At the time this book was written, the bill had been referred to the House Committee on the Judiciary and its subcommittee on crime.

The powerful Hollywood lobby of celebrities has to date had more luck in its own backyard than in Washington, D.C. In October 1998, the then–California governor, Pete Wilson, signed into law a controversial piece of legislation designed to discourage paparazzi-like invasions of privacy. Not surprising, that new law was endorsed by the Screen Actors Guild and a number of celebrities. The law's primary targets? The paparazzi and their use of telephoto lenses and other enhancement devices for taking long-range photographs and long-distance sound recordings—the very kind of devices that capture vérité voyeurism moments.

The California law provides that a person may be held liable for what it calls a "constructive invasion of privacy" even if there is no physical trespass or entry onto another's property. Essentially, the law expands the trespass tort described earlier in this chapter to cover *nonphysical* entries. The statute reads in relevant part,

> A person is liable for constructive invasion of privacy when the defendant attempts to capture, in a manner that is offensive to a reasonable person, any type of visual image, sound recording, or other physical impression of the plaintiff engaging in a personal or familial activity under circumstances in which the plaintiff had a reasonable expectation of privacy, through the use of a visual or auditory enhancing device, regardless of whether there is a physical trespass, if this image, sound recording, or other physical impression could not have been achieved without a trespass unless the visual or auditory enhancing device was used.[27]

The law is extremely problematic for several reasons. First, it never defines what precisely is meant by a "visual or auditory enhancing device." To the extent that *any* camera lens enhances a photograph, it may well be that the law prohibits all photographs. It remains to be seen what this phrase sweeps up.

The new California law also allows celebrities to recover massive amounts of money—amounts far beyond what is necessary to compensate them for harm. Specifically, the law provides that plaintiffs may recover "up to three times" the amount of money necessary to compensate them for injuries that flow from the photographer's conduct. A brief hypothetical illustrates the danger of what might be thought of as this "bonus" damages provision.

A freelance photographer—nearly all of the photographs in a publication such as the *National Enquirer* are taken by freelancers, who broker their work through clearinghouses such as Gamma Liaison—uses a telephoto lens to capture a photograph of a celebrity's wedding. The photograph is taken from a hillside about 200 yards away from the celebrity's home where the wedding is held in the backyard. Remember, the photographer does not need to physically enter the celebrity's property to be held accountable under the California law.

If a jury found that the celebrity was harmed in the amount of $100,000 by the photographer's "offensive" use of a telephoto lens, the jury is entitled to triple this amount to $300,000. What is more, the statute also provides that the photographer will be forced to give up whatever profits he or she made from selling the photograph to a publication. On top of all this, the jury has the discretion to award what are called punitive damages—damages designed to punish the photographer for the wrongdoing, as opposed to compensate the celebrity for actual injuries sustained. Punitive damages, in fact, amount to a windfall for the celebrity. Jurors have vast discretion in awarding punitive damages and they often abuse it to punish the very tabloid publications that they do not want to admit to reading or purchasing themselves. Punitive damages often exceed the money given to compensate the plaintiff for real injuries. Thus, if the jury hits the freelancer up for $500,000 in punitive damages—a not-unrealistic sum given past jury bashing of the media—the celebrity in this hypothetical gets to keep this amount on top of the $300,000 and whatever money the photographer made in selling the photograph. The practical impact, of course, is that this will drive freelancers out of business or force them to do business in another state without such a Draconian law. That, of course, is the goal of the Hollywood lobby.

Legislation like that adopted in California and proposed in Congress today affects far more than just the voyeuristic tendencies of the paparazzi to capture real moments of celebrities' lives when they least expect it. As the First Amendment attorneys Anne E. Hawke and Bruce D. Brown wrote in *The Legal Times* in 1999, "A media that now routinely smothers the likes of a Betty Currie [President Clinton's secretary] making her way out of a federal courthouse has just as much to lose from these legislative initiatives as any supermarket screamer."[28] The line, in other words, between the mainstream media and the paparazzi has blurred almost to the extent of being nonexistent. Both attempt to bring us unguarded images of celebrities and political figures.

The real danger of paparazzi legislation, of course, is to the First Amendment freedom of the press. A restriction that targets the paparazzi will have a spillover, or ripple, effect on other members of the media. Carving out a law to regulate one class of photographers leads down a slippery slope of legislative bodies creating more and more statutory exceptions to press freedom. Our right to be voyeurs of the very people who make their living being watched is transgressed by the paparazzi legislation.

Testifying in the same hearing as Fox and Reiser was Robert D. Richards, a professor of journalism and law at Pennsylvania State University. Unlike that pair of actors, however, Richards was not there to endorse the proposed legislation. Taking the side of First Amendment press freedom, Richards argued that to expose the paparazzi "to federal criminal and civil penalties for doing their job would have a deleterious effect not only on the news gathering process but also on the information the American public receives." He spelled out the dangers of the unintended consequences of legislation such as Gallegly's proposal:

Although these measures are designed to prohibit a type of improper behavior, their language may sweep into the law's reach other than news gathering activities not contemplated in this legislation. For example, in the hubbub of activity surrounding a news story about a public official, camera crews from what we consider mainstream media oftentimes have to chase after sources seeking to avoid the public scrutiny. If enough camera crews encircle the source, that individual may indeed momentarily fear for his or her safety.[29]

Paul Tash, the executive editor of the *St. Petersburg Times* and chair of the Freedom of Information Committee of the American Society of Newspaper Editors, echoed Richards's arguments. Tash told members of the Judiciary Committee that despite the bill's optimistic goal of protecting celebrities from the tabloid press, it "would protect villains, frauds, and scoundrels against diligent photojournalists who would bring them and their activities to light."[30]

Richards points out in a forthcoming law journal article still another potential danger of paparazzi legislation. He argues that because the legislation restricts the ability of photographers to capture pictures, it may in fact drive up the market value of those photographs that are snapped. Photographers, in turn, may engage in even more dangerous and risky conduct to capture images of celebrities, given the photographs will be more valuable. In brief, marketplace forces may cause the very legislation intended to protect celebrities to in fact subject them to more threatening situations.

One more point should be made about the anti-voyeuristic, anti-paparazzi legislation. Much of this legislation arose in anger and haste over public response to one tragic incident—the death of Princess Diana. Just as tough cases can make for bad laws, so can legislative reaction to media hype over one extreme and unusual event. The Philadelphia assistant district attorney Irene L. Kim writes in a recent law journal article, "Abridging free speech and press, the most basic of constitutional rights, with statutes that are no more than figments of public opinion is a dangerous and untrustworthy response to a newsworthy event."[31] What is more, the practical effect of the legislation is elitist, primarily designed to protect a certain class of individuals—celebrities—who make their money off of the public's attention. It will be remembered that the bills pending in Congress pertain only to those who seek to capture photographs for commercial purposes. Celebrities, of course, would like a slice of that money for themselves.

The lines are clearly drawn between the right to privacy and the right to a free press. The right to a free press, in turn, serves our interest in voyeurism. Clearly, the legal backlash against the actions of the paparazzi threaten both the press and voyeurism. Moreover, the behavior complained of by the proponents of the paparazzi legislation is already proscribed by other laws, such as trespass and intrusion into seclusion, described earlier in the chapter, as well as measures against harassment and stalking adopted by most states. It is, then, legislative overkill to attack mediated voyeurism with additional legislation.

As the next section suggests, the paparazzi are far from the only producers of mediated voyeurism under legal attack today.

The Upending of Upskirting

Stephen W. Glover of Monroe, Louisiana, was a videotape voyeur, or so claims his former neighbor, Susan Wilson. In April 1999, Wilson testified before Louisiana's House Committee on the Administration of Justice about the trauma that she said she experienced at the hands—more precisely, at the eyes of the surveillance cameras—of Glover in 1998. Glover, Wilson alleges, for six months secretly videotaped Wilson and her family in private moments—moments in her bedroom and bathroom, no less—with mini cameras that he had secretly placed in the attic of her home.[32] When police searched Glover's home in June

1998, they found and confiscated four videotapes containing images of Susan Wilson and her husband, Gary.

Although peeping in windows is a crime in Louisiana, using a camera to record a person's activities in his or her own home was not at the time these incidents occurred. In other words, if Glover had watched in person by peering through a window or a hole in a wall, his conduct would have been illegal. Louisiana law, however, like laws in many other states, had not kept up with changing technology and the growing trend of video voyeurism. Glover thus had to be charged under an alternative theory—unauthorized entry into an inhabited dwelling. He pleaded guilty and ultimately received three years probation and a $2,000 fine to pay for damages done to the house.

Wilson, who said she "felt raped" by Glover's actions, lobbied the Louisiana legislature to amend its laws to deal with video voyeurs. In June 1999, the Louisiana House voted 101–0 in favor of a bill authored by Willie Hunter, a representative from Monroe, that would make video voyeurism a crime if one tapes for "lewd and lascivious" purposes. The state Senate followed suit by a 32–3 vote, sending the bill on for approval by the governor, who signed the legislation in summer 1999.

Susan Wilson, however, is far from alone as a victim of video voyeurism in a state that did not have an appropriate law to protect her privacy interests. Take the case of John Humphreville, a student at Cheshire High School in Connecticut. In 1998, he allegedly used a hidden camera to videotape at least four girls changing into their swimsuits at two pool parties. When one of the girls reportedly came across friends who were watching a video of her undressing, the school suspended Humphreville. Prosecutors reacted more slowly—Connecticut, it seemed, had no laws that addressed video voyeurism.[33] He was ultimately charged with breach of the peace for distributing and playing the videos, *not* for taping them.

As in Louisiana, the Connecticut voyeurism case caught the eye of that state's legislature. In June 1999, a video voyeurism

bill passed in the Connecticut Senate and in the House of Representatives.[34]

As described earlier in the book, the World Wide Web is
awash with sites that cater to precisely the type of sexual
voyeurism involved in both the Louisiana and Connecticut
cases. Most victims of such voyeurism probably would be surprised to learn how public their lives—and bodies—have become.

There are today web fetish sites dedicated to displaying photographs that capture women and men as they change and undress. As discussed earlier, they also feature photographs
known as upskirts—pictures taken with a hidden camera placed
in a shopping bag that is directed upward under a woman's
skirt. These upskirt images often are captured in public places
such as shopping malls or fairgrounds.

For instance, in March 1999, twenty-seven-year-old Kenneth
James Hofbauer of Tampa, Florida, pleaded no contest to
charges of videotaping up women's skirts at a mall.[35] According
to investigators, Hofbauer spent Labor Day in 1998 at the mall
with a video camera that he placed in a black nylon bag and set
down by women's feet as they shopped. Fortunately for the victims of Hofbauer's actions, a law had gone into effect in that
state in July 1998 to target just such conduct. Florida's law provides that "a person commits the offense of voyeurism when he
or she, with lewd, lascivious, or indecent intent, secretly observes, photographs, films, videotapes, or records another person when such other person is located in a dwelling, structure
or other conveyance and such location provides a reasonable
expectation of privacy."[36]

The state of Wisconsin, however, did not have a similar law
in July 1998 when local law enforcement officials accused a
forty-one-year-old man of allegedly hiding a video camera in a
backpack, cutting a hole in it for the camera lens to be exposed,
and then aiming it up the skirts of about six female store clerks
as they helped him.[37] Although Wisconsin had recently adopted

a law banning videotaping a person in the nude without that person's consent, the focus in this case did not involve nudity—underwear and pantyhose apparently were the target. The suspect thus could only be charged with disorderly conduct when he allegedly peered directly under a sixteen-year-old girl's skirt as she stood on a ladder at a J. C. Penny store.

In May 1998, police in Alexandria, Virginia, nabbed a nineteen-year-old man who was using a VHS camera to take pictures under women's dresses in the china department at a Hecht's store. Two weeks later, police in nearby Fairfax arrested a twenty-one-year-old man at a Tower Records store who was holding a palm-sized video camera under a woman's dress.[38] Similar stories of such upskirting now abound across the country.

In addition to web sites that display the "public" voyeurism of upskirting, other sexual voyeurism sites show pictures of women as they shower at home, often captured by a crafty landlord or a clever boyfriend who places a camera under a pile of towels, behind a mirror, or in the ceiling. A Weymouth, Massachusetts, man was arraigned in May 1999 on charges of possession of child pornography after he allegedly used a hidden camera to videotape his baby-sitters—one was only thirteen years old at the time—as they showered or undressed in the bathroom in his home.[39] This is precisely the kind of material that often finds its way to the web. According to one article, there were more than 100 web sites devoted to photographs of such sexual voyeurism in April 1999.[40]

All of this, of course, once again pits the audience's interest in voyeurism against the unsuspecting individual's interest in privacy. Louis Mizell Jr., a former special agent and intelligence officer in the U.S. Department of State, argues in his 1998 book *Invasion of Privacy,* "Secret videotaping may very well be the single greatest threat to personal privacy. More than 20,000 women, men, and children are unknowingly taped every day in situations where the expectation and the right to privacy should be guaranteed, i.e., while showering, dressing, using a public rest room, or making love in their own homes."[41]

Many states have statutes that restrict or limit secretive audio recordings, thus protecting the privacy interest. Most famously, Linda Tripp found herself in legal hot water when she secretly recorded the words of her former friend Monica Lewinsky without her consent. Under Maryland law, it is a crime to record a private conversation without the consent of all parties, unless there is a law enforcement purpose.

But recording audio is *not* the same as recording video. Many wiretapping or eavesdropping laws regulate audiotaping or recording but are silent as to videotaping. If sound is not recorded when a videotape is made, then prosecutors must seek other remedies to punish video voyeurs. What is more, the so-called Peeping Tom penal statutes that exist in most states relate to peering into private dwellings or physically trespassing, not videotaping up skirts in public places such as shopping malls, parks, and fairgrounds.

This raises an important question that affects the victims of upskirt voyeurs seeking civil recovery under tort law: Can a person have an expectation of privacy in a public place? Unfortunately for some of the victims of upskirt voyeurism, the answer under civil law initially appears to be an emphatic no.[42] The law professor Andrew Jay McClurg writes in an excellent law journal article calling for a theory of liability for intrusions in public settings, "One lesson of modern privacy law in the tort arena is that if you expect legal protection for your privacy, you should stay inside your house with the blinds closed. Tort law clings stubbornly to the principle that privacy cannot be invaded in or from a public place."[43]

Under this general principle, victims of upskirt voyeurism that takes place in a public location such as a park or shopping mall would be left remediless under the privacy theory called intrusion into seclusion.[44] To maintain a cause of action for intrusion into seclusion, one must have a reasonable or legitimate expectation of privacy.[45] If there is no expectation of privacy in the place or location where a photograph or video is taken, the plaintiff will generally lose under this theory.

The drafters of the *Restatement (Second) of Torts* amazingly seemed to predict the rise of upskirt voyeurism decades before it became a national problem. Buried in a comment relating to their articulation of the intrusion tort, the drafters wrote that "even in a public place, however, there may be some matters about the plaintiff, *such as his underwear or lack of it,* that are not exhibited to the public gaze; and there may still be an invasion of privacy when there is intrusion upon these matters."[46]

The Original Upskirt:
Flora Bell Graham

The illustration the *Restatement* framers used to inform the comment set forth above is drawn from a real case decided by the Alabama Supreme Court over thirty-five years ago, *Daily Times Democrat v. Graham.*[47] Unlike the covert upskirt voyeurism cases of today, this case involved a dress that was, quite literally, already up and underwear that was plainly visible to the public. Flora Bell Graham, then a forty-four-year-old housewife, was attending the Cullman County Fair in Alabama in October 1961.[48] As she was leaving the fun house with her two young children, air jets blew up underneath her dress à la Marilyn Monroe in the 1957 Billy Wilder film *Seven Year Itch* and, as the Alabama Supreme Court put it, "Her body was exposed from the waist down, with the exception of that portion covered by her 'panties.'"[49] As misfortune would have it, a photographer for the *Daily Times Democrat* snapped a picture of Graham at that precise moment and the newspaper had the bad taste and profoundly poor journalistic judgment to later publish it on its front page.[50] As a result of that publication, Graham claimed to become "embarrassed, self-conscious, upset and was known to cry on occasions."[51] She filed a lawsuit claiming her privacy was invaded.

One of the central questions faced by the Supreme Court of Alabama was whether Flora Bell Graham possessed a reasonable expectation of privacy at the time the photograph was taken at the fun house.[52] The newspaper argued that she did not, claiming that the picture was taken at a time Graham was "part of a public scene" and therefore no invasion of privacy was possible.[53]

The high court of Alabama began its analysis of the issue by acknowledging that the principle that one does *not* possess a reasonable expectation of privacy in a public place "is established by the cases."[54] Yet it chose not to follow this general rule in Flora Bell Graham's case. Apparently not wanting to deprive Graham of legal recourse for an obviously embarrassing photograph, the court observed that "a purely mechanical application of legal principles should not be permitted to create an illogical conclusion."[55] The court then reasoned that it would be illogical to conclude that a person who "is involuntarily and instantaneously enmeshed in an embarrassing pose forfeits her right of privacy merely because she happened at that moment to be part of a public scene."[56]

In reaching this conclusion in Graham's favor, the Alabama Supreme Court created a rule that if followed by courts today, would appear to provide modern-day victims of video voyeurism in public places—upskirt and downblouse victims in malls, parks, and amusement parks—with a line of reasoning necessary to provide a reasonable expectation of privacy in a public place. The rule? The court wrote,

> Where the status he [the plaintiff] expects to occupy is changed without his volition to a status that is embarrassing to an ordinary person of reasonable sensitivity, then he should not be deemed to have forfeited his right to be protected from an indecent and vulgar intrusion of his right to privacy merely because misfortune overtakes him in a public place.[57]

It may be possible, then, to claim an expectation of privacy in some cases of upskirt voyeurism that occur in public places. But the *Graham* case applies only to *civil* liability issues of tort law. What about *criminal* liability for upskirt video voyeurism in public places? Even when there are state criminal laws that directly target video voyeurism, loopholes can be found that frustrate privacy advocates and facilitate voyeurs. For instance, the former special agent and intelligence officer quoted earlier, Louis Mizell, observes that some states have laws that regulate secret videotaping, but only when the taping occurs in particular locations, such as a store dressing room.[58]

In April 1999, lawmakers in California were concerned with just such a problem with that state's law against video voyeurism. That is when Dick Ackerman, assemblyman from Fullerton, began ardently pushing a bill to close a gap in Section 647(k) of that state's penal code.[59] The then-current section prohibited recording via a video camera in the interior of "a bathroom, changing room, fitting room, or tanning booth, or the interior of any other area in which the occupant has a reasonable expectation of privacy," but said nothing about recording in public places such as shopping malls and amusement parks. Indeed, at least one incident was investigated at Disneyland in Ackerman's own turf of Orange County, in which a man allegedly spent hours sneaking videotape of women. In 1999, the California governor, Gray Davis, signed Ackerman's legislation tightening the screws on the gathering of sexually prurient mediated voyeurism.

As in California, many state legislative bodies today are concerned that voyeurism is overtaking privacy interests and that technological developments have outstripped the evolution of existing surveillance and Peeping Tom statutes. They are starting to take steps to amend and update their laws. In June 1999, a bill that for the first time would make it a crime to photograph, film, or videotape, without their consent, persons undressing or having sex was pending in the New Jersey Assembly.[60] Until now, prosecutors in the Garden State have been forced to rely on wiretap statutes to prosecute video voyeurs, but those statutes are effective only if an audio recording is made along with the video.

Finally, it should noted that the legal privacy implications are substantially reduced, if not eliminated, in the case of web cam sites like those hosted by Jennifer Ringley and Voyeur Dorm, described in Chapter 1. In these cases, the individuals willingly consent to being watched and thus can claim no expectation of privacy. They are, as Chapter 1 notes, akin to exhibitionists. The real concern, then, must be with unsuspecting victims of upskirt voyeurism and all other forms of taping unconsenting subjects.

Summary

The legal tension between privacy and voyeurism is far from resolved. As Chapters 5 and 6 have made clear, there are existing laws as well as pending legislation designed to protect an individual's interest in privacy against mediated voyeurism. Courts and legislative bodies thus do recognize limits to a First Amendment freedom of the press and corporate speech that would otherwise provide blanket protection to voyeurism. On the other hand, courts also allow the publication of private and embarrassing information as long as it is deemed newsworthy, and they give vast deference to journalistic judgment and editorial discretion on this issue. What is more, the First Amendment freedoms of speech and press protect not just individuals but large corporations that engage in mediated voyeurism for profit.

Whether the voyeurism value eventually captures or embodies the heart of First Amendment jurisprudence may in the future depend on the theoretical reasoning and arguments that justify mediated voyeurism as a protected form of free expression. In the next chapter, the voyeurism value is briefly contrasted with more traditional theories that are used to support freedom of expression in the United States.

7

Seeing Voyeurs in First Amendment Theory

The First Amendment commands, quite simply and eloquently, "Congress shall make no law . . . abridging the freedom of speech, or of the press." That speech and press are protected by the Constitution says nothing, however, about *why* expression ranging from the political protest of flag burning to the pornographic photographs of *Hustler* magazine deserves protection. Surely there must be some rationale or reason for awarding speech and press protected status under the First Amendment.

The law professors John Garvey and Frederick Schauer observe that "inquiring into the purposes served by the freedoms of speech and press has been a major preoccupation of scholars and judges."[1] It should not be too surprising, then, that a veritable laundry list of reasons to protect expression has emerged over the years. The freedoms of speech and press, for instance, have been said variously to promote and to protect discovery of truth,[2] democratic self-governance,[3] self-realization,[4] dissent,[5] tolerance,[6] and honest government.[7] Kathleen Sullivan and Gerald Gunther, two of the nation's foremost constitutional law scholars, housed at Stanford University, argue that the "three principal values" served by free speech are the opening ones on that list: the discovery of truth in the metaphorical marketplace

207

of ideas, the promotion of wise and informed decisionmaking in a self-governing democracy, and the development and fulfillment of an individual through speech.[8]

No one of these theories for protecting speech, however, is necessarily better or more correct than any other. As the law professor Rodney A. Smolla writes, "Acceptance of one rationale need not bump another from the list, as if this were First Amendment musical chairs."[9] If that is the case, then adding another chair—read, another First Amendment theory—to the game might be a beneficial exercise.

In particular, it might help to uncover some value of speech or principle of expression that we have been overlooking or forgetting in extant First Amendment theories. Alternatively, it might simply serve as a point of contrast for reinforcing or reinvigorating traditional First Amendment values. The very proposal and rejection of a new free speech value thus may serve an important purpose—answering more completely why, at the dawn of the twenty-first century, we value and therefore protect expression.

Surely the plethora of speech values mentioned above is not and need not be exhaustive or exclusive. Concomitantly, the explication of a new First Amendment value need not deny or preclude the existence of others. It may simply serve to complement, supplement, or round out current First Amendment theory. Proffering another value of speech to be debated and critiqued—accepted or rejected—thus makes sense.

It makes particular sense given the glaring weaknesses with some of the free speech principles and policies now embraced in the First Amendment. Those theories often seem antiquated, naïve, and sorely out of touch with the reality of the modern communications environment. Even a cursory examination of two of the most established free speech theories—the marketplace of ideas and democratic self-governance—makes this clear.

Consider first the time-worn metaphor of the marketplace of ideas. With discovery and testing of the truth as its telos, this theory "consistently dominates the Supreme Court's discussions of freedom of speech."[10] Justice Oliver Wendell Holmes Jr. firmly implanted it in First Amendment jurisprudence more than eighty years ago when he wrote, in a dissenting opinion, "The best test of truth is the power of the thought to get itself accepted in the competition of the market."[11] The origins of the marketplace theory, in fact, predate Holmes's oft-quoted aphorism. It finds "its roots in John Milton and John Stuart Mill," observes the First Amendment scholar Lucas A. Powe Jr.[12] Milton, more than three centuries ago in his *Areopagitica,* penned the now-famous lines: "And though all the winds of doctrine were let loose to play upon the earth, so Truth be in the field, we do injuriously by licensing and prohibiting to misdoubt her strength. Let her and falsehood grapple; who ever knew truth put to the worse in a free and open encounter?"

Those words from 1644 assume a robust yet fair "grappling" of all ideas. Today, however, the marketplace of ideas is anything but fair. The winds of speech do not blow so freely—the airwaves, in fact, are quite expensive to access—and the metaphorical field to which Milton referred tilts decidedly in favor of a few powerful corporate and special interest voices. Specifically, the marketplace of ideas is controlled by a handful of megamedia conglomerates that, as Ben Bagdikian writes, represent "a new communications cartel within the United States."[13] What are the ramifications for the marketplace metaphor? Todd Gitlin writes that these "effective monopolies" permit and deny access to the marketplace of ideas as they choose, often based on bottom-line considerations.[14] Smolla concurs, observing that the marketplace of ideas, just like the economic marketplace from which the metaphor springs, "will inevitably be biased in favor of those with resources to ply their wares."[15]

One need think no further than the merger of AT&T with TCI, the purchase of CBS by Viacom, or the unification of radio giants Clear Channel Communications and AMFM Inc. at the close of the twentieth century to understand this unfortunate reality. The voices of AT&T and Viacom are loud and powerful in the marketplace of the new millennium, drowning out others with their sheer might and domination. Clear Channel and AMFM now boast a combined total of 830 radio stations, dominating that medium.[16] The marketplace of ideas is controlled by a few corporate entities that stifle, or at least overwhelm, the expression of others.

In October 1999, the United States Supreme Court Justice Stephen G. Breyer astutely acknowledged this simple fact during oral argument in a case involving state-imposed caps on campaign contributions. "A big megaphone can drown out the smaller ones," the erudite Clinton appointee remarked.[17] Many academics readily agree with this sentiment. For instance, Mark Crispin Miller of New York University lamented after the announcement in September 1999 of the Viacom-CBS deal, "It seems to me that this is, by any definition, an undemocratic development. The media system in a democracy should not be inordinately dominated by a few very powerful interests."[18]

But there are troublesome flaws with the modern-day application of the marketplace metaphor beyond questions of access and power. The problems lie in the very ideas that are produced, displayed, and sold as commodities. In particular, the marketplace of ideas is polluted by media content that seemingly does precious little to further an idealistic search for the truth—if truth, in fact, ever can be discovered in these days of ethical and moral relativism and uncertainty—and, more often than not, panders to emotions and amusement rather than furthering the rational discourse and discussion necessary to arrive at the truth. The tell-all voyeurism of Jerry Springer's popular "talk" television show illustrates this point. The appeal is the voyeuristic eavesdropping on the often freakish and outlandish private-turned-public lives of others. Springer's fans ritualistically chant "Jer-ry, Jer-ry" not to discover or test any truth, but because they are caught up in the emotional satisfaction of the contrived spectacle before them. The late Kurt Cobain of the pioneering grunge rock band Nirvana seemed to get the value of free speech right for many people when he sang, "Here we are now, entertain us." And although Cobain's often angst-ridden lyrics—"I feel stupid and contagious"—are a far cry from Holmes's eloquent judicial opinions, the former's words about the desire to be entertained and amused—"I wish I was like you, easily amused"—ring perhaps more realistic today than the latter's when it comes to the reasons why people value speech.

The marketplace of ideas metaphor, however, is not the only theory of free speech today that although appealing in the abstract is in reality riddled with flaws. The democratic self-governance theory articulated by the late philosopher-educator Alexander Meiklejohn, for instance, holds that the ultimate aim of protecting speech is "the voting of wise decisions."[19] He believed, "The principle of the freedom of speech springs from the necessities of the program of self-government."[20] This theory thus privileges political speech above all other types of expression, advocating a hierarchical approach to First Amendment jurisprudence in which nonpolitical speech receives less protection.

Today's political reality suggests the theory of democratic self-governance is far from relevant to most people. Voting apparently is not taken seriously by the many who ignore the opportunity to cast a ballot, and politics, as described in Chapter 3, often is reduced to sexual voyeurism or a mediated spectator sport in which we watch—we spectate—gadfly pundits who pontificate pointlessly. Political speech often appears to exist only for the purposes of lining the pockets of pundits and for the entertainment interests of the audience. Ronald Collins and David Skover thus are squarely on point when they remark in *The Death of Discourse,* "The modern obsession with self-amusement can trivialize public expression and thereby under-mine the traditional aims of the First Amendment."[21]

But there are additional problems with seeing political speech as the primary reason for protecting expression. Many people today simply may not care about politics enough to participate in the voting of wise decisions—Meiklejohn's goal of free speech. The electorate, for instance, is shrinking. The turnout of the voting-age population in the 1996 presidential election was only 49 percent, less than half of all potential voters and the lowest figure since 1924.[22] To put that figure in perspective, more people—about 95 million—watched on television the slow-speed pursuit of O. J. Simpson in the white Bronco during the summer of 1994—itself a classic spectacle of mediated voyeurism under the definition used in this book—than voted in the 1996 presidential election.[23]

Voter turnout for the presidential election in 1988 was just 50.1 percent of the voting-age population.[24] Although the figure was a slightly higher 55.2 percent in 1992, this is still far less than the voter turnout during the elections of 1960, 1964, and 1968, each of which topped more than 60 percent.[25] There has been, writes the Columbia University communications scholar James W. Carey, a steady "evacuation of the public realm."[26]

Apathy toward politics is reflected in the attitude of a whole new generation of college students. That observation is based on more than one professor's unscientific assessment of his or her own students. In particular, a recent UCLA survey found that freshmen entering college in 1997 were less interested in politics and social issues than any class in a generation.[27] In 1997, about 27 percent of incoming freshmen reported that keeping up to date with politics was important, whereas at the start of the 1990s the figure was over 40 percent.[28] Alexander Astin, a UCLA professor who helped to conduct the survey, called the numbers "part of a larger pattern of disengagement of the American people from political and civic life in general."[29]

The marketplace, in a nutshell, is rigged, and political participation is passé. Traditional theories of free speech are no longer sufficient, by themselves, to justify protecting expression that we care about in our mediated and visual society. Those theories do not match reality, do not even come close. The uses that we often make of speech today—be it watching sit-coms on television or surfing the Internet for on-line e-Bay bargains, for instance—are far removed from discovery of truth or wise and informed politics.

This is not to say, of course, that discovering the truth and voting wisely are not important tasks or that speech that serves these purposes does not deserve protection. Those clearly are significant interests served by free expression. Rather, it is to say that many people today value or prize speech that on its face serves neither of these noble goals and that this speech is nonetheless very important to these individuals even if its primary purpose is not discovery of the truth or insightful voting. There is, in other words, speech that many people find meaningful today and worthy of protection that is radically separated from the intellectual moorings of Oliver Wendell Holmes's marketplace of ideas metaphor and Alexander Meiklejohn's theory of democratic self-governance. In the somewhat trendy academic parlance of the late 1990s, there is a "disconnect" between free speech theory and free speech reality.

Adding a Voyeurism Value to First Amendment Theory

Much of First Amendment theory today seems highly irrelevant on a daily basis for protecting the kinds of speech in which many people are most interested. The fact is that our current state of free speech theory, as Collins and Skover write, is ill equipped to deal with "the public's insatiable appetite for amusement."[30] They rightly suggest, "We cannot retain our old constitutional prerogatives in a world transformed" and therefore we must articulate First Amendment principles to suit a new cultural environment.[31] Realism about the nature and uses of speech and, in particular, visual images must transpire if our First Amendment jurisprudence is to have any relevance for a large segment of American society in the twenty-first century. Collins and Skover thus contend, "We need to develop a *bottom-up* approach to the First Amendment, an approach going directly to our communicative experiences rather than to imaginative theories."[32]

In this book, I have asserted that many of our "communicative experiences" with the media today are voyeuristic. From reality police shows like *Cops* to MTV's pseudo-documentary-turned-soap-opera series *The Real World,* from television newsmagazines such as *Dateline* that take us inside other people's private lives to the tell-all talk shows like *Ricki* that expose others' private garbage, we are a nation of mediated voyeurs. As Amy Carr of the *Chicago Daily Herald* accurately observed in a June 1999 column, "There's a little bit of voyeur in all of us. Our eyes are drawn to the illicit, the outrageous and the shocking."[33] A major purpose served by free speech today—a purpose relevant, at least, to many people—therefore is the protection of mediated voyeurism.

With this in mind and employing the bottom-up approach to free speech theory advocated by Collins and Skover, we should be able to construct and assert a new, emerging First Amendment value in the postmodern, mediated visual age of television, the Internet, and the hidden camera. It should be possible to assert the existence of a *voyeurism value* of free expression—a theory that is specifically designed to protect, and hence "value," mediated voyeurism and its many uses described in Chapter 2. After all, if it can been argued that one category of speech—political expression—should be singled out for heightened First Amendment protection as it is under Meiklejohnian theory, then why not carve out another category of expression—mediated voyeurism—for increased constitutional protection? A voyeurism value theory of freedom of expression would exist to support protection for this latter category of expression.

The principles and tenets of the voyeurism value articulated here are still rough. They are offered up in this venue as much for commentary, consideration, and criticism as they are for establishing a new set of free speech precepts. The fact is, however, as Chapters 5 and 6 just suggested, that courts and legislative bodies today *are* actively shaping and refining our right to engage in mediated voyeurism as they consider issues such as hidden camera investigations and ride-along journalism.

If mediated voyeurism is to thrive and its uses and purposes described in Chapter 2 are to be supported by courts and legislatures, then it might help to articulate the particular aspects of it that necessitate First Amendment protection. In doing so, it is particularly useful to contrast the aspects of free speech embraced in mediated voyeurism with those found in more traditional theories such as the marketplace of ideas, democratic self-governance, and self-realization. Why? These theories may already provide sufficient rationales and principles for protecting mediated voyeurism. In that case, we simply might borrow from established theories to provide theoretical support for the creation and distribution of mediated voyeurism. Articulating a distinct theory devoted to protecting a category of speech called mediated voyeurism would prove unnecessary.

It will be recalled from the Introduction that this book defines mediated voyeurism as the consumption of revealing images of and information about others' apparently real and unguarded lives, often yet not always for purposes of entertainment but frequently at the expense of privacy and discourse, through the means of the mass media and Internet. There are many purposes or reasons why people are attracted to mediated voyeurism, as Chapter 2 described. These include (1) a search for truth and reality, (2) a quest for justice and reinforcement of social norms, (3) knowledge and power, and (4) hedonism and personal pleasures. What protection must the First Amendment freedoms of speech and press provide if mediated voyeurism is to thrive and these uses are to be valued?

A number of characteristics of mediated voyeurism described at various points in this book emerge that help to answer this question. In particular, if mediated voyeurism is to flourish, then First Amendment theory must embrace and protect—it must, in other words, value—the following principles and interests:

- The gathering of information, visual or otherwise, about people's lives.
- The receipt of visual images of and information about people's lives.
- The ability of an audience to watch others without obligation to them.
- Real-life images of people transformed into entertainment for others.
- Corporate profit made on the distribution of real-life images.

These are the ingredients that make up a voyeurism value theory of free expression. Conversely, First Amendment theory must *devalue* certain principles and interests if mediated voyeurism is to be thoroughly protected. These include the individual privacy interests of people who are the focus of our mediated voyeurism and the value placed on discourse and interaction with others.

Chapters 5 and 6 early on explicated the tensions between some of these interests. These chapters later used recent legal cases and legislation to illustrate conflicts between the aggressive gathering of images and privacy, and between an audience's implied First Amendment right to know and an individual's ability to control the flow of information about himself or herself. Chapter 3 highlighted the economic interests at stake in mediated voyeurism as a form of low-cost, high-profit programming. And Chapter 2 suggested that the audience's entertainment interests, as well as other wants and needs, are serviced by mediated voyeurism.

With these interests, principles, and tensions in mind, we articulate in step-by-step fashion a voyeurism value theory of freedom of expression. First, the purpose of a voyeurism value theory is to protect mediated voyeurism as a form of expression. Second, the theory holds that it is important to protect mediated voyeurism as a form of expression primarily because many people enjoy this form of speech and secondarily because of the multiple uses that it provides to those people and society at large. Third, the theory itself posits that if courts and legislative bodies provide expansive protection to media corporations and other entities for the gathering, producing, and distributing of images of and information about the apparently real lives of people and if they impose no obligations or responsibilities on the recipients of those images and information to interact with the people whose images and information are distributed, then mediated voyeurism is allowed to thrive as a form of expression.

How does the voyeurism value theory of freedom of expression compare with established free speech theories? The next sections explore this issue.

Mediated Voyeurism and the Free Speech Tradition

In the field of communications research and theory, traditional linear models of communication include at least four basic components: (1) the *source* of a message, (2) the *message* itself, (3) the *channel* through which the message is conveyed, and (4) the *receiver* of or audience for the message. Keeping an eye on the source-message-channel-receiver components of communication is helpful for gaining a better understanding of a voyeurism value theory of free expression. In particular, this section uses these four elements to compare the voyeurism value with other, more traditional theories for protecting expression in First Amendment jurisprudence. It starts at the end of the chain with what is the most important part, at least from the perspective of the mediated voyeur: the receiver link.

The Receiver Link:
Focusing on the Audience's Rights

The central interest at the heart of a voyeurism value theory of free expression would seem to be the ability of the audience to receive speech and, in particular, to receive, consume, and make use of mediated voyeurism as a brand or category of speech. It thus is the right of the audience—the receiver in the source-message-channel-receiver model of communication—that must be paramount if First Amendment theory is to value and therefore protect mediated voyeurism.

To watch revealing images of others' apparently real and unguarded lives—to be a mediated voyeur under the definition of that concept adopted in this book—is to view them, to see them, to ogle them through the means of mass communication and the Internet. Protection of mediated voyeurism thus compels protection of mediated messages—in particular, voyeuristic images—for the benefit of the audience. The rights of the audience to receive a message must be privileged, over and above the privacy rights and abilities of the person who is the subject of the message—the focus of the mediated voyeur's gaze and attention—to control its dissemination to the audience. Put more bluntly, a voyeurism value theory must protect the rights of the *watcher*, not the rights of the *watched*.

The right of the audience to receive messages is not unique to a voyeurism value theory of free expression. It also is important in a number of traditional theories. For instance, the marketplace metaphor pivots on the ability of the audience to receive the information that it needs to discover the truth or, at least, to test conceptions of the truth. Likewise, Meiklejohn's theory of democratic self-governance privileges the rights of the audience over the speaker in the quest for wise and informed decision-making. As Meiklejohn famously wrote, "The point of ultimate interest is not the words of the speakers, but the minds of the hearers."[34] And under the free speech theory of self-realization, people must be able to receive speech—they need access to information—to fully develop their mental capacities as individuals and to shape their identities. As the First Amendment theorist Thomas Emerson put it, self-realization requires "the right of the individual to access knowledge."[35] The need to receive speech thus cuts across what Sullivan and Gunther, mentioned earlier in the chapter, consider the three principal values of expression.

But as mentioned earlier in the chapter, the audience's desire to receive speech often appears today to have nothing to do with promoting the lofty goals of truth discovery or wise voting. It may also have very little to do with fully developing our capacities as evolved, intellectually engaged human beings. Instead, our desire to watch often appears to have much to do with the pleasurable *experience* of watching others—the experience of seeing something private or revealing. The experience may be hedonistic or prurient, or it may simply be the thrill of watching others—without obligation, moral or otherwise, to interact with them—that is so attractive. Whatever the case, the end, or telos, of the receipt of speech by the audience sometimes seems far removed from considerations about the internal quality of the speech—its strength of argument, its informational value—or its instrumental worth in serving a purpose to society as a whole.

It therefore bears recognizing that although many theories of free speech justify protecting the audience's right to *receive* speech, the goal of the receipt of speech in those theories may be very narrow. In contrast, there are multiple uses and gratifications, as Chapter 2 made clear, for mediated voyeurism, some seemingly more noble than others. Some of these uses may overlap with the uses protected by established theories of free expression, but others may not. Thus, although it may be that the mediated voyeur watches video vérité voyeurism to learn about the reality of police work or to discover the truth about police abuse—goals protected by the marketplace theory's emphasis on truth discovery—these are not always the uses or purposes of such voyeuristic content. It may be consumed, instead, simply for racist pleasure, as Chapter 2 suggested.

Likewise, it may be that consuming mediated voyeurism about a politician's sex life informs the voting of wise decisions in line with Meiklejohnian theory, but there are more uses to mediated voyeurism than the political. And it may be, as Chapter 2 suggested, that we watch mediated voyeurism to learn about ourselves—how we might react, for instance, if we faced situations similar to those we watch. Yet there are purposes for consuming mediated voyeurism far beyond self-realization.

To enhance the audience's right to be mediated voyeurs, First Amendment theory would be used broadly to support government measures enhancing the right to receive speech. Taken to its extreme, First Amendment theory in service of mediated voyeurism would call for a media version of the chicken-in-every-pot/car-in-every-garage vision of the American dream. In brief, the government could provide every citizen—every potential mediated voyeur—with a television set or a computer powerful enough to receive mediated voyeurism. The government could equip the audience with the tools necessary to receive the speech that it wants to watch. That high-cost measure obviously is not likely to occur in the near future, and it clearly is not supported in either past or present First Amendment jurisprudence.

The Source Link:
Protecting Sources to Protect Voyeurs

Alternatively, and surely more realistically than providing every mediated voyeur with a television set, the legislative and judicial branches of both the state and federal governments can revise or reinterpret existing laws and create new ones that make mediated voyeurism easier. Rather than providing the audience with the tools necessary to receive mediated voyeurism, these changes would entail increased protection to the *sources*—media corporations and journalism organizations, in particular—that gather and disseminate voyeuristic expression.

For instance, changes might occur that provide media outlets that serve up voyeuristic fare with increased *access* to places and events that we traditionally think of as private. Privacy, a social construction described in Chapter 2 that varies from time to time and from place to place, thus would be reconceptualized and diminished in the name of mediated voyeurism and the voyeurism value in First Amendment jurisprudence. Heightened access to places that permit revealing images of others' apparently unguarded lives to be captured means, in turn, decreased privacy rights for those others. The talismanic reasonable-expectation-of-privacy standard used to determine privacy in tort law would shift, with the reasonable expectations of yesteryear becoming unreasonable today. Privacy expectations would change to comport with both the new technological developments described in Chapter 4 that lessen our expectations of privacy and with our appetite—an appetite whetted and fed by those same technologies—for mediated voyeurism.

Looking back at the source-message-channel-receiver communication flow, it becomes clear that to serve the receiver's voyeuristic proclivities, the source must be afforded expanded protection both to gather and to publicize the speech—the videotape, the images, the live-action shots—the receiver wants. Courts, as Chapter 5 made clear, are asked to do this every time media organizations use the newsworthiness defense in a public disclosure of private facts case and when they claim there is no reasonable expectation of privacy in an intrusion into seclusion case.

Who, then, in the source-message-channel-receiver chain benefits from the adoption of a voyeurism value theory in First Amendment jurisprudence? Two categories of individuals or entities gain. In particular, both the message sources and the message receivers reap the benefits. The audience benefits from increased opportunities to be mediated voyeurs. The sources, in turn, net a monetary reward from providing mediated voyeurs—the audience—what they want to watch. Message sources have greater protection for gathering voyeuristic content that attracts a large audience that, in turn, attracts advertising revenue. This makes it a very profitable endeavor for message sources to gather and disseminate mediated voyeurism.

What is sacrificed in the name of the voyeurism value—privacy—relates directly to the *message* component of the source-message-channel-receiver model. In particular, the individual who is the *subject of the message*—the unsuspecting person caught on tape whose secrets or intimate moments are exposed on television or the Internet—loses. This individual's loss of privacy, of course, is the mediated voyeur's gain, as well as the message source's locus of profit. The next sections go into greater detail about the process of message flow in the source-message-channel-receiver chain as well as the nature of the content of the message itself.

The Message Flow:
Protecting Unidirectional Communication

One important characteristic that would distinguish a voyeurism value theory of free expression from other justifications for protecting speech is the one-directional, noninteractive nature of the communication. Mediated voyeurism, in particular, thrives on our ability to watch others, not to converse or to hold a discussion with them. It is the watching experience—the act of media consumption by the audience, not of conversation—that is pleasurable for the reasons identified in Chapter 2. Under a voyeurism value theory, the First Amendment thus would be called on to support one-directional, noninteractive communication.

The mediated voyeur who watches behind the one-way glass of the television set or computer screen has no obligation to correspond with the individual who is the subject matter of the communicated message. From the perspective of the audience or receiver, a First Amendment–based voyeurism value therefore must cherish what the author Curtis Bok once called "the freedom of silence."[36] Indeed, mediated voyeurs watch from a distance—a very safe and silent distance from which no interaction with the individual who is the focus of the voyeuristic message is necessary. They never interact with the individuals whose lives are exposed on the daytime tabloid television shows, whose arrests are brought to us on reality television programs, or whose crimes are captured on videotape by industrious—and sometimes duplicitous—journalists.

The freedom of silence and the freedom from responsibility in viewing may be part of the appeal of the brand of speech this book calls mediated voyeurism. We can simply watch people's problems, free from commitment to them. We can turn them off when the program ends and forget about them, much like a john who is serviced by a prostitute ceases involvement with the person when the sex act is over. He drives off to his wife and home. The difference, of course, with this analogy is that the mediated voyeur *never* has direct personal contact with the party who is the subject of the gaze.

This is not to say that mediated voyeurism does not involve feedback from the receiver/audience to the message source. The source of the message—the producer of the television program, for instance—receives plenty of feedback in the form of Nielsen ratings. Those ratings are used to set television advertising rates. Feedback, in other words, is measured in terms of audience size and demographics, profits and costs, and dollars and cents. If no one watches—watching others' apparently real and unguarded lives, after all, is what mediated voyeurism is all about—poor ratings will mean the demise of a voyeuristic program and if taken to the extreme across voyeuristic programming, the entire genre of speech called mediated voyeurism. Thus even the feedback between the audience and source is not dialogue—it is, instead, dollars.

More traditional theories of free expression, in contrast, prize dialogue and discourse. The marketplace metaphor, for instance, pivots on the robust discussion and debate of ideas to produce and challenge conceptions of the truth. A message source offers up an idea in the metaphorical marketplace and the audience then can laud or attack it, debate and discuss it, all in the name of finding or testing the truth. Meiklejohn's theory of democratic self-governance also centers heavily on discussion. In particular, it hinges on a town hall rubric in which a moderator structures and controls the flow of discussion so that, ultimately, a wise decision can be made on issues that affect the public interest.[37] The mediated voyeur, in contrast to Meiklejohn's theory, never even enters the metaphorical town hall. Instead, he or she crouches outside the walls and peers secretively through the windows at the people and events inside. The theories of democratic self-governance and the marketplace of ideas thus are readily distinct from a voyeurism value First Amendment theory on the dimension or characteristic of dialogue.

The distinction between the voyeurism value and the self-realization principle is subtler in terms of dialogue. Self-realization through speech may be accomplished, at least in some cases, *without* dialogue or conversation. The obvious example involves an individual who keeps a diary. Translating one's thoughts into a coherent, written form may help a person deal with his or her own life. The dialogue is purely internal, a distinct form of *intra*personal communication. The transcribed thoughts thus are kept in a book that by its very nature is to be kept off limits from the prying eyes of others. No one is supposed to read another person's diary or private journal. The writer thus engages in an internal monologue, reduced to tangible form, but no external dialogue with others is necessary or required for this to be a valuable or meaningful communication experience.

At first glance, this solitary use of speech for purposes of self-realization mirrors the voyeurism value's privileging of the lack of dialogue and the absence of interpersonal interaction in the communication process. There is, however, a critical difference. That difference lies in the distinction between the individuals involved in the source-message-channel-receiver process.

In the act of writing in a diary, there is a message source—the diary writer—but there is no intended receiver or audience, excluding, of course, the diary writer, who may reflect back on past entries. In fact, the presence of a receiver other than the writer frustrates the self-realization process served by putting down intimate details and thoughts about one's life and identity. As the philosopher Sissela Bok wrote in *Secrets,*

> Secrecy guards, then, the central aspects of identity, and if necessary, also plans and property. It serves as an additional shield in case the protection of privacy should fail or be broken down. Thus you may assume that no one will read your diary; but you can also hide it, or write it in code, as did William Blake, or lock it up.[38]

If a person knew there would be an audience for diary entries, self-censorship likely would occur and only blank pages or muted, restrained thoughts would result.

Mediated voyeurism, in contrast, requires the presence of an audience. A message, communicated by someone else and about someone else, must be received and viewed for an instance of mediated voyeurism to arise. The communication act is not simply internal. Indeed, the reading of a diary by illicit others—an unanticipated and unintended audience—is, perhaps, the ultimate act of voyeurism in the print medium. Insert an audience or receiver into the diary scenario and one suddenly frustrates the purpose of speech and converts an intimate act of self-realization into a vulgar act of voyeurism. The experiential pleasure of sneaking a peak at someone else's words without that someone else's permission is a form of voyeurism.

In summary, the one-directional flow of communication privileged by a voyeurism value in First Amendment theory would be distinct from both the dialogue-driven marketplace metaphor and the town hall discussion rubric of Meiklejohn's democratic self-governance theory. And although the self-realization or self-fulfillment value of free speech may be served without dialogue, it is nonetheless distinct from a voyeurism value, which requires an audience, not simply a message source, for completion.

The Message:
Serving Public Interests and Private Wants

A voyeurism value theory of free speech—a theory specifically designed to protect mediated voyeurism—guards speech that many people today want to watch. It does so regardless of whether that speech facilitates a goal for society at large, such as a collective search for the truth or a strong democracy. This becomes clear when attention focuses on the *message* step in the source-message-channel-receiver model of communication. In particular, the *content* and *function* of the message in the voyeurism value may be distinguished from those in other theories of free speech.

For instance, Meiklejohn's theory of democratic self-governance privileges speech "upon matters of *public interest*—roads, schools, poor houses, health, external defense, and the like."[39] The First Amendment, Meiklejohn writes, "protects the freedom of those activities of thought and communication by which we 'govern.'"[40] Although Meiklejohn also advocated protection of art and literature, he did so only to the extent that this speech would "lead toward sensitive and informed appreciation and response to the values out of which the riches of the *general welfare* are created."[41]

The key distinction here between the voyeurism value and the democratic self-governance principle pivots on the meaning of *public interest*. For Meiklejohn, the substance and content of the message must in some way benefit the public interest—a collective-level, "general welfare" understanding of that concept. It centers on speech that a democracy needs to function effectively and wisely. As the law professor Robert Post writes, Alexander Meiklejohn believed that the purpose of speech was "to achieve an orderly, efficient, and rational dispatch of common business."[42] In contrast, the voyeurism value protects speech that panders to the *public's interest*, meaning individual-level, autonomous wants and preferences, not collective-level needs of society or, as Post succinctly puts it, the common business.

The nude photographs described in Chapter 5 of Pamela Anderson Lee that were deemed newsworthy by a federal court illustrate this difference in the concept of the public interest. It is highly doubtful that the viewers of those photographs *needed* to see them to engage thoughtfully in democratic self-governance or to vote wisely. Rather, the viewers *wanted* to see them—the experience of seeing them itself is valuable in serving the desires of individuals who view them. A needs-versus-wants dichotomy thus separates the theory of democratic self-governance from the voyeurism value when one focuses on the message variable in the source-message-channel-receiver communication process.

In addition to the needs-versus-wants dichotomy, a second and subtler difference between the democratic self-governance theory and the voyeurism value turns on the distinction between *collectivist* and *individual* goals. Messages are privileged in Meiklejohnian theory if they serve the needs of the collective, sometimes even at the expense of individuals' rights of speech. The collective, for Meiklejohn, is democracy. Post observes that Meiklejohn's "orientation toward the needs of the collectivity, rather than the individual, underlies one of Meiklejohn's most quoted aphorisms: 'What is essential is not that everyone shall speak, but that everything worth saying shall be said.'"[43] The voyeurism value, in contrast, privileges the individual's interests in receiving speech, regardless of whether the rest of the community is interested in that speech or receives any benefits from it. The ostensible benefit of speech protected by a voyeurism value in First Amendment jurisprudence is for the individual, not for society at large. Individual gratification in any of the forms described in Chapter 2, in other words, trumps collective self-determination under a First Amendment theory that protects mediated voyeurism.

A focus on the message variable also distinguishes the voyeurism value from the marketplace theory. The idealistic marketplace of ideas has as its goal the discovery of the truth or, perhaps more precisely, the testing of accepted notions of the truth. The metaphor suggests with regard to the message component of the source-message-channel-receiver communication flow that a message must contain an idea *and* that this idea must be the kind that is subject to rational discussion and testing by others. Thus it can be said that so-called hate speech subverts or even is outside of the type of speech protected by the marketplace metaphor because it tends to be no more than an emotional appeal to hate and prejudice rather than a rational idea about race or gender.[44]

The voyeurism value may, like the metaphorical marketplace of ideas, protect speech that contains an idea that tests notions of the truth or that furthers our quest for truth, but it also protects speech that does not serve these ideals. For instance, voyeuristic video taken via hidden cameras for the television newsmagazines furthers our understanding of the truth about abusive conditions in some board-and-care homes for the elderly and may influence or shape public policies and laws relating to such homes. On the other hand, the justification for protecting the gathering and dissemination of such speech may be based on an alternative rationale that has little or nothing to do with the outcome of changing public policy or law. The video can be protected simply because people enjoy watching it—because they enjoy the consummatory or aesthetic communication experience of looking at a world they would not see or visit were it not for the undercover camera work by ABC's journalists. It may be that they enjoy seeing others exposed as part of a quest for justice or reinforcement of social norms, as described in Chapter 2.

Likewise, the vérité video for *Cops* may be protected under the marketplace rationale because the content of the message furthers our understanding of, and truths about, law enforcement and the criminal justice system. But that same video may be protected for the sole justification that people want to watch it for the pleasure of seeing others humiliated or disgraced. That we can watch and enjoy this from a distance, at home or in a bar, insulates us from fear of retaliation by or interaction with those whose lives unravel on *Cops*.

The voyeurism value thus may protect some material that the marketplace of ideas and democratic self-governance theories may not guard. The content of the nude photographs of Tommy Lee and Pamela Anderson Lee cannot be said to represent a rational or thoughtful idea that furthers truth testing, much as some feminists would argue that pornography cannot be protected by the First Amendment because it does not convey an idea. But the pleasure of seeing tattoo-covered and silicone-enhanced celebrities in the buff in apparently unguarded moments would be protected under a First Amendment theory that prizes mediated voyeurism. Individual desires to watch, not collective-level needs of democracy or truth discovery, are paramount in this voyeuristic experience.

In terms of message content, the theory of self-realization is perhaps closest to the voyeurism value. Under the principle of self-realization, all messages that in any way enhance a person's capacity to achieve his or her own intellectual potential or ability should be protected—and the audience has an affirmative right to receive them. As Thomas Emerson wrote, "The achievement of self-realization commences with development of the mind."[45]

The content of the messages necessary for developing one's mind need not have anything to do with helping society discover the truth or facilitating public voting. Thus the self-realization principle sweeps up and demands protection for a wider variety of messages than either the marketplace or democratic self-governance theories.

The self-realization principle, of course, protects more than just the *audience's right* to receive speech that may help it achieve self-fulfillment. It also protects the *speaker's right* to express himself or herself.[46] The content of the speaker's message must be protected even if it serves no value extraneous to that individual, "even when no plausible case can be made that the search for truth will be advanced."[47]

In summary, then, the self-realization principle protects message content that serves *private* interests—interests of either the audience or the speaker—that may have nothing to do with the *public* interest. To this extent it mirrors the nature of the content protected by voyeurism value—speech that serves the private interests of the audience in watching others. But as noted earlier, the function of the message content protected under the voyeurism value need not serve the noble purpose of the intellectual growth or mental development of the message source. Rather, the function of the message content may be the pure hedonistic gratification and selfish pleasure of the audience.

With the differences between a theory of free speech designed specifically to protect and privilege mediated voyeurism—a voyeurism value theory—and other established free speech theories in mind, we can consider the potential ramifications of adoption of a voyeurism value in First Amendment jurisprudence. The next part of this chapter begins to tease out some of the positive and negative consequences of embracing a voyeurism value theory.

The Implications and Ramifications of the Voyeurism Value

Initially, it must be reiterated that adoption of a voyeurism value in First Amendment theory does not deny the value or goals of other theories of free speech. As Erwin Chemerinsky, professor at the University of Southern California, observes in considering more traditional theories for protecting expression, free speech theories are not mutually exclusive.[48] Thus the voyeurism value may exist as yet another justification—a supplement or addition to traditional values—for protecting expression, another theory to be added to the laundry list set forth earlier in this chapter. To stop there, however, would be to ignore both the positive and the dangerous implications of adoption of the voyeurism value.

Privacy at What Price?

Mediated voyeurism thrives on—and the voyeurism value therefore calls for—legal constructions and interpretations that are long on protecting the audience's right to receive speech but short on protecting the privacy interests of the individuals who are the subjects of that speech. Our desire to watch, in brief, conflicts with our desire to keep private certain aspects of our lives and to control the dissemination of information about ourselves to others. A balance must be struck between protecting our voyeuristic pleasures of watching others—especially unsuspecting others and others whose lives are falling apart—and guarding our own privacy interests so that we, as audience members, do not find ourselves the subject matter of others' mediated voyeurism. A danger, then, in adopting the voyeurism value is the sacrifice of privacy and the inability to strike such a balance.

Chapter 5 highlighted a number of very recent legal cases—*Shulman v. Group W Productions, Wilson v. Layne, Sanders v. ABC*—that highlight the tension between a right to watch and a right to privacy. A fictional point of reference, however, from popular culture mentioned in the Introduction—*The Truman Show*—is worth revisiting here. It illustrates what would happen if we indeed sacrificed all privacy interests for the sake of mediated voyeurism. It clearly shows the need to control the flow of information about ourselves and the concomitant need to preserve a realm in which others are not watching us.

The movie reeks of mediated voyeurism; it portrays a man who, unknown to him, lives his entire life before hidden cameras that feed his daily activities to a mass television audience. One reviewer called it the "ultimate example of an invasion of privacy."[49] The unsuspecting protagonist is monitored twenty-four hours a day, all privacy sacrificed for the audience's pleasures in mediated voyeurism.

Aside from the obvious questions regarding privacy invasions and the tension between mediated voyeurism and privacy, two aspects of *The Truman Show* resonate with the voyeurism value. First, the film portrays, albeit mockingly, our fascination and obsession with watching others and, in particular, the importance of watching not only for the individual but, perhaps more important, for our society, our culture, and our nation. As Andrew Niccol, writer of the screenplay for *The Truman Show,* astutely observes, "Television is our community now. It has taken on the role that the church once played in medieval times. It's the thread that holds us together."[50] Our individual obsessions with watching other people, in other words, may in fact coalesce to bond and hold society together. This suggests that a deeper power of the voyeurism value as an enduring free speech principle may lie beyond providing First Amendment protection for our individual desire to watch. It may also include the maintenance of society in time. If this is the case, then it may be that mediated voyeurism serves both individual wants and societal needs.

The watching aspect of the communication process, as Niccol suggests, is what bonds us today in an otherwise often anonymous and impersonal society. *Our desire to watch sustains a sense of community when we watch the same messages.* And as Niccol points out, "There is virtually no limit as to what will be shown on TV, it seems, and there is virtually no limit on what people will watch. If there were televised executions, people would watch. I used to think this was farfetched and tongue-in-cheek, but I'm not so sure now."[51] It is the voyeurism value in First Amendment jurisprudence that may be called up to justify our individual *and* communal desires to watch. Watching not only satisfies our individual desires but also promotes community.

It can be said, of course, that any television show—voyeuristic or otherwise—may help to sustain a sense of community if enough people watch it. Fans of *Seinfeld,* for instance, shared a sense of community with each other because they had something in common to talk about—the Soup Nazi, Junior Mints, Jackie Childs. But arguably, mediated voyeurism heightens a sense of community beyond what is possible by watching a situation comedy with fictional characters or a scripted drama like *ER*. Why might this be the case?

Mediated voyeurism, as defined in this book, entails watching real people in ostensibly unguarded and revealing moments. Mediated voyeurs, in turn, learn about the lives of others. In particular, they may learn about certain lifestyles, behaviors, and activities of others that shape or influence us as a society. We may, collectively, embrace or reject the lives of others as portrayed in mediated voyeurism.

Reality television thus may police societal norms, just as the cops on *Cops* literally police societal norms by enforcing laws. Voyeuristic tell-all talk shows like Jerry Springer's bring mediated voyeurs into the world of people whose lifestyles and activities often seem far outside the norm of acceptable behavior. These shows, with what Joshua Gamson describes as their "taboo" strategies, may either reinforce or change social norms and values. That certainly is the fear of many of these shows' critics, such as Joseph Lieberman, the Democratic senator from Connecticut, who suggest that our culture is changing—changing for the worse—as a result of such "trash" programming.

There also is a certain process of identification inherent in mediated voyeurism that might not be the same as identifying with a character on a fictional situation comedy or drama; we may relate better to the real individuals that we watch. This taps into what Susan Zirinsky, the senior producer of CBS's *48 Hours,* calls the "relatability" factor, which she sometimes looks for in selecting stories for that newsmagazine.

All of this reflects some of the motivations described in Chapter 2 for our engagement with mediated voyeurism—a quest for justice and reinforcement of social norms, a desire to make comparisons of our lives with others, a need to see what really exists "out there" beyond our homes. By making comparisons with others featured in voyeuristic media content, we may as a society conclude that certain behaviors depicted in the context of mediated voyeurism fall outside the realm of acceptability. We may, alternatively, change our norms and values. What ultimately is important, then, is that mediated voyeurism may serve a purpose beyond satisfying individual viewing preferences. It may help to bind society.

This dual function certainly bolsters the case for adding a voyeurism value to First Amendment jurisprudence. A theory that protects mediated voyeurism would do more than pander to individual desires. It would be more difficult to trivialize its importance as simply a theory that protects people's sometimes-prurient desires to watch others. The theory would help protect speech that allows society to learn about itself and, in so doing, serve a collectivist function in changing or maintaining social norms and values.

The second aspect of *The Truman Show* that needs unpacking is the protagonist's name: Truman Burbank. As the name of the California city in which television shows are created by buck-raking media conglomerates, Burbank is an appropriate last name for a man whose life is conceived and lived on the airwaves. But the more important aspect, perhaps, is the name Truman. Why? It is only when we believe that we are in private, free from the glare of prying eyes, that we can be ourselves and act as we would without self-conscious circumspection, our privacy protected and others' voyeurism sacrificed. It is only then that a person can be a "true man or woman." When we know we are being watched, we are merely actors. Jim Carrey's character is the "true man"—an unsuspecting individual whose honesty makes us laugh; the other characters are merely actors, and we in television land, merely voyeurs. *The Truman Show* thus provides "a cautionary tale of unchecked voyeurism."[52]

The tension, then, is clear between individual and societal desires to watch and individual needs for privacy that promote self-identity and allow individuals to flourish and to develop outside of others' watchful eyes. Where the balance is struck will be determined by courts and legislative bodies that expand or contract existing laws or create new ones that serve either voyeurism or privacy. Should we sell out privacy for our desire to watch the lives of others?

Communication Without Dialogue, Politics Without Participation

A second concern with adoption of a voyeurism value theory, beyond threatening our sense of privacy, is the distinct lack of dialogue and conversation described earlier in this chapter. The mediated voyeur never interacts or communicates with the individual who is the focus of the message. Voyeurs need only watch; they do not interact.

For a democracy to thrive and truly be participatory, there must be dialogue and conversation so that all voices can be heard. The voyeurism value, however, is content with promoting politics as spectacle—a politics in which we watch mediated images of candidates, without interaction with them. As described in Chapter 3, it is a politics of observation, not a politics of participation. As noted previously, media coverage of politics today directly mirrors this politics-as-sports phenomenon. Our voyeuristic proclivities also underlie our fascination with the politics-as-sex stories of the Monica Lewinsky scandal.

At a time when political apathy is thriving among a new generation of young voters, one must, then, hesitate to embrace a voyeurism value in First Amendment jurisprudence. It is a value that can only further erode political participation, replacing it with political observation. It is a value that arguably trivializes the importance of free speech. It is a value that can reduce politics to a sensationalistic and salacious focus on the sex lives of our political candidates and officeholders. It is critical, then, that the premises and principles of Alexander Meiklejohn's theory of democratic self-governance not be abandoned or replaced by the voyeurism value. If the voyeurism value becomes a part of our First Amendment theory, it should be placed there merely to supplement existing theories, not to replace them.

Revisiting the
Wants-Versus-Needs Dichotomy

The voyeurism value may be criticized for pandering to individual wants and desires to watch at the expense of communal and societal needs to learn and to be informed. Media organizations will serve up whatever images we want to watch. The voyeurism value guards this transaction by protecting the media's ability to gather and disseminate these images, cloaked as news or wrapped up in the name of the public interest.

But as mentioned above, the individual-level desires to see purportedly real-life images of others *do* serve an important community-level need—sustaining a sense of shared identity and conversation around those images. If we all watch the same pictures of what reality is or may be like, we share a bond that may promote a sense of community and a sense of reality that might otherwise be lacking in anonymous urban settings in which apartment dwellers often have little or no contact with their next-door neighbors. We *can* learn from what we want to watch—the pleasure of watching does not exclude the conveyance of information and understanding. There are many reasons why people value mediated voyeurism, Chapter 2 suggested, including a quest for knowledge. The wants-versus-needs dichotomy, thus some might say, is a false dichotomy and too flimsy a rationale for rejecting outright the voyeurism value as a part of First Amendment jurisprudence.

Summary

Is it time to add a new theory to the catalogue of current free speech theories? Is it time to add a theory that actually protects the kind of speech that many people are interested in watching today? Is it time to add a voyeurism value theory—a theory specifically designed to protect mediated voyeurism—that sacrifices privacy for the multitude of uses and gratifications described in Chapter 2 that attract us to watch revealing moments from the lives of others? How much privacy are we as a society willing to give up to learn about those lives? These are questions that one author alone cannot answer but that require consideration from others, not only from the readers of this book but from all of the viewers of mediated voyeurism as well as those who may find themselves the targets of a mediated voyeur's gaze.

This chapter has attempted to show how such a theory may be different from extant free speech theories and it has tried to show the pros and cons of adding a voyeurism value theory. It seems clear that some of the uses of mediated voyeurism described in Chapter 2—the quest for knowledge and search for truth—that would be protected by a voyeurism value are already protected by other theories. On the other hand, other uses of mediated voyeurism are valuable to individuals even if they do not serve collectivist goals of truth discovery or better democracy. Likewise, principles of self-realization overlap the interests protected by a voyeurism value, yet, as this chapter has attempted to show, there are differences between these theories.

Ultimately, it is difficult to articulate a theory of freedom of expression in one chapter in one book. In this chapter, I have simply tried to sketch the beginnings of such a theory and to compare it with other established theories, some of which seem to have lost their real-world relevance in the daily lives of many people. The simple fact is that many people today enjoy mediated voyeurism and that these individuals thus value it as a form of speech. By articulating the conditions that are necessary to allow mediated voyeurism to thrive, this chapter has suggested there is room under the tent of free speech theory to protect this popular form of speech.

Conclusion

Most genres of popular television programming wax and wane. The initial success of one top-rated show often breeds a legion of imitators attempting to capture its hit formula. Witness the proliferation in early 2000 of prime-time television quiz shows that were spawned by the November 1999 runaway success of the Regis Philbin–hosted program *Who Wants to Be a Millionaire?* Eventually, however, after the proliferation and imitation, the audience's interest starts to melt away. The shows begin to fade from the screen and the genre declines.

There is little reason, we might think on first reflection, to suppose that this will not be the case with mediated voyeurism as we know it today on the tell-all talk shows, television newsmagazines, reality police programs, and even the Internet. The year 2000 brought to U.S. television two new voyeuristic treats, *Survivor* and *Big Brother.* But we may grow weary of consuming the lives of other people as a form of entertainment, knowledge, power, or other use or gratification. We may eventually switch off the set when we feel that the shows have gone too far in exploiting the trials and tribulations of others for ratings. Maybe we will turn it off if our sense of respect for the privacy of others feels violated—if we sense that our right to watch infringes on the privacy interests of the people who are the focus of our gaze and spectatorship.

This, after all, is the nature of the marketplace accountability that largely dominates the media system in the United States. We hold media outlets accountable with our remote control

wands, changing to another channel—another genre of programming even—when we have had enough. Taken in the aggregate, all of those clicks away from one show will lead to
lower ratings and, concomitantly, its demise. This is how we in
television land can control mediated voyeurism.

Although most television genres come and go (and later come
back again), is there any reason to think that mediated
voyeurism might somehow be immune from this cycle? Is it
possible that when the stars of the show are not celebrities or
high-paid actors but real people, our fascination will not re-
cede? Is there a qualitative difference, in other words, between
images of reality involving ordinary people and images of fiction featuring actors that will allow mediated voyeurism to
avoid falling prey to the invention-imitation-decline cycle of
programming? We may grow tired of watching celebrities, but
will we grow weary of watching ourselves? Only time will answer these questions and tell us if marketplace accountability
will lead to the downfall of mediated voyeurism.

What does seem clear, however, is that legal accountability
will not be sufficient standing alone to check mediated
voyeurism or to force it off the air. Although the United States
Supreme Court's *Wilson v. Layne* and *Hanlon v. Berger* decisions, described in Chapter 6, may put a damper on one form of
mediated voyeurism—the presence of media cameras inside a
person's home during the execution of a warrant—they far
from deal a death blow to ride-along shows like *Cops* that do
not depend on this footage. And the October 1999 decision of a
federal appellate court in favor of ABC, protecting its use of
fraudulent news-gathering methods, clearly is a victory for mediated voyeurism generally and, in particular, for the hidden
camera reporting of television newsmagazines. If all that Food
Lion can recover for attacking the news-gathering efforts of
ABC is a *de minimis* sum of two dollars, then there is little in-
centive for ABC or other media outlets not to engage in similar
tactics, such as lying on résumés to gain the access necessary to

obtain hidden camera videotape. The tape justifies the lies, the ratings justify the deception. ABC, of course, was forced to spend large sums of money in attorneys' fees to defend itself, but Food Lion too had to shell out vast sums of money to litigate its claims. It is not likely in future cases that corporations situated similarly to Food Lion will be willing to put up massive amounts of money for a legal fight if all that awaits at the end of the battle is two dollars.

Another model of media accountability that might hinder mediated voyeurism—in addition to the marketplace and legal models described above—involves self-policing by media organizations. This may occur through the adoption of, and subscription to, codes of ethics like those presently in place at many newspapers and television stations. Consider, for instance, the ethics code adopted by the Society of Professional Journalists and revised in 1996. It has a provision that specifically covers the use of deceptive news-gathering methods, including hidden cameras. It reads: "Avoid undercover or other surreptitious methods of gathering information except when traditional open methods will not yield information vital to the public. Use of such methods should be explained as part of the story."[1]

Although this provision clearly does not govern all types of mediated voyeurism, it should nonetheless affect the hidden camera techniques used today to gather some voyeuristic images. It should make journalists and others pause to consider whether the images they are gathering really are "vital to the public"—a phrase suggesting the difference between a *need* to know and a mere *want* or curiosity to know described earlier in the book—and whether "traditional methods" would not uncover the same information. There is a major problem, however, with the concept of traditional methods as a check on unbridled mediated voyeurism. It is that the use of hidden cameras itself is already becoming a traditional method of gathering images.

Another tenet of the Society of Professional Journalists' ethics code may better check mediated voyeurism, if adhered to voluntarily. It admonishes journalists to "minimize harm" and to "recognize that gathering and reporting information may cause harm and discomfort. Pursuit of news is not a license for arrogance."[2] Indeed, the gathering of some voyeuristic images, by journalists or others, on videotape may cause great harm— harm to privacy, harm to trust—to its targets. Ultimately, the harm caused by some forms of mediated voyeurism may go beyond that caused to the target of hidden cameras or the individual whose life is exploited for our viewing pleasure.

In particular, deceptive gathering of images may erode public trust generally in the media, in turn affecting the ability of journalists to play a legitimate watchdog function. As the media defense attorney Bruce Sanford writes in his most recent book, *Don't Shoot the Messenger,* "The canyon of distrust between the public and the media" may eventually silence journalists, hurting us all in the process.[3] The deception also may affect society's general expectations of privacy, reducing them to the point where they detrimentally affect our sense of self and identity.

It must be emphasized here that almost all of the media conduct described in the legal cases in Chapter 5 can also be analyzed through nonlegal principles of media ethics. Just because something may be legal does not make it ethical. The law, as the journalism professor Jay Black of the University of South Florida and his colleagues write in *Doing Ethics in Journalism,* merely "is a bottom-line, minimalistic enterprise that tells us what we *can* do or what we *can* get away with."[4] In contrast, ethics is about what we *ought* to do, what we *should* do.

Just because the media can, under the law, use hidden cameras in many cases does not mean that they should use them. Just because ABC may be legally liable for only two dollars to Food Lion does not mean that the conduct of its employees—lying on job applications, concealing cameras in clothing—was ethical. Lying harms trust, which, in turn, harms credibility. If journalists will lie to those they investigate, how can we be sure they will not lie to us, the audience?

Just because the California Supreme Court holds that watching the severely injured Ruth Shulman is newsworthy as a matter of law does not make it ethical for journalists or other media professionals to audiotape or videotape the aftermath of her car accident. The high court in California even noted that although "the broadcast *could* have been edited to exclude some of Ruth's words and images," this was not determinative of the legal question of newsworthiness.[5] In other words, although it might have been ethical to edit out images, what is ethical does not determine what is legal.

Although this book is neither a treatise on nor an introduction to media or journalism ethics, it should be clear that law and ethics may provide alternative frameworks for analyzing the same type of conduct. Instances of mediated voyeurism that involve deception and lying and that affect privacy may be considered from both perspectives. Perhaps the "bottom-line, minimalistic enterprise" of law, as Jay Black and his colleagues put it, is not enough to curtail mediated voyeurism. Maybe the "higher line" of ethics and self-policing is necessary to perform this feat.

The portion of the Society of Professional Journalists' ethics code quoted earlier in the Conclusion provided that the use of undercover and surreptitious methods of gathering information "should be explained as part of the story."[6] This is an important point that should not be overlooked in considering the ethical implications of mediated voyeurism. Perhaps if the media told us—explained to us—*why* it is that we see so much mediated voyeurism today, we would be able to better decide whether the conduct that leads to its creation is ethical. Media accountability, after all, is promoted through public explanation of the practices, processes, and beliefs that shape media content. If we purchase the product of mediated voyeurism, then surely we should be entitled to know something about the production process.

In summary, there are marketplace, legal, and ethical systems of media accountability in place that could check the development of mediated voyeurism. But even if this category of speech fades from television sets in the near future, it has exposed our fascination with viewing images of and information about others' apparently real lives. Maybe there has always been a Peeping Tom inside each of us. But it has taken the age of videotape and the miniature camera to unearth and clearly reveal our voyeuristic proclivities. Technology simply makes voyeurism all that much easier and safer. We no longer need to be physically present to play the role of Peeping Tom. We now are mediated voyeurs and our fellow citizens are the targets of our gaze. The price we pay is that we too may be watched, just as we do our own watching. The price, in other words, is privacy.

That our Peeping Tom proclivities would ever lead to the highly *un*private world of Truman Burbank seems unlikely. But it is important to keep in mind that movie character's life. It was lived on tape for all to see, and when he discovered that his life was simply a television series, he tried desperately to escape his televised life. It seems clear that we have the power both to prevent this situation and to lead to its creation. It is only when we keep in check our desire to see others' lives unfold that we will stop the development of a Burbankesque world. All the world may indeed be a stage, but we certainly do not all need to be players for others' viewing enjoyment.

Notes

Introduction

1. Philip Wuntch, "Trapped in the Box," *Dallas Morning News,* May 31, 1998.

2. Rita Kempley, "Theatre of the Observed," *Washington Post,* June 5, 1998.

3. Edward Guthmann, "Remote Control Jim Carrey Is a Born TV Star in The Truman Show," *San Francisco Chronicle,* June 5, 1998.

4. Neal Gabler, *Life the Movie: How Entertainment Conquered Reality* (New York: Alfred A. Knopf, 1998), p. 6.

5. Jeanne Hall, "Realism As Style in Cinema Vérité," *Cinema Journal* 30 (Summer 1991): 24.

6. Some would argue that the fly-on-the-wall technique is better described as "direct cinema" rather than cinema vérité. Brian Winston, "The Documentary Film As Scientific Inscription," in Michael Renov, ed., *Theorizing Documentary,* pp. 40–47 (New York: Routledge, 1993).

7. Mark Fishman, "Ratings and Reality: The Persistence of the Reality Crime Genre," in Mark Fishman and Gray Cavender, eds., *Entertaining Crime: Television Reality Programs* (New York: Aldine De Gruyter, 1998), p. 71.

8. Stephen D. Easton, "Cameras in Courtrooms: Contrasting Viewpoints: Whose Life Is It Anyway: A Proposal to Redistribute Some of the Economic Benefits of Cameras in the Courtroom from Broadcasters to Crime Victims," *South Carolina Law Review* 49 (1997): 1, 5.

9. Gray Cavender and Mark Fishman, "Television Reality Crime Programs: Context and History," in Fishman and Cavender, *Entertaining Crime,* p. 4.

10. Andrew Culf, "BBC Defends 'Voyeuristic' Crime Series," *London Guardian,* June 23, 1993, p. 6.

11. Ibid.

12. Joshua Gamson, *Freaks Talk Back* (Chicago: University of Chicago Press, 1998), p. 220.

13. Tom Rosenstiel and Bill Kovach, "And Now ... the Unfiltered, Unedited News, " *Washington Post,* February 28, 1999.

14. Leslie Phillips, "Clinton-Flowers Ad Assailed, Called 'Voyeurism,'" *USA Today,* July 10, 1992.

15. Douglas Rushkoff, *Media Virus!: Hidden Agendas in Popular Culture* (New York: Ballantine Books, 1996), p. xi.

16. Ronald K.L. Collins and David M. Skover, *The Death of Discourse* (Boulder: Westview Press, 1996).

17. Stanley Fish, *There's No Such Thing As Free Speech* (New York: Oxford University Press, 1994), p. 231.

18. Lee v. Penthouse International Ltd., 25 Media Law Reporter 1651 (C.D. Cal. 1997).

19. Wilson v. Layne, 119 S. Ct. 1692 (1999).

Chapter One

1. Thomas B. Edsall, "Key Conservative Surrenders in Culture War, but Fight Continues," *Washington Post,* February 18, 1999.

2. Robert D. Richards, *Freedom's Voice* (Washington, DC: Brassey's, 1998), p. 67. Emphasis added.

3. Joseph I. Lieberman, "The Jurisprudence of Ratings Symposium Part I: Reflections on the Ratings Craze," *Cardozo Arts & Entertainment Law Journal* 15 (1997): 147.

4. Joseph I. Lieberman, "'Revolt of the Revolted' Revisited: America's Values Vacuum and What to Do About It," *Harvard Journal on Legislation* 35 (1998): 51, 52

5. Joshua Gamson, *Freaks Talk Back* (Chicago: University of Chicago Press, 1998), p. 6.

6. Stacy Davis and Marie-Louise Mares, "Effects of Talk Show Viewing on Adolescents," *Journal of Communication* 48 (Summer 1998): 69, 84.

7. Ibid., p. 82.

8. Graeme Turner, *British Cultural Studies: An Introduction* (New York: Routledge, 1992), p. 15.

9. Walter Lippmann, *Public Opinion* (New York: Harcourt Brace, 1922).

10. Peter Keough, ed., *Flesh and Blood: The National Society of Film Critics on Sex, Violence, and Censorship* (San Francisco: Mercury House, 1995), p. 2.

11. Richard Kilborn, "How Real Can You Get? Recent Developments in 'Reality' Television," *European Journal of Communication* 9(4) (December 1994): 424.

12. Joanne Ostrow, "TV Mag Repellant Needed," *Denver Post,* December 2, 1998.

13. World's Wildest Police Videos site. http://www.fox.com/police2/show.htm (site visited March 19, 1999).

14. Cops web site. http://www.tvcops.com/pages/behind_the_scenes/john_langley.html (site visited March 19, 1999).

15. Kathy Kiely and Steve Marshall, "Poll: Monica Changed Few Minds," *USA Today,* March 5, 1999.

16. Heather Svokos, "Monica Tells All, and It's Just Really Bad," *Lexington Herald-Leader,* March 4, 1999.

17. Kathy Kiely, "Monica Mania: Do We Envy 'Everywoman'?" *USA Today,* March 3, 1999.

18. Transcript, "Women Behind Bars," *20/20,* March 14, 1999.

19. Frazier Moore, "Elian's Misfortunes Feed Voyeuristic Pop Culture," *Associated Press File,* April 26, 2000.

20. Paula Span, "MTV, Making Its Own Reality," *Washington Post,* May 7, 1992.

21. *The Real World Diaries* (New York: MTV Books, 1996), p. 4.

22. Ibid., p. 5.

23. Gaile Robinson, "The Unreal Amenities of MTV's 'Real World,'" *Los Angeles Times,* July 8, 1993.

24. Melanie McFarland, "Real World: Seattle Wraps a Successful Season," *Seattle Times,* November 3, 1998.

25. Caryn James, "The Eighth Roommate: A Camera," *New York Times,* June 16, 1998, p. E9.

26. Sally Beatty, "A Real Tailspin, in Weekly Episodes," *Wall Street Journal,* October 14, 1999.

27. John Maynard, "MTV's 'Road Rules': Rough Riding," *Washington Post,* July 19, 1995, p. D10.

28. Beatty, "A Real Tailspin," p. B1.

29. Ibid.

30. Ibid.

31. Ibid.

32. Jay Black et al., *Doing Ethics in Journalism,* 3rd ed. (Boston: Allyn & Bacon, 1999), pp. 28–30.

33. Paula Bernstein, "'Real Families' Live at Lifetime," *Hollywood Reporter,* January 6, 1999.

34. Hugh Dauncey, "French 'Reality' Television: More Than a Matter of Taste," *European Journal of Communication* 11(1) (March 1996): 83.

35. Mark Woods, "Reality Bites TV Auds," *Variety,* April 28–May 4, 1997, p. 68.

36. Judith Matloff, "Russian TV Viewers Cry 'Go, Thief,'" *Christian Science Monitor,* January 30, 1998.

37. Ronald Aquilla and Patrick A.E. Day, *Lady Godiva: Images of a Legend in Art and Society* (Coventry, UK: City of Coventry Leisure Services, 1982).

38. A. C. Spearing, *The Medieval Poet As Voyeur* (Cambridge, UK: Cambridge University Press, 1993), p. 1.

39. Dorothy Kelly, *Telling Glances: Voyeurism in the French Novel* (New Brunswick, NJ: Rutgers University Press, 1992).

40. Ibid., p. 1.

41. Ibid., p. 2.

42. Elizabeth Lynne Flocke, "Tabloids," in Margaret A. Blanchard, ed., *History of the Mass Media in the United States* (Chicago: Fitzroy Dearborn Publishers, 1998), p. 629.

43. Michael Emery and Edwin Emery, *The Press and America: An Interpretive History of the Mass Media,* 8th ed. (Boston: Allyn & Bacon, 1996), p. 287.

44. Simon Michael Bessie, *Jazz Journalism: The Story of Tabloid Newspapers* (New York: E. P. Dutton, 1938), p. 17.

45. Ibid., p. 49.

46. Flocke, "Tabloids," p. 630.

47. Andie Tucher, "Television Did Not Invent Mass Voyeurism," *New York Times,* May 22, 1985.

48. Bessie, *Jazz Journalism,* p. 49.

49. Allen Funt, *Eavesdropper at Large* (New York: Vanguard Press, 1952), p. 175.

50. Candid Camera web site. http://marketing.cbs.com/primetime/candid-camera (site visited March 26, 1999).

51. Philip Rosen, "Document and Documentary: On the Persistence of Historical," in Michael Renov, ed., *Theorizing Documentary* (New York: Routledge, 1993), pp. 58–89.

52. Roger Ebert, "Peeping Tom," *Chicago Sun-Times,* May 2, 1999.

53. Norman K. Denzin, *The Cinematic Society* (London: Sage Publications, 1995), p. 1.

54. Laura Mulvey, "Visual Pleasure and Narrative Cinema," in Patricia Erens, ed., *Issues in Feminist Film Criticism* (Bloomington: Indiana University Press, 1990), p. 31.

55. Denzin, *The Cinematic Society,* p.118.

56. Ibid., p.121.

57. Funt, *Eavesdropper at Large,* p. 205.

58. Isabel Cristina Pinedo, *Recreational Terror: Women and the Pleasures of Horror Film Viewing* (Albany: State University of New York Press, 1997), p. 52.

59. Ibid.

60. Elisabeth Bronfen, "Killing Gazes, Killing in the Gaze: On Mike Powell's Peeping Tom," in Renata Salecl and Slavoj Zizek, eds., *Gaze and Voice As Love Objects,* (Durham, NC: Duke University Press, 1996), pp. 59–89.

61. *Webster's Ninth New Collegiate Dictionary* (Springfield, Mass: Merriam-Webster, Inc., 1983), p. 435.

62. JenniCam.Org. http://www/jennicam.org/faq/general.html#b (site visited March 17, 1999).

63. Voyeur Dorm. http://www.voyeurdorm.com (site visited August 1, 1999).

64. Ibid.

65. Steve Huettel, "Voyeur Dorm Is Test of Cyberlaw," *St. Petersburg Times,* April 26, 1999.

66. Walt Belcher, "'20/20' Takes Look at City's 'Voyeur Dorm,'" *Tampa Tribune,* August 11, 1999.

67. David Pedreira, "Voyeur Dorm Cyber Zone Denied," *Tampa Tribune,* August 27, 1999.

68. Ibid.

69. Sigmund Freud, *Three Essays on the Theory of Sexuality,* translated and newly edited by James Strachey (New York: Basic Books, 1962), p. 23.

70. American Psychiatric Association, *Diagnostic and Statistical Manual for Mental Disorders,* 4th ed. (Washington, DC: American Psychiatric Association, 1994), p. 532.

71. Bradley S. Greenberg et al., "Daytime Television Talk Shows: Guests, Content and Interaction, " *Journal of Broadcasting and Electronic Media* 41 (Summer 1997): 418–419.

72. Anne Barnard, "Athletes Caught on Secret Tape," *Philadelphia Inquirer,* April 5, 1999.

73. Barb Albert, "Patients' Medical Records Inadvertently Posted on Net," *Indianapolis Star,* March 30, 1999.

Chapter Two

1. Robert Abelman, *Reaching A Critical Mass: A Critical Analysis of Television Entertainment* (Mahwah, NJ: Lawrence Erlbaum, 1998), p. 97.

2. Stanley J. Baran, *Introduction to Mass Communication: Media Literacy and Media Culture* (Mountain View, CA: Mayfield Publishing, 1999), p. 325.

3. Werner J. Severin and James W. Tankard Jr., *Communication Theories: Origins, Methods, and Uses in the Mass Media,* 3rd ed. (White Plains, NY: Longman, 1992), pp. 272–273.

4. Geraldine E. Forsberg, *Critical Thinking in an Image World* (Lanham, MD: University Press of America, 1993), p. 4.

5. Sissela Bok, *Lying: Moral Choice in Public and Private Life* (New York: Vintage, 1989), p. 4.

6. Ibid.

7. Jay Black, Bob Steele, and Ralph Barney, *Doing Ethics in Journalism: A Handbook with Case Studies,* 3rd ed. (Boston: Allyn & Bacon, 1999), p. 6.

8. Clifford G. Christians et al., *Media Ethics: Cases and Moral Reasoning,* 5th ed. (New York: Longman, 1998), p. 53.

9. James S. Ettema and Theodore L. Glasser, *Custodians of Conscience: Investigative Journalism and Public Virtue* (New York: Columbia University Press, 1998), p. 11.

10. Ibid., p. 131.

11. Jeremy Iggers, *Good News, Bad News: Journalism Ethics and the Public Interest* (Boulder: Westview Press, 1998), pp. 46–47.

12. Carlin Romano, "The Grisly Truth About Bare Facts," in Robert Karl Manoff and Michael Schudson, eds., *Reading the News* (New York: Pantheon Books, 1986), p. 73.

13. Mary Beth Oliver, "Influences of Authoritarianism and Portrayals of Race on Caucasian Viewers' Responses to Reality-Based Crime Dramas," *Communication Reports* 9 (Summer 1996): 141, 142.

14. Aaron Doyle, "'Cops': Television Policing As Policing Reality," in Mark Fishman and Gray Cavender, eds., *Entertaining Crime: Television Reality Programs* (New York: Aldine De Gruyter, 1998), pp. 95, 107.

15. Joe Schlosser, "'Jerry Springer': Scraps or Scripts?" *Broadcasting & Cable,* April 27, 1998, p. 10.

16. Gini Graham Scott, *Can We Talk?: The Power and Influence of Talk Shows* (New York: Insight Books, 1996), p. 261.

17. Vicki Abt and Leonard Mustazza, *Coming After Oprah: Cultural Fallout in the Age of the TV Talk Show* (Bowling Green, OH: Bowling Green State University Popular Press, 1997), p. 108.

18. World's Most Amazing Videos home page. http://www.nbc.com/tvcentral/shows/worldsmostamazingvideos (site visited April 21, 1999).

19. Paul Farhi, "'Jenny Jones' Show Found Negligent in Murder Case," *Washington Post,* May 8, 1999.

20. Viktor E. Frankl, *Man's Search for Ultimate Meaning* (New York: Insight Books, 1997), p. 140.

21. Ibid., p. 142.

22. Michael J. Sniffen, "Murders, Other Serious Crimes Drop for 6th Year," *Washington Post,* November 23, 1998.

23. Mary Beth Oliver, "Influences of Authoritarianism and Portrayals of Race," pp. 141, 142.

24. Mary Beth Oliver and G. Blake Armstrong, "Predictors of Viewing and Enjoyment of Reality-Based and Fictional Crime Shows," *Journalism and Mass Communication Quarterly* 72 (Autumn 1995): 559, 665.

25. Gray Cavender and Mark Fishman, "Television Reality Crime Programs: Context and History," in Fishman and Cavender, *Entertaining Crime,* pp. 3, 7.

26. Norman K. Denzin, *The Cinematic Society* (London: Sage Publications, 1995), p. 208.

27. Joshua Gamson, *Freaks Talk Back: Tabloid Talk Shows and Sexual Nonconformity* (Chicago: University of Chicago Press, 1998), p. 19.

28. Ibid., p. 220.

29. Tom R. Tyler and Heather J. Smith, "Social Justice and Social Movements," in Daniel T. Gilbert et al., eds., *The Handbook of Social Psychology, Vol. 2,* 4th ed. (Boston: McGraw-Hill, 1998), p. 597.

30. Jennifer Crocker et al., "Social Stigma," in Daniel T. Gilbert et al., *The Handbook of Social Psychology,* Vol. 2, p. 524.

31. Constantine Sedikides and Michael J. Strube, "Self-Evaluation: To Thine Own Self Be Good, to Thine Own Self Be Sure, to Thine Own Self Be True, and to Thine Own Self Be Better," in Mark P. Zanna, ed., *Advances in Experimental Social Psychology,* Vol. 29 (San Diego: Academic Press, 1997), p. 217.

32. Abt and Mustazza, *Coming After Oprah,* p. 109.

33. Phil Davis, "Slow . . . Gawkers Ahead," *Los Angeles Times Home Edition,* May 28, 1998.

34. Severin and Tankard, *Communication Theories,* p. 300.

35. Carl Sessions Stepp, "The X Factor," *American Journalism Review* 18(9) (November 1996): 34–38.

36. Felicity Barringer, "Steady Growth of Revenue Is Energizing Newspapers," *New York Times,* June 29, 1998.

37. Frank Newport and Lydia Saad, "A Matter of Trust," *American Journalism Review* 20(6) (July-August 1998): 30–33.

38. David Croteau and William Hoynes, *Media/Society: Industries, Images and Audiences* (Thousand Oaks, CA: Pine Forge Press, 1997), p. 203.

39. Ronald K.L. Collins and David M. Skover, *The Death of Discourse* (Boulder: Westview Press, 1996), p. xxii.

40. Ibid., p. 5.

41. Ellen Hume, "The New Paradigm for News," *Annals of American Academic Politics & Social Science* (July 1996): 141, 147. Italics added.

42. Robert H. Bork, *Slouching Towards Gomorrah* (New York: Regan Books, HarperCollins, 1996), p. 5.

43. Ibid., p. 137.

44. Robert I. Simon, "Video Voyeurs and the Covert Videotaping of Unsuspecting Victims: Psychological and Legal Consequences," *Journal of Forensic Sciences* 45 (September, 1997): 884.

45. Ibid.

46. Bork, *Slouching Towards Gomorrah,* p. 128.

47. Abt and Mustazza, *Coming After Oprah,* p. 9.

48. Ibid., p. 46.

49. Bork, *Slouching Towards Gomorrah,* p. 125.

50. Gamson, *Freaks Talk Back,* 4.

51. Marc Sandalow, "The Race to Report Scandals," *San Francisco Chronicle,* April 14, 1999.

52. Sissela Bok, *Secrets: On the Ethics of Concealment and Revelation* (New York: Vintage Books, 1989), pp. 10–11.

53. Erving Goffman, *Relations in Public: Microstudies of the Public Order* (New York: Basic Books, 1971) pp. 38–39.

54. Samuel D. Warren and Louis D. Brandeis, "The Right to Privacy," *Harvard Law Review* 4 (December 1890): 193.

55. Gary Gumpert and Susan J. Drucker, "The Demise of Privacy in a Private World: From Front Porches to Chat Rooms," *Communication Theory* 8 (November 1998): 409.

56. Howard Kurtz, "Media Blitz Raises Coverage Questions," *Washington Post,* April 22, 1999.

57. Lisa de Moraes, "Denver, We Have a Problem," *Washington Post,* April 27, 1999.

58. Gamson, *Freaks Talk Back,* p. 16.

59. Ibid., p. 18.

60. Robin Anderson, *Consumer Culture & TV Programming* (Boulder: Westview Press, 1995), p. 160.

61. "Parents Sue Producers of TV Program for Showing Son's Body," Freedom Forum Online. http://www.freedomforum.org/press/news/970818.asp (site visited April 22, 1999).

62. Valerian J. Derlega et al., *Self-Disclosure* (Newbury Park, CA: Sage Publications, 1993), p. 1.

63. Dalmas A. Taylor, "Motivational Bases," in Gordon J. Chelune, ed., *Origins, Patterns, and Implications of Openness in Interpersonal Relationships* (San Francisco: Jossey-Bass Publishers, 1979), p. 111.

64. Valerian J. Derlega and Janusz Grzelak, "Appropriateness of Self-Disclosure," in Chelune, *Origins, Patterns, and Implications of Openness in Interpersonal Relationships,* pp.154–162.

65. Patricia Joyner Priest, *Public Intimacies: Talk Show Participants and Tell-All TV* (Cresskill, NJ: Hamilton Press, 1995), p. 14.

66. Ibid., pp. 27–35.

67. Ibid., p. 45.

68. Ibid., p. 46.

69. Gamson, *Freaks Talk Back,* p. 215.

70. Ibid.

71. Priest, *Public Intimacies,* p. 115.

72. Scott, *Can We Talk?* p. 293.

73. Abt and Mustazza, *Coming After Oprah,* p. 51.

74. Jeffrey R. Young, "Higher 'EDtv': Dorm Cams Features Lots of—Well, Studying," *Chronicle of Higher Education On Line,* May 12, 1999. http://chronicle.com/free/99/05/99051201t.htm (site visited March 12, 1999).

75. Priest, *Public Intimacies,* p. 49.

76. Mark Crispin Miller, *Boxed In: The Culture of TV* (Evanston, IL: Northwestern University Press, 1988), p. 19.

77. Ibid.

Chapter Three

1. Richard Weir, "Neighborhood Report: Greenwich Village; Candid Camera: Some Smile, Some Frown," *New York Times,* February 28, 1999.

2. Bruce Lambert, "Secret Surveillance Cameras Growing in City, Report Says," *New York Times,* December 13, 1998.

3. "Surveillance Cameras for Streets of Everett," *Seattle Times,* May 6, 1999.

4. "Surveillance Cameras Canned," *San Diego Union-Tribune,* June 17, 1999.

5. Quentin Burrows, "Scowl Because You're on Candid Camera," *Valparaiso University Law Review* 31 (Summer 1997): 1079.

6. Stuart Silverstein, "Employee Finds Hidden Camera in Bathroom," *Los Angeles Times,* September 12, 1997.

7. Sandra Stokley and Patricia A. Gonzalez, "Inland Firm Caught by Own Spy Cameras," *Press-Enterprise,* September 12, 1997.

8. Stuart Silverstein, " Trucking Company Avoids Prosecution," *Los Angeles Times,* November 11, 1997.

9. *Cheaters* home page. http://www.cheaterstv.com (site visited August 27, 1999).

10. Ibid.

11. Jim Henderson, "Busted?" *Houston Chronicle,* June 13, 1999.

12. Ibid.

13. Richard Campbell, *Media and Culture: An Introduction to Mass Communication* (New York: St. Martin's Press, 1998), p. 135.

14. Mark Fishman, "Ratings and Reality," in Mark Fishman and Gray Cavender, eds., *Entertaining Crime: Television Reality Programs* (New York: Aldine de Gruyter, 1998), p. 68.

15. Susan King, "Weekend TV: Pax Debuts New Reality Series," *Los Angeles Times,* August 26, 1999.

16. "Court TV Adds Cops to Prime Time," *Media Week,* May 31, 1999.

17. Kevin V. Johnson, "Reality-Check: Home-Video Shows Retrench," *USA Today,* June 11, 1999.

18. Vicki Abt and Charles Mustazza, *Coming After Oprah: Cultural Fallout in the Age of the TV Talk Show* (Bowling Green, OH: Bowling Green State University Popular Press, 1997), p. 9.

19. Gini Graham Scott, *Can We Talk?: The Power and Influence of Talk Shows* (New York: Insight Books, 1996), p. 228.

20. Greg Spring, "Buyers Slice, Dice Newsmagazines," *Electronic Media,* April 12, 1999.

21. Ibid.

22. Doris A. Graber, "Whither Televised Election News? Lessons from the 1996 Campaign," *Harvard International Journal of Press/Politics* 3 (Spring 1998): 117.

23. Abt and Mustazza, *Coming After Oprah,* p. 106.

24. Adam Sandler and Cynthia Littleton, "High Court Handcuffs Media on 'Ride-Alongs,'" *Daily Variety,* May 25, 1999, p. 4.

25. Theodore L. Glasser, "Objectivity Precludes Responsibility," *Quill,* February 1984, p. 16.

26. Carlin Romano, "The Grisly Truth About Bare Facts," in Robert Karl Manoff and Michael Schudson, eds., *Reading the News* (New York: Pantheon Books, 1986), p. 39.

27. Michael Schudson, "The Sociology of News Production," in Dan Berkowitz, ed., *Social Meanings of News* (Thousand Oaks, CA: Sage Publications, 1997), p. 7.

28. Dean Alger, "Megamedia, the State of Journalism, and Democracy," *Harvard International Journal of Press/Politics* 3 (Winter 1998): 126.

29. Richard M. Cohen, "The Corporate Takeover of News," in Erik Barnouw, ed., *Conglomerates and the Media* (New York: New Press, 1997), p. 32.

30. Ibid., p. 33.

31. Neil Hickey, "Money Lust: How Pressure for Profit Is Perverting Journalism," *Columbia Journalism Review* (July-August 1998): 30.

32. Franklin D. Gilliam Jr. et al., "Crime in Black and White: The Violent, Scary World of Local News," *Harvard International Journal of Press/Politics* 1 (Summer 1996): 7.

33. Phyllis Kaniss, "Bad News: Too Few Reporters," *American Journalism Review* (September 1993): 20.

34. Jamie Malanowski, "Bad News: Murder Travels," *American Journalism Review* (September 1993): 22.

35. Ibid.

36. Howard Rosenberg, "Bad News: The Cult of Personality," *American Journalism Review* (September 1993): 18.

37. Lawrence K. Grossman, "Why Local TV News Is So Awful," *Columbia Journalism Review* (November-December 1997): 21.

38. Steve McClellan, "Grades Improve for Local News," *Broadcasting & Cable,* September 21, 1998, p. 50.

39. Andie Tucher, "'Your News': It's Not Your Father's Newscast Anymore," *Columbia Journalism Review* (May-June 1997): 27.

40. Jacqueline Starkey, "The Diana Aftermath," *American Journalism Review* (November 1997): 20.

41. Jules Witcover, "Where We Went Wrong," *Columbia Journalism Review* (March-April 1998): 18.

42. "Dirty Laundry," from the album *I Can't Stand Still* (Elektra Entertainment, 1982).

43. Rick Kushman, "Breaking News Hypnotizes Those Who Watch, Those Who Broadcast," *Sacramento Bee,* September 3, 1999, p. G1.

44. Ibid., p. G5.

45. Ibid.

46. "The Erosion of News Values: A Debate Among Journalists over How to Cope," *Columbia Journalism Review* (March-April 1998): 44.

47. Ibid., p. 45.

48. Neil Postman and Steve Powers, *How to Watch TV News* (New York: Penguin Books, 1992), p. 161.

49. Hickey, "Money Lust: How Pressure for Profit Is Perverting Journalism," p. 30.

50. 47 U.S.C. §307(c) (2000).

51. FCC v. WNCN Listeners Guild, 450 U.S. 582 (1981).

52. Brian Lowery et al., "Networks Decide Diversity Doesn't Pay," *Los Angeles Times,* July 20, 1999.

53. Robert Britt Horwitz, *The Irony of Regulatory Reform* (New York: Oxford University Press, 1989), p. 4.

54. Jon Lafayette, "Who Owns the Airwaves?: Ownership Ranks Rapidly Thinned by Consolidation," *Electronic Media,* May 18, 1998.

55. In Re: Applications for Renewal of Licenses of Television Stations at Denver, Colorado, http://www.fcc.gov/Bureaus/Mass_Media/Orders/1998/tvautho.txt. The four television stations are KCNC-TV, Channel 4 (CBS); KMGH-TV, Channel 7 (ABC); KUSA-TV, Channel 9 (NBC); and KWGN-TV, Channel 2 (WB).

56. Rocky Mountain Media Watch home page. http://www.oneimage.com/~rmmw/index.html (site visited June 15, 1998).

57. Paul Klite et al., "Local TV News: Getting Away with Murder," *Harvard International Journal of Press/Politics* 2 (Spring 1997): 102.

58. Ibid.

59. Clay Calvert, "Toxic Television, Editorial Discretion and the Public Interest: A Rocky Mountain Low," *Hastings Communications and Entertainment Law Journal* 21 (Fall 1998): 180.

60. In Re: Applications for Renewal of Licenses of Television Stations at Denver, Colorado, http://www.fcc.gov/Bureaus/Mass_Media/Orders/1998/tvautho.txt.

61. Ibid.

62. In re: Honorable Ronald Reagan, 38 F.C.C.2d 378 (1972).

63. Philip Patterson and Lee Wilkins, *Media Ethics: Issues and Cases,* 3rd ed. (New York: McGraw Hill, 1998), pp. 220–221.

64. In re: Hunger in America, 20 F.C.C.2d 143, 151 (1969).

65. Galloway v. FCC, 778 F.2d 16, 20 (D.C. Cir. 1985).

66. Ibid.

67. In re: Hunger in America, 20 F.C.C.2d 143, 151 [1969]).

68. John F. Stacks, "Is Nothing Private?" *Time,* August 23, 1999, p. 80.

69. Alexander Meiklejohn, *Political Freedom: The Constitutional Powers of the People* (New York: Harper & Brothers, 1960), p. 25.

70. Alicia C. Shepard, "White Noise," *American Journalism Review* (January-February 1999): 22.

71. Ibid.

72. Deborah Tannen, "TV's War of Words," *Brill's Content,* September 1999, p. 88.

73. Ibid., p. 89.

74. James Fallows, *Breaking the News: How the Media Undermine American Democracy* (New York: Pantheon Books, 1996), p. 16.

75. Ibid., p. 20.

76. Alicia Shepard, "White Noise," p. 23.

77. Bartholomew H. Sparrow, *Uncertain Guardians: The News Media As a Political Institution* (Baltimore: Johns Hopkins University Press, 1999), p. 48.

78. Joseph N. Cappella and Kathleen Hall Jamieson, *Spiral of Cynicism: The Press and the Public Good* (New York: Oxford University Press, 1997), p. 36.

79. Ibid., p. 230.

80. Ibid., p. 231.

81. Ibid., p. 239.

Chapter Four

1. *World's Wildest Police Videos.* http://www.fox.com/police/show.htm (site visited October 22, 1999).

2. Sanders v. American Broadcasting Companies, 978 P.2d 67 (Cal. 1999).

3. Shulman v. Group W Productions, 955 P.2d 469 (Cal. 1998).

4. Food Lion v. Capital Cities/ABC, 194 F.3d 505 (4th Cir. 1999).

5. Felicity Barringer, "Appeals Court Rejects Damages Against ABC in Food Lion Case," *New York Times,* October 21, 1999.

6. Robert Salladay, "California Crusade on Video Peeping," *Arizona Republic,* April 11, 1999.

7. Andrea Simakis, "Lawmaker Planning Bill for Stronger Voyeur Law," *Plain Dealer,* September 17, 1999.

8. Ibid.

9. Ellen Alderman and Caroline Kennedy, *The Right to Privacy* (New York: Vintage Books, 1997), p. 225.

10. Hidden Camera Solutions. http://www.concealedcameras.com (site visited October 18, 1999).

11. Spy Company. http://spycompany.com/video.htm#ghz24 (site visited October 18, 1999).

12. Gadgets By Design. http://www.jeffhall.com (site visited October 18, 1999).

13. Eyetek Surveillance. http://www.eyetek.com (site visited October 18, 1999).

14. See-it Surveillance Company. http://www.seeitvideo.com (site visited October 18, 1999).

15. ISIS Surveillance Systems & Equipment Company. http://www.surveillancecam.com (site visited October 18, 1999).

16. Hidden Camera Solutions catalogue. http://www.concealedcameras.com/catalogue/main.html (site visited October 18, 1999).

17. Hidden Camera Solutions. http://www.concealedcameras.com (site visited October 18, 1999).

18. Gadgets By Design catalogue. http://www.jeffhall.com/cgi-local/webcart.cgi (site visited October 18, 1999).

19. Ibid.

20. Patricia Davis, "Video Peeping Toms Seeing More Trouble," *Washington Post,* June 7, 1998.

21. Gadgets By Design catalogue. http://www.jeffhall.com/cgi-local/webcart.cgi (site visited October 18, 1999).

22. Spy Company Video Clock. http://spycompany.com/video.htm#clock (site visited October 18, 1999).

23. Ibid.

24. All Secure Camera Systems Covert Wall Picture. http://www.camera-site.com/wireless/covert/covertpic.htm (site visited September 20, 1999).

25. Eric Fidler, "A Voyeur's Delight: Tiny Cameras Go Anywhere," *Atlanta Journal & Constitution,* August 13, 1999.

26. ISIS Surveillance Systems & Equipment Company Body Worn Sun Glass Cam. http://www.surveillancecam.com/Surv_cams.html (site visited October 18, 1999).

27. SpyCentre.com Body Worn Video. http://www.spycentre.com/body-worn.htm (site visited October 20, 1999).

28. Ibid.

29. Ibid.

30. Louis R. Mizell Jr., *Invasion of Privacy* (New York: Berkley Books, 1998), pp. 25–26.

31. "Bay State Wrap: Man Allegedly Films Teens in Bathroom," *Providence Journal-Bulletin,* May 27, 1999.

32. Ibid.

33. "Man Accused of Taping Baby Sitters Indicted," *Patriot Ledger,* July 20, 1999.

34. Ed Hayward, "Weymouth Man Charged with Videotaping Babysitters," *Boston Herald,* May 16, 1999.

35. Ibid.

36. John Kuehner, "Principal May Face Voyeur Charges," *Plain Dealer,* September 14, 1996.

37. Ibid.

38. "Principal Guilty of Spying on Girls," *Columbus Dispatch,* April 15, 1997.

39. "School Fires Official Jailed for Voyeurism," *Cincinnati Enquirer,* June 17, 1997.

40. Ibid.

41. James Ewinger, "Peeping Principal Settles with Cheerleader," *Plain Dealer,* September 17, 1998.

42. Upskirt Heaven. http://www.upskirtheaven.com (site visited July 30, 1999).

43. Upskirt Pictures. http://www.upskirt-pictures.com (site visited on July 30, 1999).

44. The VoyeurWeb. http://www.voyeurweb.com (site visited August 13, 1999).

45. Cf. Panty Man. http://www.pantyman.com/contribute (site visited July 31, 1999).

46. Online Voyeur. http://www.onlinevoyeur.com/pics/hidden/hidden.html (site visited July 31, 1999).

47. Diego Bunuel, "Naked Truth: Voyeur Sites Are Hottest Thing on Net," *Arizona Republic,* February 28, 1999.

48. Ibid.

49. Alderman and Kennedy, *The Right to Privacy,* p. 225.

Chapter Five

1. Eve Klindera, "Qualified Immunity for Cops (and Other Public Officials) with Cameras: Let Common Law Remedies Ensure Press Responsibility," *George Washington Law Review* 67 (1999): 401.

2. Christopher Meyers, "Justifying Journalistic Harms: Right to Know vs. Interest in Knowing," *Journal of Mass Media Ethics* 8 (1993): 133, 134.

3. Cohen v. Cowles Media, 501 U.S. 663 (1991).

4. Ibid., p. 670.

5. Branzbrug v. Hayes, 408 U.S. 665, 681 (1972).

6. Matthew D. Bunker, Sigman L. Splichal, and Sheree Martin, "Triggering the First Amendment: Newsgathering Torts and Press Freedom," *Communications Law and Policy* 4 (Summer 1999): 290.

7. Shulman v. Group W Productions, 955 P.2d 469 (Cal. 1998).

8. Ibid., p. 474.

9. Roe v. Wade, 410 U.S. 113 (1973).

10. 18 U.S.C. §2710 (2000).

11. Robert C. Post, *Constitutional Domains: Democracy, Community, Management* (Cambridge, MA: Harvard University, 1995), p. 73.

12. Reid v. Pierce County, 961 P.2d 333 (1988).

13. Sean M. Scott, "The Hidden First Amendment Values of Privacy," *Washington Law Review* 71 (1996): 683, 700.

14. Diane L. Zimmerman, "Requiem for a Heavyweight: A Farewell to Warren and Brandeis's Privacy Tort," *Cornell Law Review* 68 (1983): 291, 353.

15. Ibid., p. 353.

16. Geoff Dendy, "The Newsworthiness Defense to the Public Disclosure Tort," *Kentucky Law Review* 85 (1996): 147, 152.

17. Donald M. Gillmor, *Fundamentals of Mass Communication Law* (Minneapolis, MN: West, 1996), p. 92.

18. Kathleen Hall Jamieson and Karlyn Kohrs Campbell, *The Interplay of Influence*, 4th ed. (Belmont, CA: Wadsworth Publishing, 1997), p. 4.

19. C. Edwin Baker, "Giving the Audience What It Wants," *Ohio State Law Journal* 58 (1997): 311, 313.

20. Anonsen v. Donahue, 857 S.W.2d 700, 702 (1993).

21. Sipple v. Chronicle Pub. Co., 154 Cal.App.3d 1040, 1048 (1984).

22. Ibid.

23. Lee v. Penthouse International Ltd., 25 Media Law Reporter (BNA) 1651, 1655 (1997).

24. Michaels v. Internet Entertainment Group, Inc., 27 Media Law Reporter (BNA) 1097, 1101 (1998).

25. Weber v. Multimedia Entertainment Inc., 26 Media Law Reporter (BNA) 1377, 1380 (S.D.N.Y. 1988) (holding that the newsworthiness defense, under New York law, can apply to television talk shows).

26. Anonsen v. Donahue, 857 S.W.2d 700 (1993) (extending the newsworthiness defense in the context of a cause of action for public disclosure of private facts arising from a revelation on *Donahue*).

27. Shulman v. Group W Productions, Inc., 955 P.2d 469 (Cal. 1988).

28. Maura Dolan, "The Right to Know vs. the Right to Privacy," *Los Angeles Times*, August 1, 1997.

29. Shulman v. Group W. Productions, 955 P.2d 469, 478 (Cal. 1998).

30. Ibid., p. 481.

31. Ibid.

32. Ibid.

33. Ibid., p. 485.

34. Ibid.

35. Ibid. Emphasis added.

36. Ibid.

37. Ibid., p. 488.

38. Ibid.

39. Lee C. Bollinger, *The Tolerant Society* (Oxford, UK: Oxford University Press, 1986).

40. Ibid., p. 77.

41. Lovell v. Griffin, 303 U.S. 444, 452 (1938).

42. Branzburg v. Hayes, 408 U.S. 665, 704 (1972).

43. Near v. Minnesota, 283 U.S. 697 (1931).

44. Ibid., p. 704.

45. Ibid., p. 718.

46. Ibid., p. 719.

47. Miami Herald Publishing Co. v. Tornillo, 418 U.S. 241 (1974).

48. Ibid., p. 243.

49. Ibid., p. 258.

50. Ibid., p. 256.

51. Columbia Broadcasting System v. Democratic National Committee, 412 U.S. 94 (1973).

52. Ibid., pp. 124–125.

53. "In 1959, the Federal Communications Commission—a federal regulatory agency—was directed by Congress to define 'bona fide news' programs, a definition broadcast journalists were to follow to be excluded from certain equal-time regulations." Samuel P. Winch, *Mapping the Cultural Space of Journalism: How Journalists Distinguish News from Entertainment* (Westport, CT: Praeger, 1997), pp. 73–74. *See* 47 U.S.C. §315(a) (1988) (providing that bona fide newscasts, bona fide news interviews, bona fide news documentaries, and spot coverage of bona fide news events do not trigger the equal opportunities requirements imposed on broadcasting stations for legally qualified candidates for public office).

54. Winch, *Mapping the Cultural Space,* p. 92.

55. Todd Gitlin, "Not So Fast," *Media Studies Journal* (Spring-Summer 1996): 6.

56. C. Edwin Baker, "Turner Broadcasting: Content-Based Regulation of Person and Presses," *Supreme Court Review* (1994): 80.

57. "Ticker," *Brill's Content,* September 1998, p. 148.

58. Owen M. Fiss, "Free Speech and Social Structure," *Iowa Law Review* 71 (1986): 1410.

59. Ibid.

60. Herbert I. Schiller, *Information Inequality: The Deepening Social Crisis in America* (New York: Routledge, 1996), p. 7.

61. Kathleen M. Sullivan, "Free Speech and Unfree Markets," *UCLA Law Review* 42 (1995): 958.

62. Desnick v. American Broadcasting Companies, Inc., 44 F.3d 1345 (1995).

63. Ibid.

64. Ibid., p. 1352.

65. Ibid.

66. Jonathan D. Avila, "Food Lion and Beyond: New Developments in the Law of Hidden Cameras," *Journal of Media, Information, and Communications Law* 16 (Winter 1999): 22.

67. Victor Kovner et al., "Recent Developments in Newsgathering, Invasion of Privacy, and Related Torts," in *Communications Law 1997* (New York: Practising Law Institute, 1997), p. 539.

68. Wilkins v. NBC, 71 Cal.App.4th 1066 (1999).

69. Ibid., p. 1078.

70. Medical Laboratory Management Consultants v. American Broadcasting Companies, Inc., 30 F.Supp.2d 1182 (1998).

71. Ibid., p. 1185.

72. Ibid., p. 1188.

73. Ibid.

74. Ibid., p. 1190.

75. Sanders v. American Broadcasting Companies, Inc.,978 P.2d 67 (Cal. 1999).

76. Ibid., p. 70.

77. Ibid., p. 71.

78. Ibid., p. 72.

79. Ibid., p. 76.

80. Ibid., p. 78.

81. Ibid., p. 76.

82. Ibid., p. 77.

83. Ibid.

84. Robert A. Bertsche, "$5.5M Ruling Against ABC Highlights Growing Risks of Undercover Reports," *TIPS Committee News* 4(1) (Winter 1997): 7.

85. Food Lion v. Capital Cities/ABC, 194 F.3d 505 (4th Cir. 1999).

86. Felicity Barringer, "Appeals Court Rejects Damages Against ABC in Food Lion Case," *New York Times,* October 21, 1999.

87. Ibid.

88. Lisa de Moraes, "ABC Won't Pay Food Lion's Share," *Washington Post,* October 20, 1999.

Chapter Six

1. Semayne's Case, 77 Eng. Rep. 194, 195 (K.B. 1604).

2. Wilson v. Layne, 119 S.Ct. 1692 (1999).

3. Brief for Respondents Paul W. Berger and Erma R. Berger, Hanlon v. Berger, 1997 U.S.Briefs 1927, p. 5.

4. Ibid., p. 6.

5. Berger V. Hanlon, 129 F.3d 505, 508 (9th Cir. 1997).

6. Ibid., p. 515.

7. Ibid.

8. Ibid., p. 510.

9. Ibid., p. 517.

10. Brief for Petitioners, Wilson v. Layne, 1998 U.S.Briefs 83, p. 5.

11. Reply Brief for Petitioners, Wilson v. Layne, 1998 U.S.Briefs 83, pp. 2–3.

12. Ibid., p. 8.

13. Brief for Federal Respondents, Wilson v. Layne, 1998 U.S.Briefs 83, p. 13.

14. Wilson v. Layne, 119 S.Ct. 1692 (1999).

15. Ibid., p. 1697.

16. Ibid., p. 1698.

17. Ibid., p. 1699.

18. Ibid.

19. Ibid., p. 1701.

20. Karl Vick, "Made-for-TV Tragedy," *Washington Post,* December 14, 1997.

21. California Highway Patrol, General Order 100.42 (Rev. Sept. 1997), p. 4. Emphasis added.

22. Letter to the author from Lawrence Schultz, June 25, 1999.

23. Committee on the Judiciary—Fox Statement. http://www.house.gov/judiciary/10142.htm (site visited May 21, 2000).

24. Committee on the Judiciary—Reiser Statement. http://www.house.gov/judiciary/10143.htm (site visited May 21, 2000).

25. Committee on the Judiciary—Masur Statement. http://www.house.gov/judiciary/10147.htm (site visited May 21, 2000).

26. Protection from Personal Intrusion Act. http://thomas.loc.gov (site visited May 21, 2000).

27. California Civil Code §1708.8 (Deering's 2000).

28. Anne E. Hawke and Bruce D. Brown, "Anti-Paparazzi Legislation Threatens All Those Paid to Take Photos," *Legal Times,* February 15, 1999.

29. Committee on the Judiciary—Richards Statement. http://www.house.gov/judiciary/10151.htm (site visited May 21, 2000).

30. Committee on the Judiciary—Tash Statement. http://www.house.gov/judiciary/10148.htm (site visited May 21, 2000).

31. Irene L. Kim, "Defending Freedom of Speech: The Unconstitutionality of Anti-Paparazzi Legislation," *South Dakota Law Review* 44 (1999): 277–278.

32. Ed Anderson, "Video-Voyeur Victim Lobbies for New Law," *Times-Picayune,* April 8, 1999; Ed Anderson, "House OKs Ban on Video Voyeurs," *Times-Picayune,* April 10, 1999.

33. Janice D'Arcy, "Teen Named in Warrant in Cheshire Voyeur Case," *Hartford Courant,* January 8, 1999.

34. 1999 Ct. ALS 143.

35. Sue Carlton, "Tampa Video Voyeur Gets Probation," *St. Petersburg Times,* March 30, 1999.

36. Florida Statute §810.14 (1999).

37. Lisa Sink and Linda Spice, "Man Accused of Videotaping Under Skirts," *Milwaukee Journal Sentinel,* July 11, 1998.

38. Patricia Davis, "Video Peeping Toms Seeing More Trouble," *Washington Post,* June 7, 1998.

39. Ed Hayward, "Weymouth Man Charged with Videotaping Babysitters," *Boston Herald,* May 26, 1999.

40. Robert Salladay, "California Crusade On Video Peeping," *Arizona Republic,* April 11, 1999.

41. Louis R. Mizell Jr., *Invasion of Privacy* (New York: Berkley Books, 1998), p. 23.

42. "The appearance of a person in a public place necessarily involves doffing the cloak of privacy which the law protects." Cefalu v. Globe Newspaper Co., 8 Mass.App.Ct. 71, 77 (1979).

43. Andrew Jay McClurg, "Bringing Privacy Law Out of the Closet: A Tort Theory for Intrusions in Public Places," *North Carolina Law Review* 73 (1995): 990.

44. The public voyeurism situation of upskirts in malls and parks should be distinguished from the more private video voyeurism that takes place with cameras hidden in dressing rooms, bedrooms, and bathrooms. These places are generally considered private locations in which people have an expectation of privacy unless they are given notice that a camera may be watching their movements. See, People for the Ethical Treatment of Animals v. Berosini, 111 Nev. 615, 635 (1995) (writing that a private bedroom, a restroom, and a dressing room are places "traditionally associated with a legitimate expectation of privacy").

45. As the Supreme Court of California recently observed: "To prove actionable intrusion, the plaintiff must show the defendant penetrated some zone of physical or sensory privacy surrounding, or obtained unwanted access to data about, the plaintiff. The tort is proven only if the plaintiff had an objectively reasonable expectation of seclusion or solitude in the place, conversation or data source." Shulman v. Group W Productions., Inc., 18 Cal.App.4th 200, 232 (1998).

46. *Restatement (Second) of Torts* §652B cmt. c (1977). Emphasis added.

47. Daily Times Democrat v. Graham, 276 Ala. 380 (1964).

48. Ibid., p. 381.

49. Ibid.

50. Ibid.

51. Ibid., p. 382.

52. Ibid., p. 383.

53. Ibid.

54. Ibid.

55. Ibid.

56. Ibid.

57. Ibid., pp. 383–384.

58. Mizell, *Invasion of Privacy,* pp. 23–24.

59. Mark Gladstone, "Bill Would Ban Surreptitious Taping by 'Video Voyeurs,'" *Los Angeles Times,* April 7, 1999.

60. Seamus McGraw, "Authorities Have to Get Creative in Dealing with Video Voyeurs," *Bergen County Record,* June 1, 1999.

Chapter Seven

1. John H. Garvey and Frederick Schauer, *The First Amendment: A Reader,* 2nd ed. (St. Paul, MN: West Publishing Co., 1996), p. 35.

2. "The best test of truth is the power of the thought to get itself accepted in the competition of the market." Abrams v. United States, 250 U.S. 616 (1919) (Holmes, J., dissenting).

3. Alexander Meiklejohn, *Political Freedom: The Constitutional Powers of the People* (New York: Harper & Brothers, 1960).

4. C. Edwin Baker, *Human Liberty and Freedom of Speech* (New York: Oxford University Press, 1989).

5. Steven H. Shiffrin, *The First Amendment, Democracy and Romance* (Cambridge, MA: Harvard University Press, 1990).

6. Lee C. Bollinger, *The Tolerant Society* (New York: Oxford University Press, 1986).

7. Vincent Blasi, "The Checking Value in First Amendment Theory," *American Bar Foundation Research Journal* (1977): 521.

8. Kathleen M. Sullivan and Gerald Gunther, *First Amendment Law* (New York: Foundation Press, 1999), p. 4.

9. Rodney A. Smolla, *Free Speech in an Open Society* (New York: Vintage, 1992), p. 5.

10. Baker, *Human Liberty,* p. 7.

11. Abrams v. United States, 250 U.S. 616 (1919) (Holmes, J., dissenting).

12. Lucas A. Powe Jr., *The Fourth Estate and the Constitution* (Berkeley: University of California Press, 1991), p. 237.

13. Ben H. Bagdikian, *The Media Monopoly,* 5th ed.(Boston: Beacon Press, 1997), p. ix.

14. Todd Gitlin, "Introduction," in Erick Barnouw et al., eds., *Conglomerates and the Media* (New York: New York Press, 1997), p.12.

15. Smolla, *Free Speech,* p. 6.

16. Elizabeth A. Rathbun, "Count 'em: 830," *Broadcasting & Cable,* October 11, 1999, p. 64.

17. David G. Savage, "Justices Pick at Campaign Donor Limits," *Los Angeles Times,* October 6, 1999.

18. Paul Farhi, "Viacom to Buy CBS, Uniting Multimedia Heavyweights," *Washington Post,* September 8, 1999.

19. Meiklejohn, *Political Freedom,* p. 26.

20. Ibid., p. 27.

21. Ronald K.L. Collins and David M. Skover, *The Death of Discourse* (Boulder: Westview Press, 1996), p. 4.

22. Eric Schmitt, "Half the Electorate, Perhaps Satisfied or Bored, Sat Out Voting," *New York Times,* November 7, 1996. The decrease in voter turnout is especially troublesome because registration is probably at its highest level since 1968.

23. David Cay Johnston, "Voting, America's Not Keen On. Coffee Is Another Matter," *New York Times,* November 10, 1996.

24. Jon R. Sinclair, "Reforming Television's Role in American Political Campaigns: Rationale for the Elimination of Paid Political Advertisements," *Communication & Law* (March 1995): 65, 84.

25. Ibid., p. 84.

26. James W. Carey, "The Press, Public Opinion, and Public Discourse," in Theodore L. Glasser and Charles T. Salmon, eds., *Public Opinion and the Communication of Consent* (New York: Guilford Press, 1995), p. 374.

27. Rene Sanchez, "Freshmen Apathetic, Survey Shows," *Washington Post,* January 12, 1998.

28. Ibid.

29. Ibid.

30. Collins and Skover, *The Death of Discourse,* p. 3.

31. Ibid.

32. Ibid., p. xxi.

33. Amy Carr, "Admit It—You Like to Look," *Chicago Daily Herald,* June 22, 1999.

34. Meiklejohn, *Political Freedom,* p. 26.

35. Thomas Emerson, *Toward a General Theory of the First Amendment* (New York: Vintage, 1966), p. 5.

36. Curtis Bok, "The Duty of Freedom," in Robert B. Downs, ed., *The First Freedom* (Chicago: American Library, 1960), p. 457.

37. Meiklejohn, *Political Freedom,* p. 24.

38. Sissela Bok, *Secrets: On the Ethics of Concealment and Revelation* (New York: Vintage Books, 1989), p. 13.

39. Meiklejohn, *Political Freedom,* p. 24.

40. Alexander Meiklejohn, "The First Amendment Is an Absolute," *The Supreme Court Review* (1961): 255.

41. Meiklejohn, "The First Amendment," p. 257. Emphasis added.

42. Robert C. Post, *Constitutional Domains: Democracy, Community, Management* (Cambridge, MA: Harvard University Press, 1995), p. 274.

43. Post, *Constitutional Domains,* p. 270.

44. Smolla, *Free Speech,* p. 7.

45. Emerson, *Toward a General Theory*, pp. 4–5.

46. Smolla, *Free Speech*, p. 9.

47. Ibid.

48. Erwin Chemerinsky, *Constitutional Law: Principles and Policies* (New York: Aspen Law & Business, 1997), p. 756.

49. Philip Wuntch, "Trapped in the Box," *Dallas Morning News,* May 31, 1998.

50. Ibid.

51. Ibid.

52. Christina Cheakalos et al., "Take Two," *People,* June 29, 1998, p. 117.

Conclusion

1. Jay Black, Bob Steele, and Ralph Barney, *Doing Ethics in Journalism: A Handbook with Case Studies,* 3rd ed. (Boston: Allyn & Bacon, 1999), p. 6.

2. Ibid., p. 7.

3. Bruce Sanford, *Don't Shoot the Messenger: How Our Growing Hatred of the Media Threatens Free Speech for All of Us* (New York: Free Press, 1999), p. 10.

4. Black et al., *Doing Ethics,* p. 5.

5. Shulman v. Group W Productions, 955 P.2d 469, 488 (Cal. 1998).

6. Black et al., *Doing Ethics,* p. 6.

Index

DATE			